The Progressive M-

About Policy Network

{
} policy network

Policy Network is an international think-tank launched in December 2000 with the support of Tony Blair, Gerhard Schröder, Giuliano Amato and Göran Persson following the International Progressive Summits in New York, Florence and Berlin.

} *A Progressive Network*

Policy Network's objective is to facilitate the exchange of progressive ideas among the centre-left in Europe and the world, working with those who look to forward a progressive agenda through its unique network of organisations and experts.

} *Our Common Challenge*

Progressive governments and politicians across the globe are, more than ever, facing the same problems. Rising fears for security, both economic and political, the revolution in information technology, and the contradictions of traditional welfare and employment policies are among the new challenges that affect countries in increasingly similar ways. Often, governments and parties had worked independently to resolve these problems. But, even where particular national challenges exist, we now find that we can learn much from the experience of others on the kind of approach that is likely to prove most effective. There is a growing consensus about the need to pay greater attention to policies tried and tested in other countries, to look creatively at new means to achieve traditional progressive goals, and to support modernisers.

} *Working Together*

Policy Network works with governments, parties, experts, and decision-makers from over 25 different countries, providing them with a range of tools to promote debate, share ideas, and make it easier to find solutions. Policy Network widens the debate by involving the broader policy community, practitioners, business, trade unions and the public in each country. We address a broad range of themes, including: globalization, modern public services, Welfare State reform, employment in a knowledge society, pension reform, new industrial relations, immigration and inclusion, education, inequality, the future of Europe, and EU–US relations.

Policy Network
2nd Floor, Tower Building
11 York Road, London
SE1 7NX, United Kingdom

T + 44 (0) 20 7981 0300
F + 44 (0) 20 7981 0301

W www.policy-network.net

The Progressive Manifesto

New Ideas for the Centre-Left

Edited by
Anthony Giddens

polity

First published in 2003 by Polity Press in association with Blackwell Publishing Ltd

Editorial office:
Polity Press
65 Bridge Street
Cambridge CB2 1UR, UK

Marketing and production:
Blackwell Publishing Ltd
108 Cowley Road
Oxford OX4 1JF, UK

Blackwell Publishing Inc.
350 Main Street
Malden, MA 02148, USA

A catalogue record for this book is available from the British Library.

Library of Congress Cataloging-in-Publication Data
The progressive manifesto : new ideas for the centre-left / edited by Anthony Giddens.
    p. cm.
    ISBN 0-7456-3294-7 (alk. paper) — ISBN 0-7456-3295-5 (pb : alk. paper)
1. Capitalism.   2. Socialism.   3. Right and left (Political science)
4. Globalization.   I. Title: New ideas for the centre-left.   II. Giddens, Anthony.
    HB501 .P73 2003
    335—dc22
                                                      2003018450

Typeset in 10.5 on 12pt Sabon
by Graphicraft Limited, Hong Kong
Printed and bound in Great Britain by MPG Books, Bodmin, Cornwall

For further information on Polity, visit our website: www.polity.co.uk

Contents

Contents

Contributors

Anthony Giddens is former Director of the London School of Economics and Political Science (LSE).

John Kay is one of Britain's leading economists. He was elected a fellow of St John's College, Oxford at the age of 21, a position that he still holds.

Folke Schuppert is a Professor of Constitutional and Administrative Law at Humboldt University, Berlin.

Tom Bentley has been Director of Demos since 1999 and was a former adviser to David Blunkett MP – then Secretary of State for Education.

David Halpern is a senior adviser at the UK Prime Minister's Strategy Unit.

Gøsta Esping-Andersen is Professor of Sociology at Universidad Pompeu Fabra, Barcelona, Spain.

Nicola Rossi MP is Professor of Economics at the University of Rome and is currently Secretary of the Parliamentary Group of the Democratic Left in Italy.

Contributors

David Held is Graham Wallas Professor of Political Science at the London School of Economics.

Rebecca Willis has been Director of the UK think tank, Green Alliance since 1998. Previously, she was a policy adviser at the European Parliament.

James Wilsdon is Head of Strategy at Demos. Prior to joining Demos in November 2001, James was senior policy adviser at Forum for the Future.

Preface

The contributions in this book were prepared for the summit of progressive political leaders held in London on 11–13 July, 2003. The authors did not write their articles in isolation. The ideas developed were a result of several months of collaboration and discussion based upon a series of seminars held at the London School of Economics during the early months of 2003. I should like to thank all those who contributed to the seminars, which without exception were intensive and constructive.

Special thanks must go to those at Policy Network who made all of this possible. I should like to thank especially Matt Browne, Yasmin Holzkamm, Joanne Burton, Paul Thomson and Nick Bent. Thanks go to Sandra Byatt and her colleagues at Polity. Several others were very involved and supportive, including David Held. I should also like to express my gratitude to colleagues at the LSE who were so helpful in organising the seminars – in particular Alan Revel.

Anthony Giddens
July 2003

Introduction

Neoprogressivism. A New Agenda for Social Democracy

Anthony Giddens

It is said that anyone who goes to a restaurant should never make a joke to the waiter about the food or the menu. The waiter's smile will inevitably be forced, because he will have heard the same observation many times before. I feel much the same about the third way. I have been to many countries discussing third way politics. I have lost count of the number of times people have said what we really should be looking for is a fourth way. I have usually answered that we are already on the fifteenth way, meaning that the third way discussion is a continuing and evolving debate, which it is.

But now I have come to see that in a certain sense they are right. At this juncture in political thinking and policy-making, we have to go beyond where third way thinking has got so far. There are two reasons. The main one is simply that the world has moved on since the late 1980s and early 1990s, the time at which third way ideas, in their contemporary guise, were initiated. The second is that there were some weaknesses in these ideas, understandable in the context in which they developed, but that also now need to be remedied.

The Third Way: What It Was and Is

Let me first of all comment upon some misconceptions about the third way debate. The third way, at least in my understanding of it, is *not* a programme specifically linked to the New Democrats in the US or to New Labour in Britain. It is not, in other words, a label for a distinctively Anglo-Saxon approach to political analysis and policy-making. The notion stretches much more widely, to the efforts of social democratic parties across the world to rethink their policies in the post-1989 period. Another word for the third way is simply progressivism. Third way politics stands in traditions of social democratic revisionism that stretch back to Eduard Bernstein and Karl Kautsky.

The third way is *not* a 'middle way' – specifically, it is not an attempt to find a halfway point between the Old Left and free market fundamentalism. It seeks to transcend both of these. Neither of these earlier two 'ways' is adequate to cope with the social and economic problems we face today. The third way is a distinctively left-of-centre project – it is about the modernisation of social democracy. When I wrote my book *The Third Way* in 1998,[1] I gave it the subtitle 'The Renewal of Social Democracy', and that to me is what the third way means. Finally, the third way is *not* an empty PR exercise. On the contrary, from its beginnings it has been a policy-driven response to change. We live in a world marked by rapid and dramatic transformations – globalisation being the most important – and it is the role of third way thinking to seek to show how to cope with them.

Third way thinking has been directed to two main aims. One is *electoral recovery*. By the early 1990s, social democratic parties had been out of power in some of the leading industrial countries, such as the UK, Germany and France, for a long while. In the US, until Bill Clinton came to office in 1993, there had been no Democratic president for twelve years. Left of centre parties had been slow to adjust to a society in which their traditional constituency, the working class, was shrinking away. A generation ago, in the EU countries, over 40 per cent of the labour force worked in manufacture; that proportion has dwindled to 16 per cent, and it is still declining. The old industrial economy has increasingly been replaced by a knowledge-based economy, in a society where the middle class is easily the dominant grouping.

Second, the centre left had to respond to the *crisis of Keynesianism*, the counterpart in Western countries to the dissolution of East

European state socialism. Globalisation was the prime force behind
both of these transitions. It is not possible to have national demand
management in a globalised marketplace. At that time, free market
fundamentalism – the belief that most of our problems can be
resolved through the spread of markets – seemed triumphant, even
in those countries that did not directly experience Thatcherite or
neoliberal rule. The third way developed essentially as a critical riposte
to neo-liberalism, and it was a highly effective one. The emerging
synthesis stressed that active government is an essential prerequisite
both for successful economic development and social justice. But it
recognised that some established notions and policies of the left had
to be rejected or rethought.

Contrary to what some critics say, the policy framework of the
third way is coherent and intellectually powerful. It can be sketched
out in brief as follows. Government and the state need thorough-
going reform, to make them faster moving, more effective and responsive, and to reflect the need for greater transparency and diversity
in a society where consumer choice has become a prime force. The
state should become more of an enabler rather than a direct provider
or producer. 'Command and control' has visibly failed, not only in
the Soviet Union, but also in its milder versions in Western societies,
where it took the shape of nationalisation of the 'commanding heights'
of the economy. The emphasis of the state should now be upon
helping people to help themselves.

Public investment, however, has to be geared to what a society can
afford. 'Tax and spend' in the past for the left often meant 'tax and
overspend'. In place of this attitude modernising social democrats
place an emphasis upon fiscal discipline, and upon improving the
conditions of economic competitiveness. Economic development and
social justice can go hand in hand if we concentrate upon promoting
high levels of job creation. A society with a high proportion of people in work is likely to be increasingly prosperous, but is also able to
free up resources to pay for public investment. Having a job, above
the floor of a decent minimum wage, is the best route out of poverty
for anyone able to work.

These ideas presume a new citizenship contract, based upon responsibilities as well as rights. The state helps provide citizens with

the resources to make their own lives, but in return they have to recognise their obligations to the community. T. H. Marshall's famous citizenship triad, the classical source for traditional social democratic thought, mentioned only rights – social, political and economic.[2] Today we should recognise that most rights are conditional. People who claim unemployment benefits, for example, should have the obligation to look for work.

We have to add a further citizenship right to those mentioned by Marshall – the right to live free from the fear of crime. In third way thinking, there should be no policy areas accepted as the inevitable terrain of the right. Voters in the past have tended to trust social democrats on issues such as welfare and education, but not with questions to do with crime, immigration and defence. The point is not, or should not be, for social democrats to take over rightist policies on these issues, but to offer persuasive left of centre approaches and solutions to them.

Finally, the third way framework is internationalist. It is not naively 'pro-globalisation'. It recognises that globalisation produces insecurities, tensions and conflicts alongside its benefits. Yet many of these benefits, including those generated by free trade, are real. Globalisation is also intrinsically related to the spread of democracy. It isn't only in the industrial countries that people are becoming more active citizens, wishing to have more control over what they do, and less inclined than in the past to accept the dictates of authority.

Third way type parties registered a string of successes during the 1990s. At one point, the Democrats held the White House, while 13 out of 15 EU countries were ruled by centre left parties or coalitions. As of 2003, by contrast, the Republicans rule the roost in the US, holding not only the presidency, but both houses of Congress too. Only some six countries in the EU are now governed from the left of centre. The last few years have also seen the rise of far right populism in Europe, with some far right parties polling heavily among erstwhile social democratic voters.

The implications of these changes for the third way have to be put into perspective. In the US election of 2001, the Democratic candidate Al Gore won a higher percentage of the popular vote than George Bush, and but for a few thousand dimpled chads would have been

4

president. Some of the reverses suffered by the centre left in EU countries resulted from tactical errors rather than from swings in public consciousness. Mr Jospin, for instance, lost the chance to get into the presidential run-off in France because the left of centre vote in the first stage became too fragmented. In Italy, following the period of government of the Olive Tree Coalition, the left was also divided, allowing Mr Berlusconi to come through for victory. We should also note that centre left coalitions have recently won power in a number of East European countries, including Poland, the Czech Republic and Hungary.

The electoral setbacks of the centre left came not from the fact that the third way failed, but because it was not embraced actively enough. Governments or parties that did not move sufficiently in a third way direction either fell from power or were not able to attain it. Some governments, for example, were unwilling or unable to push through labour market reforms. As a result, unemployment remained higher than it needed to be. The Lisbon programme in the EU was heavily influenced by third way thinking, and is crucial to a resumption of economic growth and to job generation in Europe – yet it has by no means always been endorsed in practice. The Lisbon summit set a target of 70 per cent or more of the labour force in work by 2010. Progress thus far has been slow. The employment ratio of the EU countries in 2002 was 64 per cent – compared to over 75 per cent in the US.

Some parties failed to respond to voter concerns about crime and immigration. They tried to tack on new policies in these areas only after the rise of the far right had shaken them out of their complacency – and too late to register effectively with the voters. Al Gore might very well have emerged a clear winner had he stuck more closely to the policies that helped generate such exceptional economic prosperity in the US during the Clinton years.

I have no doubt at all in my mind that many of the core ideas of the third way are valid and should be sustained. The third way was right to challenge traditional leftist thinking. It was successful wherever it managed to reach out to the new middle class groups and embrace individual aspiration. It was right to reject old-style tax and spend. It was right to relate rights to responsibilities as the basis of a new citizenship contract. It was right about the primacy of work over benefits and the welfare reforms needed to produce such a change of emphasis. It was right about the need to react to the changed economic conditions of the knowledge economy. And, filtered through all of these, it was right to argue that globalisation is altering fundamental aspects both of our own societies and the international arena, calling for new policy responses.

Today, nevertheless, we do stand at an important transition point. The challenges and the social context of 2003 are not those of 1993. Moreover, a certain degree of self-criticism is necessary. The third way was developed above all as a critique of the neoliberal right. It was defined too much in terms of what it was against rather than what it was for. Social democrats need, I shall argue, a greater *ideological breakout* from this situation than has been achieved so far. This ideological breakaway demands new *concepts* and new *policy perspectives*. We must continue to think *radically*, but radicalism means being open to *fresh ideas*, not relapsing back into the traditional leftism of the past. I shan't in fact call this new perspective the fourth way, although the idea is tempting. Instead I shall speak of *neoprogressivism* and the *neoprogressives* (*neoprogs*). The neoprogs need to develop a social democratic agenda as ambitious and comprehensive as the neoconservatives have done in the US and elsewhere.

We need, as I would see it, to create more *deep support* for left of centre policies than was generated by the first wave of third way policies. We should not be content with a pragmatic appeal. Deep support means touching an emotional chord among citizens, not just appealing to their pragmatic interests. It means recovering some of that capacity the left had to a much greater degree before 1989, the capacity to inspire. It means having ideals that show what we are for, rather than only what we reject. It means conveying a notion of the type of society, and the type of world, we want to create.

Ideological Breakout

What should neoprogressives stand for? My answer, in brief, would be: a strong public sphere, coupled to a thriving market economy; a pluralistic, but inclusive society; and a cosmopolitan wider world, founded upon principles of international law. Making a renewed case for public interests and public goods (nationally and internationally) seems to me the most crucial, for it is here that the reactive nature of earlier third way thinking is most evident. A healthy economy needs well-functioning markets, but it also needs a well-developed public domain, in which the state retains an essential role.

Strengthening public life does not imply returning to the nanny state. It means rethinking what the state is, and what it is for, in relation to concepts of the public interest and the public good. I call the process *publicisation*. The early post-War period was the era of the bureaucratic state. Then we had a time of privatisation and de-regulation. Now we are potentially entering another phase again – marked not by the return of the bureaucratic state, but by a more inclusive definition of the public purpose. After privatisation comes publicisation. By publicisation I mean defending the core importance of the public sphere to a decent society – one in which citizens can pursue their aspirations, but feel protected and secure. First-wave third way thinking was good at helping with the first, but was less well able to provide for the second.

Two concepts developed by those contributing to this collection are especially important in further pursuing these thoughts. One is the *embedded market*; the other is the *ensuring state*. I shall try to show that these notions mesh together closely. What follows, however, in this section and other sections is my own attempt at a synthesis. I draw on ideas suggested by the contributors, but put my own gloss on them, for which they should not be held responsible.

As John Kay says, social democrats should look to establish their own political economy of modern capitalism. We should not be content only to react critically against that provided by the neoliberals. The idea of the embedded market, a notion originally introduced by the sociologist Mark Granovetter, is a key starting point.[3] What is the embedded market embedded in? It is embedded in culture, law and mechanisms of trust. In developed market economies, formal and informal rules have grown up, permitting coordination between the vast array of people who must coordinate their activities for markets to work. The importance of markets, as Kay makes clear, is that they allow us to organise a host of transactions that no-one fully understands, above all when they are actually enacted: 'markets work because there is never a single voice'. New industries, products and services arise because markets are geared to experimentation. Most experiments fail, but in so doing they keep the momentum going for technological and product innovation. The left has long been very reluctant to accept that these qualities are necessary for economic prosperity, but they are in fact central to it. Markets institutionalise 'disciplined pluralism' – the opportunity to experiment, but with mechanisms that shut down experiments which fail.

From the perspective of the embedded market, there is no need for us to continue to pay obeisance to the idea of the minimal state – as Bill Clinton did, for instance, when he proposed that 'the era of the big state is over'. That notion was always a myth in any case. There is no industrial country in which the proportion of GDP taken by the state has declined significantly over the recent past. In developed economies, government and the state are almost everywhere, and have to be for people to lead decent, normal lives. Moreover, as Joseph Stiglitz points out on an international level, there are no cases of successful economic development where the state has not played a prominent role.[4]

In the wake of many experiences with privatisation around the world, I think we can be fairly confident about where the boundaries of the market economy should be drawn, although there will always be areas of contention around the edges – and the edges do shift, with technological change and other factors. Markets only operate successfully where there is competition. Natural monopolies therefore set natural boundaries to them. There is little reason to suppose that private companies are superior to public ones where a monopoly situation applies. In the case of health and education, markets could supply the services involved, but there are powerful reasons to do with social solidarity, equity and the public good, as to why they should be largely excluded.

We should not suddenly become hostile to privatisation. In any given country, there might well be industries or services that should be removed from state ownership or direct state control. We need not take a stance on whether the state 'in general' is superior to the market or the other way around. Both markets and the state should be subject to overriding tests of the *public interest*. The ideological justification is not 'what works', but how effective a given strategy is in promoting definable public goods. This position also implies subjecting major areas of the state and markets to continuous scrutiny. If a given service is wholly or partly privatised, for example, it does not follow that it will always stay that way. We should accept that there can be, and have been, privatisations 'too far'. For example in the UK and the Netherlands, the privatisation of what is essentially a monopoly good, the railways, proved at best problematic, and in both countries the railways have been taken back into the hands of non-profit organisations, although not renationalised.

We should distinguish between a market economy and a privatised economy – where state monopolies are simply replaced by private monopolies. To be introduced, or sustained, privatisation must go along with the promotion of competition, the possibility of entry by new firms and real consumer choice. These conditions were conspicuously ignored in many of the earlier privatisations that happened around the world. In the traditional social democratic approach, the state intervenes in cases of market failure. However, the state may often need to intervene to help markets function more effectively – by opening up new sectors to competition, encouraging technological change, and fostering flexibility in capital, product and labour markets.

The embedded market does not function most effectively by giving a licence to self-interest. On the contrary, the penetration of this view into business, especially into the outlook of many business leaders, is one of the reasons for the current crisis of public confidence in business and in stock markets. 'It is not true', John Kay remarks, 'that profit is the purpose of a market economy, and the production of goods and services is a means to it: the purpose is the production of goods and services, and profit the means.'

Third way authors – again, quite rightly – dropped the hostility to business and the corporation so prominent among some on the more traditional left. Businesses, after all, are the wealth producers, and business success is necessary for economic development to occur at all. But being business friendly has sometimes meant accepting the self-definitions of business leaders themselves – including a good deal of self-aggrandising behaviour. The 1990s were a period of the worship of the business hero, a tendency from which third way social democrats were not entirely immune. But all of that looks different now. Many of the erstwhile heroes have fallen from grace altogether; some others have made massive miscalculations, losing their companies millions or billions of pounds. The corporate excesses of the 1990s have been such that they are threatening business's very public 'licence to operate'.

The way to approach the issues, I would say, is again via the route of the public sphere and citizenship. After the years of deregulation, business is dealing with issues that concern large arenas of the public interest, but in effect denying its responsibilities in the public space. In the US, institutional investors, such as pension and mutual funds, now own some 70 per cent of all equity. Those whose money is in there, and whose futures depend upon the actions of their managers, are asking, 'who are these people running our lives?' Public pressure on business, and on massive CEO payouts, is building up sharply. I do not think this is a temporary phenomenon, to do only with the problems of the stock market and a weak economy. Something of a sea change is happening in how people view business and its legitimacy. The shareholder model of capitalism is undermining itself.

A survey carried out in the UK in 2003 by the polling organisation MORI showed major changes happening in public attitudes towards business, not just recently but over an extended period.[5] In the 1960s, nearly 60 per cent of the population agreed with the statement: 'The profits of large companies help make things better for everyone who uses their services.' There has been a decline year on year in the numbers endorsing the proposition since then. In 2003 the proportion of the public agreeing had fallen to only 27 per cent. Four-fifths of citizens believe that companies have responsibilities towards the wider society, but they are highly sceptical about whether most are living up to them. 61 per cent say the 'large companies don't really care about the long-term environmental and social impact of their actions'. MORI has for some while asked how important the social responsibility of a company is to individuals in their behaviour as consumers. The proportion who say it is 'very important' to them has doubled over the period 1998–2003.

I would compare the changing attitudes towards business today with what happened to perceptions of the state thirty years ago. Business is under a cloud not just because of corporate scandals and the problems of the world economy, but because it has overrun the limits of its own legitimacy. Just as in the case of the state, I don't think things can go back to how they were before. Companies that don't take their environmental and social obligations seriously will face increasingly serious resistance, both from consumers and from NGOs.

Traditional models of stakeholder value are inadequate to meet the challenge. They depend too much upon the corporation identifying its own stakeholders and defining its responsibilities towards them. I would suggest that a useful notion for neoprogs here (although not discussed by any of the contributors) might be that of the *civil economy*, a concept proposed by the business guru Stephen Davis.[6] He argues that business firms are being propelled into more public and socially responsible roles by a string of agencies now surrounding them. Government can help shape the influence such groups have, in order to create a more effective framework of business responsibility. The civil economy is an analogue to civil society, and in part an extension of it, but focused upon the marketplace. Davis starts from the premise I mentioned earlier – that, after and as a result of two decades of neoliberal dominance, the business world is threatening to erode its own mandate to operate. We need to build a civil economy in order to recover legitimacy for business activity, but also to ensure that business acknowledges its wider social responsibilities.

Nationalisation may have been ineffective and inefficient, but it did mean that services 'belonged' to the public – they were part of a wider setting of democracy and public activity. Privatised industry, and business more generally, have to respond to regulators, but regulation usually concentrates upon economic criteria. We need to recover the public space that has been ceded.

A civil economy cannot be created wholly through the state alone. Government can give the lead, through a diversity of means, including tax incentives, best practice company law, and guidelines and laws promoting accountability. But other agencies are required, and are in fact everywhere becoming more active. The agencies of responsibility in civil society are an independent judiciary, a free press, voluntary associations and so forth. In a civil economy they are active shareholders, auditors, professional associations and civil society groups engaged with marketplace issues. As elsewhere, the state should seek to intervene but not dominate.

Shareholder activists – including institutional shareholders – are likely to play an increasingly important role in the civil economy, particularly in the Anglo-Saxon countries. Executive pay packages will be one of their chief concerns. It is simply a fiction that the massive salaries now commonly paid to CEOs are the result of market forces. They are set by remuneration committees, usually composed of their peers from other businesses. Moreover, the severance arrangements of CEOs mean that they are protected whatever happens to the firm – they bear virtually none of the risk they ask their employees to shoulder.

A survey of the 500 largest firms in the US in the financial year 2001–2 showed that CEOs negotiated severance packages worth an average $16 million. These arrangements have become a particular focus of shareholder anger. At a whole range of firms in the US – Tyco, Hewlett-Packard, United Technologies, Alcoa, Union Pacific and many others – investors have passed resolutions pressing companies to put such deals to a vote of shareholders. In the UK, rules allowing shareholders to vote each year on executive salaries have just been introduced. One of the first results was a vote rejecting a pay package, reputed to be worth £25 million, offered to J. P. Garnier of GlaxoSmithKline.

With the passing of the age of the business hero, such deals can be seen as the scandal they are. They should be of major concern to social democrats, because they bear directly on issues of solidarity, equality and citizenship. The point is not so much the stratospheric nature of the salaries themselves, but the signals they send to employees and to society as a whole. Self-discipline on the level of salaries is an indicator of the acceptance of citizenship responsibilities and obligations.

The Ensuring State

A basic organising concept for the neoprogressive agenda should be that of the ensuring state. It is a more compelling and assertive idea for social democrats than the enabling state. The concept of the enabling state was itself an advance over more traditional conceptions. The central idea of the enabling state is that the state should empower its citizens – the state should provide resources that allow individuals to develop their own lives, rather than being told what to do or how to act. However, the notion was again formed mainly as a reaction to the neoliberal approach. It finds a role for the state beyond the minimal state, but the state is conceived of mainly as a facilitating agency. The implication is that, once having been provided with resources, citizens are going to be left to fend for themselves. The responsibilities of the state would seem to end at the point where people have sufficient resources to live autonomous lives.

We should not drop the idea of enabling, of course. The concept of the ensuring state, however, recognises that the state also has obligations of *care and protection* for citizens, and that some of these obligations should be provided as *guarantees*. The concept of the ensuring state does not mark a return to any sort of command and control perspective. It recognises that many services once delivered directly by the state are now provided by non-state agencies.

What should the ensuring state ensure? How does it differ from the enabling state? The ensuring state takes responsibility for the delivery of policy outcomes, and for the coordination of services, many of which it does not directly organise. It is not only responsible for providing citizens with resources – access to education, health care, welfare services and so forth – but for guaranteeing standards of delivery. The ensuring state is a regulatory state, but its orientation differs from the traditional bureaucratic state. Given the range of agencies involved – civil society groups, voluntary associations, not-for-profit corporations and others – 'regulation' normally does not mean direct control but standard setting and the offering of incentives for behaviour relevant to public purposes. 'Enabling' certainly remains important, but it is recognised that the state has responsibilities after that point. These responsibilities are often 'double responsibilities' – they are responsibilities for making sure that others behave responsibly.

For example, it is very much contrary to the public interest that, as happens in the UK, a quarter of eleven-year-olds cannot read and write properly, that too many drop out of school when they are sixteen, and that 50,000 pupils a day are playing truant, many of them tangled up with the law. The state cannot directly ensure that this situation is remedied, but what it can and must do is seek to get parents and young people to take action themselves. It has to forge a contract of rights and responsibilities with them, and help – to some extent constrain – them to live up to it.

Processes of devolution and decentralisation expand the scope of the ensuring state at the same time as the directive control of the centralised state becomes less marked. 'Disciplined pluralism' is as appropriate a term here as in the sphere of the market, but it is important to see that the regulatory mechanisms are different. Except where public goods are delivered directly through market mechanisms, the 'discipline' in disciplined pluralism cannot be delivered through the fact that those who fail will go to the wall.

First-wave third way ideas about the reform of the state were strongly influenced by the New Public Management (NPM), also known as 'reinventing government'. The NPM undoubtedly marked a step forward compared to more traditional approaches. According to the NPM, state-based organisations should learn from best practice in business. They should move towards flattened hierarchies, the setting up of quasi-markets, local responsibility for budgets, and assessment by outcomes rather than process. Some of these emphases are important, but this is another area where we need to stake out a different perspective.

There are crucial differences between businesses and state agencies. Business must respond to the vagaries of the market. For the reasons John Kay describes, markets are directionless – no one knows where they will take us. Public agencies cannot be like this. They must of course react to change, hopefully in a rapid and effective way. But they also have to have a sense of purpose and direction that is adhered to whatever the external circumstances. A school system, for

14

instance, must adapt to relevant innovations, such as the use of computers in classrooms, but is mainly geared to overall public purposes set by the democratic process.

Concepts for the centre left (1)

The Embedded Market – State and market necessarily intertwine; economic exchange that becomes too geared to egoism undermines business's 'licence to operate'

The Ensuring State – The state provides resources, but also offers performance guarantees

The Civil Economy – A framework of agencies and institutions monitoring business activity

---

Producing disciplined pluralism in the public services must depend upon what Schuppert calls 'regulated self-regulation'. The centre must to a large degree let go, but must regulate the conditions under which local autonomy is exercised. We should want those working in the public services to be free to take initiatives, experiment where possible and be honest about their mistakes. Their efforts have to be audited, but auditing should be strategic – those who are doing well should be free of persistent intrusion. The experience of different countries, such as the Netherlands or the UK, shows that heavy-handed auditing methods can be actively counter-productive. Such methods produce 'Soviet-style' responses – everything becomes twisted to the meeting of targets. Targets that are set should be generated from below as well as from above.

Developing the ensuring state will take a good deal of capacity building and structural transformation. Even where there is some decentralisation, in most countries bureaucracies are still driven mainly by functional specialisation and process control. They have been used to managing public programmes in a direct way. It is not easy to find a balance between devolved agencies and the political centre. Moreover, there can be problems of 'horizontal control' – there has to be coordination between groups working on different aspects of what used to be integrated through bureaucratic management at the top. Yet the advantages are clear and very considerable.

Take as an illustration the history of the Federal Emergency Management Agency (FEMA) in the US.[7] The agency was once a typical version of a slow-moving, bureaucratic department. One of the jokes passed around about it was that every natural disaster in fact became two. One was the disaster itself, a hurricane, flood, or earthquake; the other was when the FEMA officials arrived on the scene. Then in the early 1990s, a new administrator was appointed, who introduced more autonomy and responsibility at local level. He greatly speeded up the claims process, the arrival of relief payments, and the processing of information. FEMA officials had traditionally arrived after a disaster to provide help and assistance. The new arrangements focused much more on a preventative strategy, through combining state agencies and local groups.

For instance, instead of waiting for a hurricane to hit, FEMA worked closely with local organisations to improve prior plans for evacuation. Partnerships were developed with construction firms to design houses that would be resistant to damage in natural disasters. FEMA moved, in other words, 'from a limited form of direct service delivery to a complex network-based approach that stretched from the federal government into state and local governments and the private sector'. The result was said to be a '180 degree turnaround' in effectiveness.

The notion of the ensuring state, as this example implies, presumes a different concept of *citizenship* from that formerly involved with third way thinking. The third way emphasises the active citizen – summed up in the principle 'no rights without responsibilities'. It was a crucial innovation, but we need to specify where the responsibilities come from. Do they come from the individual, or are they set by the state? One reason for a certain authoritarian element in some third way policy-making is that it has sometimes been assumed that it will be mainly set by the state.

We should instead speak of shared responsibilities, or what some have called the *co-production* of public goods. That is to say, there should be collaboration between the state and the citizen in the production of socially desirable outcomes. In the example given by Schuppert, good environmental policy is in the first instance a responsibility of everyone. How far people recycle paper, take to public transport, cycle or walk rather than use a car, and many other practices directly influence environmental goals. These goals in some part need to be set locally and collaboratively. Co-production should be taken to cover both the establishing and the implementation of policy. The state has the role of ensuring that a certain range of outcomes is achieved, but (as an ideal) through a process of local involvement and dialogue.

As David Halpern and Tom Bentley show, the issues surrounding such an approach to citizenship are complex. There are difficult problems, for example, in relation to the conditionality of citizenship obligations. Thus it is widely agreed that unemployment benefits should be conditional – but what mixture of incentives and sanctions should be used to produce effective and equitable results? As they point out, we cannot concentrate only upon the relation between the state and the individual. Individuals may have only limited capacities to produce desired outcomes – we must include social capabilities too.

Choice, Pluralism and Inequality

Choice and *competition*, where they can be achieved, are as important in public services as in the private sector. The possibility of choice, social democrats should accept, is always in principle desirable, since it is a measure of autonomy and freedom. Competition normally expands the range of available choices and has obvious economic virtues too. However we cannot treat goods such as education and health care merely as commodities; the mechanisms for expanding choice and competition have to be different from those of the marketplace. Moreover the public services also cover natural monopolies, where choice barely enters in at all.

Consumer choice in a market context is the very mechanism of both quality and trust. Public services cannot be merely another setting for the exercise of consumer choices, for they are defined in large part by their explicit connection to rights and responsibilities

Anthony Giddens

of citizenship. Choice depends more upon prior guarantees of trust and involvement than it does in the marketplace. Quality and trust in the sphere of public services have to rest more than in the commercial world upon the *integrity* of those who work in them, an integrity backed directly by appeal to democratic mechanisms. The public service ethos is not just a myth. Indeed, it is difficult to see how public services could supply what citizens want without it.

In the market sphere, I want to argue, the individual functions as a *consumer-citizen*. In market-provided goods and services, there is open competition and high product diversity. The consumer regularly and continually makes choices, although neither producer nor consumer acts as a pure market agent, since all market transactions relate to, and are affected by, wider aspects of the civic and regulatory environment. In the domain of public services, by contrast, the individual is more of a *citizen-consumer*. Greater choice and diversity have to be introduced into public services, but in the context of clearly defined public purposes. We have to show that *decentralised non-market models* can be created that are both equitable and responsive to consumer needs.[8]

The issues involved can be illustrated from the field of health care. Health care cannot be provided for in the open market because there is imperfect information for consumers to act upon. No one knows when he or she might fall ill, or what treatments might be required. The consumer cannot, as in an orthodox market, find the best products at the most efficient price. Hospitals cannot be allowed to open or shut at the whims of consumer demand. Although the private sector should play a role, even a fairly important one, health care must be based on a system of public insurance, however that might be structured, and a pooling of risks.

Yet it does not follow that such a system has to be centralised or uniform. Social insurance systems allow users to choose which GP, and to some extent which specialist, to see. Parallel choices can and should be introduced into tax-funded systems; diversity can be encouraged by devolution and the expansion of local accountability. Where a system has in the past been highly centralised, as in the UK, radical changes need to be contemplated. The Labour government is quite right to push for the devolution of budgets, the introduction –

18

and subsequent generalisation – of foundation hospitals, the tailoring of services to local needs, and the promotion of greater patient choice through walk-in centres and NHS direct.

In Scandinavia since the mid-1990s a range of schemes has been set up to expand consumer choice, including the use of vouchers.[9] Very few if any such schemes employ physical coupons. Rather, they involve user subsidies or special tax credits. Sweden and Denmark, for example, have both introduced vouchers for the disabled, with the Swedes leading the way. The voucher schemes make it possible for disabled people to hire their own personal assistance to allow participation in social and cultural activities outside the home. Similar arrangements have been introduced for elderly people, making it possible for them to choose between different suppliers of food, cleaning or washing. Coupons that are not used can be saved. The recipient is entitled to change providers at will. Vouchers are also used in education. In Denmark, for instance, public-per-user subsidies allow disabled children to attend schools of their parents' choice.

In public services that operate in monopoly or near-monopoly conditions, such as the railways, roads or fire services, efficiency and accountability by definition cannot be facilitated mainly either through choice or competition. These qualities have to be generated through a public service ethic, good management, democratic surveillance, and effective regulation. A fundamental emphasis here must be to prevent *producer capture*.

Public sector reform in practice is a battleground. It is one that pits left against left as much as left against right. Many on the more traditional left actively resist moves towards restructuring. They are last-ditch defenders of the centralised, bureaucratic state, which they see as an instrument of equality and protection of the public purpose. Quite often they have powerful allies in the shape of the labour unions. How should the centre left respond?

Two issues should be separated here. One is the relation between public sector interest groups and the public interest; the other is that between pluralism and inequality. So far as the first of these goes, social democrats must spell out the ambiguity of the word 'public' in 'public services'. 'Public services' actually means state-based services. As with other aspects of the state, it is an open question how far such services, and the actions of those who provide them, conform to the public interest. Public service workers form vested interest groups if they act in bad faith – if they use an appeal to public goods and values to advance or protect their own sectional interests. This is what the phrase 'producer capture' means. Leftists are also in bad faith if they endorse such a position. Of course, producer groups in the public services may seek to block change for good reasons, but if so these reasons have to be articulated and defended in the public domain. Difficult though it may be, neoprogs must be prepared to take on vested interest groups – even among their 'natural support-ers' – wherever such reasons do not apply.

Critics from the traditional left argue that pluralism and devo-lution should be resisted because they produce rising inequalities, particularly where they are coupled to greater consumer choice. But a compelling case can be made to the effect that exactly the opposite is true. Supposedly uniform systems turn out on inspection to be highly inequitable. In the UK, for example, which until now has had one of the most centralised health care systems, performance data show clearly that the poorest people get the worst services – and the least choice or control over how they are provided. The better off have more choice, since they can opt out of state-based provision.

Generalising choice means that poorer people get some of the same choices available to the more affluent. Choice can also improve equity, especially where an element of competition is involved, since it puts pressure upon the low-quality public providers that the poor are currently obliged to rely on. Finally, expanding choice and diver-sity is crucial to limiting middle-class opt-out. In the area of health care, such diversity should include the availability of options to pay for superior services. I would propose that we should look to create a social 'effort-bargain' between the more affluent and the underprivi-leged. I shall call this *controlled inequality*. What I mean by it is that we should accept some inequalities in order to prevent worse ones developing.

Affluent groups normally expect a higher level of provision, and a greater range of consumer choices, in the public service arena than those offered to the majority. They should be allowed to have them, within certain limits, because it is likely to be the price of their continued involvement with the public sector. It makes sense to allow for users to purchase special privileges should they wish to do so. Insistence upon bureaucratic uniformity is counter-productive, since the more privileged simply desert the state system – a consequence that not only heightens inequality, but is socially divisive too.

New Policy Perspectives

We need to rethink our policies in the area of welfare – this process should form a core part of our ideological breakout. Of course, the problems involved here are extensive, but two basic ideas suggest themselves from this collection. One is the need for social policy to focus far more than in the past upon the *life course*. There is more than one reason for this shift of emphasis. In societies marked by far higher levels of individualism than in the past people, rich and poor alike, have *life projects* that define their identities and aspirations. Policy-making that does not recognise and adapt to this change is likely often to miss the mark.

Just as important, many of the statistics upon which political thinking and policy-making rely are of the snapshot variety – they do not reflect, or even often even allow us to analyse, the different trajectories peoples' lives follow. We cannot design appropriate poverty strategies, for example, if we don't track how many people move in and out of poverty over periods of time. Recent research indicates that there is far more fluidity in most industrial countries than we used to think. Thus a study showed that 40 per cent of the population of working age in Germany have been below the poverty line at some point in their lives, although the large majority move out again after a relatively short period.[10]

A second, related idea is that, in looking for innovative strategies to combat inequality, social democrats should concentrate upon the persistence of *social inheritance* – the transfer of inequalities from generation to generation. We might even take as our slogan: abolish social inheritance! The aim might seem a wholly utopian one – until we realise that some countries, notably the Scandinavian countries, have already come close to achieving it.

The distribution of risks, and therefore the dynamics of poverty and social exclusion, have changed greatly over the past two or three decades. A generation ago, life careers were more stable and predictable. Most men expected a long working life, often spent in the same industry or same job. Women generally left the labour force at the birth of a first child, and most did not return. Welfare provisions were slanted towards the old.

Today, when much of this has changed, welfare risks are cascading down towards the young. Children, especially in single parent families or in workless households, increasingly make up a large percentage of the poor. Moreover, in most industrial countries, particularly in Europe, there is an alarming fertility problem, the birth rate in some societies having fallen to less than 1.2 children. The implications for future welfare funding, particularly of pensions, are fearsome. Esping-Anderson points out that this situation is not because people don't want larger families – surveys show that Europeans want on average more than two children per family. Their economic circumstances deflect them from this goal.

The new welfare risks, it is important to mention, are not only the result of economic globalisation. Some of the societies coping best with them, such as the Netherlands, Denmark or Sweden, are among the most open of industrial economies. They are the result also of the demographic patterns just mentioned, in combination with technological change.

In reforming the welfare state, Esping-Andersen argues, we should move away from income transfers and concentrate more upon the needs of families. We should focus in particular on the *employed mother*, since the large-scale employment of women is the single most important change affecting family structure today. The causes of disadvantage, especially in terms of social inheritance, today cluster around these family circumstances, as of course do problems of low fertility.

In third way thinking, investment in education was seen as the prime means of contesting inequality of opportunity. 'Education, education, education' was the watchword. No one would gainsay the importance of high educational standards. But the weight of the sociological evidence is that educational reforms do little to weaken social inheritance. We should therefore turn our attention to what happens in children's lives before they get to school, in their families of origin.

In Denmark or Sweden, social inheritance is remarkably low. Why? Their low levels of child poverty are certainly a factor. But the most significant influence is the almost universal system of day care for pre-school children. Investment in day care has multiple benefits, short- as well as long-term. It helps women get into work – and having a high proportion of women in work is the best protection against poverty, above all for single mothers. Moreover, it is also directly relevant to the fertility problem. Women have twice as many children in Denmark as in Italy, since the level of social and economic sacrifice is significantly lower. These considerations also point up the importance of policies for flexible working conditions. To make sure that parents are not denied time with their children, liberal and flexible parental leave provision is needed.

It might be objected that the Scandinavian welfare state cannot be reproduced anywhere else – Esping-Andersen himself has emphasised this point in his *Three Worlds of Welfare Capitalism*.[11] It is not just that tax levels are higher in Scandinavia than elsewhere, but that there are structural differences also from other welfare systems. How far other countries can duplicate what has been achieved in Scandinavia is of course questionable; but the proposed policy framework – concentration on working women, pre-school children, universal day care and work flexibility – forms a policy framework of relevance to a diversity of societies.

Although Esping-Andersen does not stress the point, concentration upon women and children does not mean ignoring the problems faced by boys and young men. However, young men are not helped by the traditional emphasis of welfare policy upon the male breadwinner. In impoverished areas they are becoming marginalised precisely because that role is no longer available to them. For them, too, early childhood experience is decisive, strongly affecting how far they can make the adaptations needed to achieve a different identity and outlook.

One should also stress that such an emphasis does not mean downplaying lifelong learning, or what I would prefer to call a politics of *second chances*. We have to be concerned not only with early

experiences, but with the many situations in later life where individuals have to overcome barriers and move on. In a society that has
become much more aspirational and fast moving than in the past, we
must try to ensure that people do not become locked into situations
from which they could and should escape. This principle applies to
schooling, personal relationships, unemployment, urban deprivation
and many other life circumstances. A politics of second chances has
to combine structural policy with the fostering of individual capacities. Thus it was a necessary step in educational reform in the UK to
abolish the 11+ examination. Those who failed the 11+ were essentially condemned to an educational ghetto – there was no second
chance of getting into the higher reaches of the educational system.
But success in education is also a function of motivation and cognitive skills. The importance of Esping-Andersen's analysis is that he
demonstrates how early on some of these traits are established and
how resistant thereafter they are to change.

Globalisation, Cultural Diversity, Technology

Globalisation, cultural diversity, technology – those who initiated
third way thinking can say: we were there first with these themes! A
concern with the nature and consequences of globalisation was the
driving force of third way revisionism. It is hard to remember now,
but in the late 1980s the term globalisation was not in wide currency.
Many, particularly on the left, doubted that the phenomenon is real.
To show their reservations, they used to put the notion in quote
marks. Some who were dubious about the reality of globalisation
have since declared themselves hostile to it, but very few now doubt
its significance.

Many of those who are 'in favour' of globalisation, and most of
those who are 'against', define the phenomenon in terms of the world
marketplace. We should recognise, however, that globalisation is by
no means wholly economic. Its origins, in my view, are not to be
found primarily in the economic sphere at all, but in the impact of
electronic communications – more accurately, in the marriage of satellite and information technology that dates from the early 1970s.

From this point onwards, instantaneous communication became possible from any part of the world to any other. Even the most iso- lationist regimes have found it hard to keep back the satellite dish, let alone the transistor radio. Different cultures are brought far closer together than ever before – producing that clash between cosmo- politanism and fundamentalism that is one of the distinctive features of our age.

Concepts for the centre left (2)

Citizenship as Co-Production – The sharing of responsibilities between the citizen and the state

Controlled Inequality – A social effort-bargain between the affluent and the underprivileged

Critique of Social Inheritance – Reducing the impact of inherited social in- equalities

Managed Diversity – A cultural effort-bargain between a host population and immigrants, with rights and responsibilities on both sides

---

Do third way policy makers need to revise their outlook towards globalisation? I would say yes – we need new ideas here too. We may have been there first, but a good deal of third way thinking about globalisation has also been too reactive – too influenced by the need to contest the 'Washington consensus'. We should form our own concept of and approach to globalisation today.

Many on the centre left have seen globalisation essentially as an external force, as a synonym for international relations – even as a synonym for issues to do with the developing world. But these em- phases are quite misleading. Globalisation is not a force that simply comes to us from the outside. We are virtually all participants in globalising processes – every time we watch television, turn on a computer or buy an item of clothing. Globalisation, in its various guises, is influencing the industrial countries just as much as the less industrialised ones. Most of the domestic issues we debate reflect it, as do the hopes and anxieties of citizens.

A key example is migration. Like globalisation itself, processes of migration at first sight look like a repeat of the late nineteenth and early twentieth centuries. There were as many people moving around the world then as now. But in both cases the differences are more important than the similarities. Current migration flows have different patterns from the past. A century ago, there was mass migration from Europe to the Americas. Today there is large-scale migration into Europe, especially into the countries of the EU. In the mid-1990s there were some 700,000 official immigrants into the US each year, compared to 1.2 million coming into the EU. A much higher proportion of immigration into both these continents is illegal than it was a hundred years ago – estimated at 500,000 a year entering the EU. Moreover, immigrants come from a very wide range of states, making the flows much more global than in the earlier period.

Just as importantly, migration has changed its very nature as a result of the globalisation of communications. Migrants at the turn of the twentieth century were forced by and large to cut themselves off from their countries of origin, as well as from the family and friends they left there. Modern communications, however, mean that many can keep in touch with their families or acquaintances almost on a daily level, or certainly when they need to. This fact is essential to understanding what immigration and cultural diversity now signify. Many immigrants are part of networks that cut across the national societies in which they find themselves. They may feel themselves part of religious or cultural diasporas covering wide swathes of the world. This point connects to what was said earlier about the life course and life projects: migration is not cut of a single cloth and cannot be reacted to as such.

Immigration and assimilation have of course emerged as core questions for the centre left, especially in Europe, given the rise of far right parties there. The questions raised for the centre left are well analysed by Nicola Rossi in this volume – I shall not pretend to cover them in any detail. Immigration is one of the main issues where the principle 'look for left-of-centre solutions to right-wing problems' applies. But it is yet another area where we should not be primarily reactive – and so far we have been. The agenda on immigration has been driven from the right, both from the far right and the more moderate right. It is also another field where the centre left could justly be accused of having little vision of the society it wishes to help create.

We should recognise that some of the worries citizens have about immigration are real. An influx of migrants can threaten the job prospects of indigenous unskilled workers, for example, in specific urban neighbourhoods. Where migrants are culturally distinctively different from locals, pre-existing habits and ways of life can come under strain. Yet many of the anxieties people have about immigration are not well founded – myths abound. For instance, it is not true that most migrants abuse the social security system, or place a major new burden upon it. Policy makers need to recognise and respond to these types of worries differently.

Managed diversity, the concept suggested by Rossi, is surely a helpful theme for the centre left. Today we must move beyond naïve multiculturalism. The way to do so is to relate the debate about immigration to that about citizenship. Legal migrants should have most of the citizenship rights of indigenous citizens immediately; but they should also be asked, or obliged, to accept a specific range of obligations too.

No one should suppose, of course, that such requirements are easy to spell out on the level of policy. As with citizenship more generally, there are problematic issues in respect of which specific political and legal decisions have to be made. The boundary lines between identity politics, universal morality and law, and national identity will always be to some extent contested. Should the veil, as a religious symbol, be banned in state schools, as has been proposed in France? Should there be sanctions, such as the potential loss of welfare benefits, to enforce the learning of the national language? How far should a liberal society be tolerant of those who openly question its codes (the dilemma raised by the populist politician and sociologist Pym Fortyn in the Netherlands)?

But the overall formula is clear. The good society should be understood as a cultural 'effort-bargain'. The host society accepts greater diversity, and recognises its energising qualities; immigrants have the obligation in return to learn core constitutional values and abide by them. Where they clash, qualities such as religious freedom, freedom of speech, and the equality of men and women, in principle override traits of cultural identity. It does not seem to me unreasonable to suppose that the degree of cultural accommodation asked of immigrants should be greater than that of the host population.

Global Tensions and Geopolitics

I agree with David Held that we need to create *global social democracy*. Our conception of social democracy on the global level must also be of a revisionist form. It should reflect many of the points made in the preceding pages. The theme of embedded markets applies on a global as well as a local level, and suggests a different model of development from free market orthodoxy. Contrary to that orthodoxy, as mentioned earlier, the state has almost always played a significant part in successful economic development. The cultivation of markets in a developing society involves far more than simply opening up its economy to global trade, since to function effectively a market economy presumes a surrounding framework of institutions. Economic growth in which poor people participate is the only known way of raising large numbers of people out of poverty, but it cannot happen through a focus on market forces alone.

Global social democracy, as Held makes clear, is not a utopian goal. There are short-term policy innovations that will promote it, as well longer-term transformations that we should hold in view. The former include, for example, making changes in the makeup and powers of some of the major international bodies, such as the UN and the WTO; the latter, the expansion of democracy above the level of the nation, the setting up of international tax mechanisms and the establishing of permanent peacekeeping forces.

On a geopolitical plane, there are quite fundamental issues that neoprogs must now face up to. One, of course, is the question of terrorism. We should recognise the differences between the *old* and the *new terrorism*. The first is familiar in Europe – in Northern Ireland, the Basque country and elsewhere. It is localised and has specific objectives, usually linked to nationalist aspirations. The new terrorism, by contrast, as Mary Kaldor rightly stresses, is geopolitical and it perpetrators have far more diffuse aims. It is closely linked to globalisation, drawing as it does upon the resources of global civil society and upon the latest communications technologies. Al Qaeda, for example, is in some respects very like an NGO. It has branches in many countries, with a loose top command structure, held together by a shared sense of mission.

Rohan Gunaratna's book *Inside Al Qaeda*, the best and most comprehensive study of the organisation, makes chilling reading. Al Qaeda, he says, 'is the first multinational terrorist group of the twenty first century . . . a world-wide movement capable of mobilising a new and hitherto unimagined global conflict'.[12] It will have no qualms about using chemical, biological, radiological and nuclear weapons against densely populated urban centres in its chosen countries of attack. According to Gunaratna, Al Qaeda can draw upon the support of 6–7 million radical Muslims across the world, some 120,000 of whom are willing to engage directly in terrorist activities. Its leadership is capable of meticulous planning, as was shown by the events of September 11.

Al Qaeda is by no means the only group of its type – there are other kinds of groups that could pose major dangers in the future. For instance, there are quasi-religious groups whose members include practising scientists whose skills could be turned to highly destructive ends. It is only relatively recently, especially of course since September 11, that we have become fully aware of the level of devastation asymmetric conflict could involve. The instruments of violence used, after all were simply aeroplanes, not even weaponry at all. Far more devastating attacks are conceivable.

It is certainly right to say that the main response to geopolitical terrorism must be multilateral. Nations and international organisations have to cooperate in the sharing of intelligence information and other measures. Yet the use of force or the threat of the use of force will sometimes be necessary. It is a capacity where the US massively outstrips every other nation or even group of nations. Many people on the centre left have in the past opted for what I would call an *easy multilateralism*. They have seen in the European Union a potential model for elsewhere – a form of cosmopolitan democracy operating above the level of the nation state. They have ignored the fact that the 'pacific transnationalism' of the EU has operated behind a defensive mantle of American military power – deployed not only within Europe itself, but in other parts of the world.

Whatever the rights and wrongs of the armed intervention in Iraq, it has brought this problem into sharp focus. It is important to stress that it connects directly with economic and fiscal concerns in the EU countries. European populations by and large are not prepared to accept increased taxation to pay for greater defence spending, nor are they willing to forgo some of their welfare benefits in order to do so. If there were greater economic growth, lowered unemployment – generating greater taxation revenue – combined with greater European military integration, the picture could look different.

Neoprogs should support the need for a coherent foreign relations strategy for Europe, and press for further integration of the EU armed forces. We should endorse a new role for NATO, sidelined by the US in the military campaign in Afghanistan and vulnerable to the accusation of redundancy. Following the Prague summit of 2002, progress has in fact been made in shifting NATO's stance, gearing up the organisation to face the threats posed by the potential spread of biochemical and nuclear weapons. Transatlantic cooperation is surely essential for the successful solution of global problems, and NATO a core part of such collaboration.

Concepts for the centre left (3)

Global Social Democracy – The application of social democratic principles above the level of the nation state

Hard-Nosed Multilateralism – Recognition of the role of force in promoting global collaboration

Predicting the Unpredictable – Coping with a world that regularly 'takes us by surprise'

Easy multilateralism should be supplanted by a *hard-nosed multi-lateralism*, which recognises that the threat or use of force will sometimes be necessary to advance the cause of cosmopolitan, liberal ideals. A multilateral outlook – focused on the UN – is more crucial than ever in an increasingly globalised world environment, but it must be one that has real purchase.

The administration of George W. Bush has explicitly pulled away from a multilateralist standpoint. According to the Bush security doctrine, the US reserves the right to act alone whenever it should deem it necessary to do so. It stresses power instead of negotiation, and effectively defines the global arena in terms of power interests. In the future, as Secretary of Defense Donald Rumsfield has proclaimed, the mission will define the coalition, not the other way around.

The doctrine is a dangerous one for the world community. Theory in international relations has the quality of a self-fulfilling prophecy. If the US defines global relations in terms of power, it is certain that others will do the same. Those hovering on the brink of nuclear capacity, for example, might very well push on to try to achieve it, whether they have previously signed up to non-proliferation agreements or not. Others might react by seeking to obtain ever more spectacular terrorist weaponry. Europe may to some degree be free-riding upon US military power. But the US, especially at the moment, is doing its own free-riding. Global cohesiveness depends upon a range of multilateral agreements, upon which the US relies, just as other nations do, but to which it currently refuses to sign up.

Here once more, the centre left seems to be tagging along behind the right. We seem again to be in a situation of saying, 'this is why you are wrong', rather than, 'this is how we would like to see the world'. The left has tended in particular to shy away from geopolitical questions, preferring to concentrate on familiar concerns with global poverty, environmental problems, and so forth. These, as it were, are held to be the 'true' causes of power divisions, conflicts and wars. There is a certain analogue here with how we used to speak about crime. Law and order was a more or less taboo topic. Crime reflected deprivation – deal with that, and crime will fade away. That view had to be adjusted, and the same should happen on the level of geopolitics.

Anthony Giddens

Predicting the Unpredictable

I come finally to the influence of science and technology, although certainly not because they are less significant than the preceding topics. Advanced military technology, concentrated in the hands of the US, after all is changing the shape of war. Science and technology more generally are altering our lives, on a global level, as much as any of the factors discussed in what went before. Moreover, environmental questions are closely and inevitably bound up with them.

I have left the topic until last because there is a general point I want to use it to make in conclusion, of which it provides especially good examples. It is that we have to learn to watch for changes coming *out of the side-field*. Social democrats come from a tradition that wanted to make the world more predictable and controllable. However, things are not turning out that way – we live in what I have described elsewhere as an erratic, runaway world.[13] Some of the most consequential events of recent years, including major technological innovations, have not been predicted by anyone. No one seriously anticipated the invention of the internet, and not even Bill Gates early on foresaw how great an impact it would have.

Perhaps more surprisingly, though, the same point applies to the social and political world. Scholarly experts spent their lives studying Soviet Communism, but no one predicted that the Soviet empire would fall as it did – almost overnight and with hardly any violence. No one fully anticipated the rise of the anti-globalisation movement, the East Asian crisis of 1998, or September 11. In the early days of the third way debate, there was much talk of thinking the unthinkable (a phrase that actually originated in the writings of the futurologist Hermann Kahn in the 1960s). Today we should speak of the need to *predict the unpredictable*.

I mean this point with some seriousness. We can't, of course do what the phrase says. But we can prepare to be taken by surprise. We can, in other words, learn to cope with unanticipated situations, because at least some of them will have a similar overall form. Consider, for instance, BSE – 'mad cow disease'. The British government at the time did not deal well with the episode, which cost the British economy an estimated £10 billion. A British minister actually went on TV with his daughter, who ate a hamburger to show that there was no reason for the population to worry about the disease attacking humans. It was as inappropriate a response as one could imagine. It presumed a certitude that did not exist. We have to get used to living with uncertainty and to coping with situations where we don't even know what we don't know.

These questions overlap very directly with environmental issues. It is sometimes assumed that we know what are the main ecological dangers that we face, but in fact uncertainty hedges around almost all of them. Consider, for example, the risks produced by the changes in agriculture happening worldwide. Farming in most countries, including the less developed, has become an enterprise in which huge tracts of land are given over to the cultivation of single crops. Fungicides and pesticides are sprayed over them in vast quantities. The so-called green revolution has helped save millions from starvation, but it has brought into being new dangers. Diseases from unknown sources have devastated crops in some areas – some have compared them to the advent of AIDS among human populations.[14] Moreover, crops have been bred in such a way as to create products that did not exist before. The bananas exported to the rich countries, for instance, are very different from those that originally grew in the wild. There is no mixing of genes as there was when many varieties of bananas grew in conjunction with one-another. The cultivated banana is sterile: farmers breed it through cloning. We know that the single crop banana is peculiarly vulnerable to insects and fungal diseases – farmers spray their crop with fungicides as many as fifty times a year. But no one knows what other consequences, short- and longer-term, might ensue.

As Rebecca Willis and James Wilsdon say, the traditional approach to uncertainty is to presume that experts have the answers to cope with new risk situations as they arise. In cases to do with disease, environmental problems, or technology, the experts are the scientists. We are used to invoking the authority of science. A positive attitude towards science is certainly essential. In many situations scientists alone can define what the problem actually is and what potential solutions suggest themselves. But often there will be inherent uncertainties and gaps in the state of our knowledge. We should adopt a new approach to risk, in which there is *acceptance of uncertainty, public involvement in decision-making*, and *the setting of decisions in a wider value context*. This approach can and should be anticipatory – as far as possible assessing ahead of time what possibilities and problems trends in scientific and technological development might create. And here, in conclusion, we rejoin the theme of co-production or collaborative citizenship. For assessing technologies 'will happen best if it is seen as a co-operative venture between people and government'.

Notes

1   Anthony Giddens, *The Third Way*, Cambridge: Polity Press, 1998.
2   T. H. Marshall, *Class, Citizenship and Social Development*, Westport: Greenwood Press, 1973.
3   Mark Granovetter, 'Economic Action and Social Structure: The Problem of Embeddedness', *American Journal of Sociology*, 91(3), 1985.
4   Joseph Stiglitz, *Globalisation and Its Discontents*, New York: Random House, 2002.
5   Stewart Lewis, *Corporate Brand and Corporate Responsibility*, MORI: MORI House, 2003.
6   Stephen Davis, 'The Civil Economy', forthcoming in the political economy issue of *Renewal*, Autumn 2003.
7   Donald F. Kettl: 'The Transformation of Governance: Polarisation, Devolution and the Role of Government'. Discussion Paper at Spring Meeting of National Academy of Public Administration, 1–3 June 2000.
8   Gordon Brown, 'A Modern Agenda for Prosperity and Social Reform', speech made at Cass Business School London, 3 February 2003.
9   Jorgen Abildgaard and Torben Vad, 'Can Vouchers Work for Health? The Scandinavian Experience', *Progressive Politics*, London: Policy Network, vol. 2, 2002.
10 Lutz Leisering and Stephan Leibfried, *Time and Poverty in the Western Welfare State: United Germany in Perspective*, Cambridge: Cambridge University Press, 1999.
11 Gøsta Esping-Andersen, *Three Worlds of Welfare Capitalism*, Cambridge: Polity Press, 1990.
12 Rohan Gunaratna, *Inside Al Qaeda*, New York: Berkley Press, 2002.
13 Anthony Giddens, *Runaway World*, London: Profile Books, 1999.
14 Mac Margolis, 'Crisis in the Cupboard', *Newsweek*, 9 June 2003.

1

The Embedded Market

John Kay

For most of the twentieth century, the left determined the language of political economy. Socialism defined the framework of debate, not only for its supporters but for its opponents.

With changing ideologies in the West, and the collapse of Communism in the East, the right has taken control of the argument. Globalisation and privatisation, not capital and class, are the terms of discourse. This is true both for those who favour these trends and for those who resist them. The claims of economic determinism and historic inevitability, once made by the left, are today made with equal strength by the right. Today, for its adherents, the version of market fundamentalism, which I describe as the American Business Model (ABM),[1] meets the same psychological need for simple, universal explanations of complex phenomena that Marxism once offered its supporters.

But the search for a new 'grand narrative' is misconceived. All modern societies that are economically successful are, in a broad sense, market economies: there are no exceptions to this rule. There are, however, many different types of successful market economy, and each is the product of its own particular history, politics and culture. The market economy is necessarily embedded in the social institutions of the society in which it is found, and cannot function outside the context of these social institutions.

John Kay

There is no end of history or any reason to think that the evolution of economic and political institutions has a unique destination, or any final destination at all. And the claim that the market economy of the United States has been substantially more successful than other market economies – specifically those of Western Europe – or that sustained and significant differences in performance have emerged in the last decade, does not bear even cursory scrutiny.[2]

The real lesson of recent experience is different. The dissemination of a facile and oversimplified model of how market economies function – the American Business Model – reached its predictable denouement in corporate corruption and the greatest speculative bubble in economic history. Both the process and the outcome undermined the legitimacy and effectiveness of market economies in the United States and abroad.

The American Business Model is a caricature which does not describe the real functioning of the successful American economy. Its fundamental weakness is that it does not acknowledge the central economic role of community, which is neither state nor market. We work and live in communities and we buy and sell in communities. The social values of communities are the principal regulator of economic life, and communities (not markets) are the primary mechanisms through which we handle the risks we encounter in daily life. The most important institution in the modern economy is the large corporation, and the successful large corporation is necessarily a community: a community of shared but not identical objectives. The politics of the corporation, like politics in society, operates best when it mediates these objectives into a common identity. If the corporation fails to achieve this it quickly ceases to be successful, losing both political legitimacy and economic effectiveness.

Communities (including corporations) do not themselves have objectives, though they do have functions. These functions meet (a subset of) the needs and aspirations of their members. Participation in communities is often one of these needs and aspirations in itself: we are social animals. Some of the communities that are important to our economic life are organisations – General Electric, Stanford University, the Transport and General Workers Union. Others are informal communities of shared values and interests[3] such as the City of London, the medical profession and Silicon Valley.

Communities of all these kinds are the mechanisms through which modern economies operate and progress. This is the economics of the embedded market, in which economic activity is conducted through social, political and cultural institutions. In an embedded market the attempt to define precise boundaries between state and market, and to impose a dichotomy between public and private action, fails to acknowledge the real and rich complexity of modern economic life.

The Boundaries of State and Market

The question 'what should be the boundaries between state and market' seems a natural starting point for any discussion of political economy. Implicit in this question is a belief that public and private institutions are of fundamentally different kinds. This difference mirrors differences in the character and motives of those who work there. Business people are risk takers, entrepreneurial but greedy: bureaucrats are risk averse, unimaginative but concerned for the public good. More extreme versions do not concede even a public service ethos to public servants, holding that government employees occupy their posts only because they lack the ability or energy to perform successfully in the private sector.

Given these fundamental differences in the character of public and private institutions, economic policy must assign different and clearly demarcated functions to each. The boundaries between state and market may be determined by regulation or by contract. Regulation may allow private, profit-making businesses to conduct activities – such as the provision of infrastructure and the production of public services – where the inevitability of monopoly and complexity had once seemed to require public ownership and control. Through contracts private profit-maximising businesses can be enabled to provide services that deliver public goods and private benefits.

This view of the nature of economic policy – that its primary purpose is to determine functions of private and public agencies appropriate to their different character – is today widely shared on both left and right. For the modern left, which recognises that direct state control of many commercial enterprises did not work well in practice, the implication is that detailed regulation of private business is needed to alleviate the many instances of market failure. The stance of the modern right differs from this only in believing that market failures are few, and that the potential weaknesses of regulation often outweigh the benefits of state action to correct these market failures.

However, the difference is one of degree, not of kind. Neither would find much to quarrel with in Milton Friedman's contention that:

> It is important to distinguish the day-to-day activities of people from the general customary and legal framework within which these take place. The day-to-day activities are like the actions of the participants in a game when they are playing it; the framework, like the rules of the game they play. . . . These then are the basic roles of government in a free society: to provide a means whereby we can modify the rules, to mediate differences among us on the meaning of the rules, and to enforce compliance with the rules on the part of those few who would otherwise not play the game.[4]

Indeed Friedman's framework is essentially that adopted by those who would substitute the goal of equality of opportunity for the traditional aspiration to equality of outcome. The state cannot ensure that everyone is a winner, but it can and must ensure that everyone comes on to a level playing field with an equal chance of success.

It seems unsporting to upset this apparent consensus. But there is not, in reality, the sharp distinction between the nature of public and private activities which this view of economic life entails. Because we live in communities, because our actions are guided by values as well as rules, there is no clear-cut division between state and market activities, or between the rules of the game and the playing of the game. To understand the reality of economic policy in an embedded market, we should begin by examining the changing functions of government itself.

The Purposes of Government[5]

The traditional functions of the state were to wage war, adjudicate disputes, and levy taxes to finance these functions. And government still does these things, but they are not now the principal things it does. The main role of government today is in the provision of goods and services, rather than the exercise of authority.

In the exercise of authority, the legitimacy of that authority and the propriety of the process by which it is exercised are fundamental. We want judges and policemen to follow the law, we want soldiers to obey orders, and we want tax inspectors to implement the tax code. But in the delivery of services, our primary concern is with outcome, not process. We want to send our children to good schools, we want the bus to come on time, the rubbish to go and the lights to stay on. We want to face retirement with confidence, and to get better when we are ill. The mechanisms by which these results are achieved are secondary. Most people are not very interested in how their hospital is run, just as they are not very interested in how their supermarket is run. Their concern in both cases is that it delivers the goods and services they want.

Systems of public management have largely failed to make the transition which this change in the nature of state functions requires. The process-oriented mechanisms needed for the proper exercise of legitimate authority are inappropriate for the effective delivery of goods and services. Judges could reach conclusions much more quickly and tax inspectors could collect revenue much more cheaply, but we do not want them to: we are concerned with how the result is achieved as much as with the result itself. But efficiency and effectiveness are the criteria we properly apply to the delivery of services.

This transition poses problems for both right and left. The right is suspicious of the state as provider of services, and wishes to limit that role: nervous of the role of government, it seeks to limit its extent by emphasising the traditional process concerns of the public adminis-trator. The left encounters a different problem, a legacy of the history of Marxist socialism.

The Legitimacy of Economic Power

Actions are legitimate if there is a good and widely accepted answer to the question 'what gives them the right to do that?' Working-class organisation and politics came into being around the issue of the legitimacy of the private exercise of economic power. The purpose of organised labour, in trades unions and political parties, was to challenge the basis on which private entrepreneurs exercised seemingly arbitrary authority over individuals and used their political power to reinforce that authority. The class struggle defined the roles of political parties and the nature of political rhetoric.

These arguments no longer have much resonance in rich Western economies. Geographic mobility and more flexible patterns of consumption, work and credit mean that competitive markets perform many of the functions which once seemed to require political action. If you don't like a job, or its pay, or its conditions of employment, you find another one. If the milkman waters the milk or the brewer salts the beer you can take your custom elsewhere. The organisation of labour and legislation to regulate economic activity helped to improve working conditions, secure product quality and fair prices: but so did competitive markets.

To the chagrin and eventual defeat of socialists, the market economy proved more effective in achieving these aims – a favourable working environment, the goods and services consumers want – than centralised political control. So in rich societies today attention has turned to the question of why the public sector's provision of goods and services cannot necessarily be relied on to produce the pace of improvement and responsiveness to changing needs that customers of private sector goods and services have come to take for granted.

Business has won legitimacy through success. We accept, even welcome, the authority of Sainsburys and Tesco in delivering our groceries because of the manifest effectiveness with which they have done this in the past. In ensuring food safety, consumers now have more trust in supermarkets, which are competing to sustain their reputation, than they have in government. There is growing concern about the undue influence of multinational companies.[6] Some of this is exaggerated, as in the frequent comparisons of the turnover of companies with the GDP of states.[7] But, to the extent that such concern is well founded, it relates to either the activities of such companies in third world countries – where neither workers nor consumers have the range of competitive options available in the rich West – or to the inappropriate exercise of political influence to advance commercial interests.

There is no similar resentment of the performance of supermarkets as they fulfil their mainstream functions of delivering groceries. This is because, in the main, we like what they do and there are alternatives if we do not. In a modern service economy, legitimacy may be earned by meeting our needs as consumers in a competitive market. What is legitimate is what works: and this is true in both public and private sectors. The traditional left position that the only source of legitimate economic authority is the ballot box fades away, and the conventional significance of the difference between public and private economic power disappears.

Motives and Functions

There is some truth in the stereotypes of the dynamic but self-interested businessperson and the public-spirited but ineffective public servant. But our objective should be to change these stereotypes rather than to build institutions around them.

Services of all kinds are best delivered by people who care about the quality of the service they provide. In the private sector, purely instrumental motivation is rarely successful in the long run. We seem to need to learn this lesson over and over again. We learned it in automobile factories where highly incentivised but boring work led to endless labour disputes and a workforce with no commitment to the final product. We have now begun to understand that complex incentive schemes for managers not only lead to fraud and rapacity but – as in those car plants – create destructive tensions within organisations.

An inappropriate emphasis on shareholder value has not only led to the destruction of great businesses like ICI and GEC, but to an environment in which banks and insurance companies have lost the confidence of their customers and the loyalty of their employees and in which pharmaceutical businesses look at pipelines largely empty of important drugs. Privatised monopolies, whose authority derives neither from democratic election nor success in a competitive marketplace, have not established the legitimacy they automatically enjoyed as public agencies.

Most people – in public or private sector – value material reward, but also value the respect of colleagues and customers, and the satisfaction of a job well done. Successful organisations – public or private – are those which effectively meet this variety of needs. In some public services – like health and education – it is particularly important to us that the service is delivered by someone who cares. These services[8] will be most effectively provided if we take advantage[8] of that ethos. But these are not substantially different from the qualities we seek in the delivery of privately provided goods and services. We learn to discount the synthetic 'have a nice day' of the fast food outlet and distinguish the smiling life insurance salesman from the trusted financial adviser.

Our purpose should be to elide rather than emphasise the differences between public and private sector organisations. In Britain and in some other countries there has been an almost obsessive attempt to shoehorn every possible activity into a corporate framework. Most of these artificial structures have subsequently failed – as in water, the railways, nuclear power and air traffic control.[9] At the same time, there is a requirement for new, more flexible organisational structures in health, education and other traditional public services. In Britain this has led to the reinvention, in a disjointed manner, of a variety of hybrid structures. We need, not two forms of organisation, but a spectrum adapted to the different kinds of services which are delivered and the different market environments and funding structures within which they operate.

The objective should be to substitute across that whole spectrum an ethos of service to the public as customers: an ethos which should replace both the instrumental motivations which are justifiably mistrusted in the private sector, and the emphasis on process over outcome still too often encountered in the public sector. This customer orientation is a major achievement of the more successful privatisations, although privatisation is neither necessary nor sufficient for this result. Public sector reform has brought about greater recognition that taxpayers should be treated as consumers in some functions – even tax collection – where privatisation is inappropriate and competition impossible.

The Origins of Innovation

We do not want our tax inspectors, judges and soldiers to be imaginative and innovative: we want them to conform to the rules and structures that have been established. But we do want these characteristics in our teachers and our doctors, and in the people who create and manage our transport infrastructure. The principal reason the private sector has a much better record of innovation than the public is not the different objectives of private and public organisations, nor the different kinds of people who work in them: it is the result of differences in the way these organisations are structured.

Centrally planned economies fell hopelessly behind market economies in consumer oriented innovation. The single voice of the planners failed relative to the disciplined pluralism of the market. Most innovations do not work, technically or commercially: most experiments fail. Large organisations, public or private, find good reasons not to embark on them. When they do, for motives which generally have a veneer of high rationality but in fact reflect a balance of political power, such innovations are undertaken on a very large scale. Feedback is poor, because decision-makers and those who report to them do not wish to hear, or pass on, bad news. The conflation of conflicting opinions into a single voice and the suppression of honest reporting – were common to the human disaster of Mao's Great Leap Forward and the commercial disaster of Britain's nuclear power generation programme[10] and are replicated, with less extreme consequences, throughout public sector organisations and large private businesses.

If the Great Leap Forward caricatures the failures of planning, the evolution of the personal computer industry exemplifies the successes of the market. Its central feature was a haphazard process of development which no one controlled. Almost all predictions of future developments were quickly falsified and most innovations – even those which ultimately proved key to the emergence of the industry we see today, such as the invention of the general purpose microprocessor, the graphical user interface, and the promotion of universal operating standards – were commercially unsuccessful for those who devised them.[11]

The process of disciplined pluralism, which allows continuous waves of incremental experiment and rapid feedback on the performance of that experiment, explains why we have the products we see today. The absence of such a process explains why, despite the Soviet Union's substantial capabilities in military electronics, no remotely comparable developments occurred there.

The difference is not the product of a difference in motivation – in practice, financial incentives seem to have played a rather minor role in major twentieth century innovations (and the financial rewards from them were correspondingly modest). The real issue is the contrast between planning and centralisation on the one hand, and pluralism and decentralisation on the other.

Disciplined Pluralism

We sometimes talk of the 'marketplace in ideas'. The metaphor identifies the most important characteristic of a marketplace: not the jingle of cash registers, but the effect of disciplined pluralism. In the marketplace for ideas new concepts are constantly floated, most of them wrong or foolish, all subject to assessment and evaluation. A few survive these tests, and knowledge advances. The modern marketplace for ideas evolved when the disciplined pluralism of scientific rationalism replaced the single voice of religious authority. It is not an accident that the development of disciplined pluralism in intellectual life was contemporaneous with innovation in commercial institutions. The co-evolution of technology with economic, social and political institutions has been the essential dynamic of Western societies since the Renaissance and Reformation.

Democracy itself is a marketplace in political leadership. Representative democracy acknowledges the need for political leadership and authority, but insists that the ideas which leaders implement and the authority they exercise is regularly contested. Ideological diversity and personal ambition provide the pluralism, the electoral process provides salutary discipline. The convergence of almost all developed societies on a democratic model which gives governments renewable tenure in office of four to five years illustrates the emergence of a particular form of disciplined pluralism through institutional evolution.

The competitive market for goods and services is the most familiar example of disciplined pluralism. By distributing economic authority, it allows free experiment in the manufacture and distribution of products and in the organisation of their production. The discipline comes from the interaction of the market for goods and services with the market for capital, which together cut off finance for experiments that fail.

The evolution of health care demonstrates two different models of disciplined pluralism. In pharmacology, we have competitive development of blockbuster innovations by corporations. The process is highly regulated and protected by patents and commercial secrecy. This is very far from the picture of a market established by the ABM: patent legislation creates an artificial but lively competition, discipline is provided by regulatory authorities and clinical choice. But it is a successful, if far from ideal, model of disciplined pluralism: by comparison, centrally planned economies performed very poorly in pharmaceutical innovation.

In surgery and treatment protocols, we have piecemeal innovation by individual practitioners and teams, with almost no formal regulation, and open sharing of methods and results in a peer review process. Both mechanisms of innovation work: a central problem of the management of health care everywhere is that organisational innovation does not keep pace with technological innovation.

The interaction of the intellectual pluralism of modern scientific thought, the political pluralism of democracy, and the economic pluralism of competitive markets, has together produced the co-evolution of institutions which is the basis of technological advance and economic growth. Anonymity is a common feature of all these mechanisms of pluralism. In the marketplace for ideas, the outcome is the verdict of many appraisers: in the marketplace for political leadership the outcome is the verdict of many voters, in the market-place for goods and services the outcome is the verdict of many consumers.

The anonymity of disciplined pluralism is infuriating to people who rail against the impersonality of market forces. And it is constantly challenged by those who would replace these competitive markets by monopolies – those in government who feel the need of the single voice.[12] Authoritarian figures on both left and right repeatedly try to dictate the course of scholarship, dominate political leadership, and control the evolution of their industries. For a time, some of them succeed. The price of progress is constant vigilance in support of free enquiry, democratic election, and genuinely competitive marketplaces.

There are many other examples of disciplined pluralism. Universities compete with each other to establish reputations. The pluralism of US higher education has massively outperformed the centralisation of Europe, and the discipline is provided, not so much through financial incentives, as by a competitive marketplace for the brightest students and the most capable faculty. This is but one example – from the not-for-profit sector – of how the disciplined pluralism involved in the creation of brands and reputations fosters innovation and raises standards. Doctors and museums, cities and sports clubs, compete with each other in similar ways.

The processes of disciplined pluralism are not necessarily fair. Priority in scientific ideas is often credited to the wrong person: the processes of peer review often reject the genuinely original. Only occasionally do pioneers in commercial innovation become leaders who build great businesses. Voters need give no reasons for casting their votes, and there is no appeal against their verdict. The absence of objective, transparent criteria is both disconcerting and important. A requirement to lay down the basis of assessment in advance necessarily runs into the common problems of socialism and regulated capitalism discussed more fully below. That basis of assessment can never be quite well enough specified. Those who are subject to targets aim at the targets rather than the objectives of the targets. We want good schools and, within a broad range, we know good and bad schools when we see them. If we knew exactly the characteristics of a good school, we would not need to entrust the task of establishing good schools to head teachers.

Disciplined pluralism is an evolutionary process. The extraordinary intellectual contribution of Darwinism outside biology itself was its demonstration that evolution could produce more sophisticated, and better adapted, organisms than could be created by design. But that analogy should be treated only as an analogy. Adaptation in institutions and in economic life is not random and the mechanisms of selection and the 'replicator dynamics' are different. Social evolution is more Lamarckian than Darwinian.

If you believe in disciplined pluralism, you believe in the merits of experiment and appraisal, but you are not confident in market outcomes, and you certainly do not assume that they are efficient simply because they are market outcomes. You worry about the concentration of too much power in the hands of Microsoft, because it threatens pluralism. You don't see a problem if one leading City of London investment bank is acquired by an American firm: you do see a problem if all are.

Decentralisation to local agencies will often be a means to pluralism, but it is not the same as pluralism, and sometimes local political control will be less pluralist than centralism. The requirements of pluralism would be better met by several autonomous state-owned hospital chains than by local monopolies of health care under local political control. If you believe in pluralism you want central government to undertake small-scale experiments – and you want it to be ready to acknowledge failure. The hallmark of successful centre-left government is what Franklin Roosevelt, probably its greatest exponent, described as 'bold and persistent experimentation'.[13]

Incentive Compatibility

It is a mistake to seek to establish a distinctive character for public and private institutions: rather we should inculcate the common virtues of disciplined pluralism in both. It is also a mistake to believe that we can define a clear boundary between state and market through regulation and contract. The attempt to decentralise social objectives in this way was pursued most extensively in the planned economies of Eastern Europe. To allocate scarce resources between competing ends – the central problem of any economic system – it is necessary to assess what it is possible to produce and what the needs of consumers and firms are. But almost all this information has to be obtained from the various proponents of the competing ends.

How can they be persuaded to assess it diligently and reveal it accurately? Most people are honest and well intentioned, and if you ask them for information they will give it. But they may discover that doing so is not to their advantage. If targets are set and resources allocated on the basis of information revealed, then you will do better if you are conservative about what is possible, pessimistic about what is needed and optimistic about the benefits which will result. But the people to whom you supply the information will realise you are doing this, and calibrate their expectations accordingly. This process became known as 'plan bargaining' in socialist economies.

No society in history offered such a wide range of rewards and punishments as the Soviet Union, from the economic and political privileges of the *nomenklatura* to the slave camps of the Gulag. The Soviet economic problem was not an absence of incentives: incentives to conform to the dictates of the centre were very strong. The Soviet economic problem was that the planners did not have good information on which to base their direction.

It was on these twin problems of information and incentives that the Soviet economy foundered; and the information problem is the more fundamental. If a powerful state could accurately calibrate both abilities and needs, it could enforce production according to abilities and assignment according to needs. That is what the Soviet state sought, and failed, to do. 'Plan bargaining' was not confined to the Soviet Union, though it was endemic there. 'Plan bargaining' is found in any planning system: in government regulation of business, in the control of public services, and in the management of large private sector organisations. When regulators supervise utilities, when governments set targets for schools and hospitals, they face the same problem: the information needed to determine the targets appropriately is held by people in electricity companies, in schools and hospitals, not people in government departments.

Lenin claimed to have found the answer to this problem: 'seize the decisive link'.[14] Because the information required to control the system completely is extensive and impossible to obtain, the centre must focus on a few supposedly key variables. But these are subject to 'Goodhart's Law'[15] – any measure adopted as a target changes its meaning. If hospitals are judged by the number of people who wait more than 12 months for an operation, then the number of people who wait more than 12 months for an operation is likely to fall, but whether the service given to patients is better or worse is another matter altogether. If corporate executives receive bonuses related to earnings per share, then reported earnings per share may rise, but whether the business is better or more valuable is, again, another question.

The inevitable result of these processes is the complication and proliferation of targets. These become confusing and inconsistent, and undermine the authority and morale of those who engage in the activities which are being planned. The problems of incentive compatibility – the desire to provide information that will yield personal advancement rather than information which is true – undermines the process of rational decision-making within the planning system itself. This is the common experience of everyone who has worked within a large centralised organisation.

Regulated Self-regulation

The fundamental problem of incentive compatibility (conflicting objectives combined with imprecise and distributed information) explains why the provision of public services, or the pursuit of social objectives, cannot be decentralised through a process of tightly defined contracts, except in narrow areas where outcomes can be precisely described and methods of achieving these outcomes are obvious and widely accepted. This view of contractualisation and decentralisation matches the experience of the private sector itself. General Motors would once distinguish sharply between customised components whose production the company must itself control, and commodity purchases which could safely be outsourced from the cheapest supplier – until Toyota demonstrated that better product quality, faster,

John Kay

leaner production, and a more flexible response to changing market conditions could be achieved by looser trust relationships among a *keiretsu* of favoured suppliers. The manufacture of complex products in a modern economy has become possible only by making permeable the boundaries between firm and market. The delivery of complex services in a modern state will be possible only by making permeable the boundaries between state and market in a similar way.

The traditional distinction between policy and implementation is therefore one which, in economic matters, can rarely be made. The idea that relationships between the state and other agents must be transparent, precisely defined, and non-discriminatory, which still, for many people seems a fundamental requirement of public administration – is incompatible with flexibility, innovation, discretion and judgement. Trust relationships are, necessarily, the product of social relationships in communities rather than legal structures.

This poses a challenging agenda. How to achieve for government the relative informality of commercial relationships between firms which is the real basis of the successful market economy, without opening the door to the corruption and arbitrariness which the legal regulation of relationships between the state and private sector is intended to prevent? The worst outcome – and a current danger – is to construct relationships between government and private firms which are formal in appearance but informal in substance: the elaborate contract is renegotiated, or set aside, whenever it comes under pressure from the inevitable occurrence of unpredicted events.

Relationships between state and market are therefore neither simply nor mainly matters of law, regulation and contract. The atmosphere in which they are conducted is critical. Economic policy is not simply, or primarily, a question of what the government should do. Government is simply one of the means by which the social context of the embedded market is expressed. Concepts such as reputation and legitimacy are equally important expressions of that context and play an equally central role in regulating economic activity.

So statutory regulation and self-regulation are not alternatives. In a properly functioning embedded market, they are complementary. Law generally can only be enforced in a democratic society if it corresponds to the behaviour most people would engage in, or at least

50

wish to see engaged in, anyway. And this is even more true of economic regulation, which cannot function by bullying recalcitrants into submission: its objectives are too complex and its subjects too sophisticated for such mechanisms to be very effective. The collapses of Enron and WorldCom were reminders, if reminders were needed (they clearly were), that detailed prescriptive rules cannot constrain those who have no intention of being bound by their substance rather than their letter. When the young Alan Greenspan wrote that 'at the bottom of the endless pile of paperwork which characterises all regulation lies a gun',[16] he was talking nonsense: if economic regulation requires a gun for its enforcement, it will inevitably fail.

We cannot achieve truth in accounting reports or securities prospectuses by rules unless these rules are internalised by private business themselves. Without elements of external regulation, self-regulation rapidly degenerates into self-congratulation – as it has in professions such as law, accountancy and medicine – but external regulation on its own can never fully secure the information or display the adaptability needed to achieve its purposes. In the financial services sector, as in others, the most powerful vehicle of regulation is mutually supportive reputation – respected traders deal only with respected traders, and confer that respect grudgingly. This mechanism was allowed to unwind in the last two decades when maximum greed within minimal rules became the credo of the market economy.

Conclusions

It is time to be humble about economic policy. It is chastening that the experience of the deliberate coordination of economic systems and of economic development demonstrated that such state coordination was generally worse than no coordination at all. The experience of economic planning under social democracy is no more encouraging, if perhaps less calamitous, than the experience of economic planning under Communism. The fundamental, and intractable, problem is that such intervention presupposes knowledge of the economic system and economic environment which no one can validly claim to have. These claims are as empty when made by the visionary leaders of private businesses whose superior insights are confirmed by their large salaries as when they come from politicians whose superior knowledge of the course of future events is established by their victory at the ballot box. Those who do claim to have such knowledge are less worthy of our trust than those who recognise the limits of human understanding.

The correct lesson to draw is that the modern market economy, necessarily embedded in a social, political and cultural context, is a sensitive instrument whose functioning we understand only imperfectly. If the dismal experience of planned economies is illuminating, so is the dismal experience of New Zealand: the country which from 1984 to 1999 followed the liberal prescriptions of the ABM more vigorously than any other developed economy, and enjoyed the worst macroeconomic performance of any developed country over the same period. The lesson of Soviet failure is not that the Marxist vision of economic organisation redesigned on entirely rationalist lines was the wrong vision, but that any attempt to implement grand economic designs is likely to end in failure.

Economic policy is properly subject- and context-specific. The institutions that are right for electricity generation are not the same as those that are right for water supply. The mechanisms of regulation appropriate for financial services are not the same as those for food retailing. But the key themes of this chapter – the role of community in supporting economic life, the absence of a sharp distinction between the nature and functions of private and public business, the overriding requirement for disciplined pluralism in every area of economic life which involves the delivery of services, and the necessity of the interaction of rules and values or 'regulated self-regulation' in the control of economic activity – provide some general principles for the development of a political economy relevant to the government of market economies for the 21st century.

Notes

1 For a more detailed account of this see Kay, J. A., *The Truth about Markets*, London, 2003.

2 See for example, Turner, J. A., *Just Capital: The Liberal Economy*, London, 2001, or his Queen's Prize lecture (http://cep.lse.ac.uk/queens/).
3 The interests referred to here encompass three different senses of interest: concern, subject or hobby, advantage or profit. Not coincidentally.
4 Friedman, M., with Friedman, R. D., *Capitalism and Freedom*, Chicago and London, 1962.
5 Osborne, D. & Gaebler, T., *Reinventing Government*, Plume, 1993.
6 Monbiot, G., *Captive State: The Corporate Takeover of Britain*, London, 2000; Klein, N., *No Logo*, London, 1999; and Hertz, N., *The Silent Takeover: Global Capitalism and the Death of Democracy*, London, 2001.
7 There is a simple economic confusion here between turnover and value added. But the more fundamental weakness of the comparison, which is directly relevant to the comparison here, is that states exercise a monopoly which corporations largely function in competitive markets: thus neither turnover nor value added is a real measure of power (including economic power).
8 This word is chosen carefully. The benefits are – and should be – shared between the individuals who provide, the customer who receives and the government which finds. Too much emphasis on any one of these stakeholders – as in all contexts – jeopardises the benefit to all.
9 For a more extensive discussion of the successes and failures of UK privatisation see, Kay, J. A., 'Privatisation: A Policy in Search of a Rationale', in *Economic Journal*, 96, March, 18–32, or in *Privatisation and Corporate Performance* ed. D. Parker, Edward Elgar, 2001.
10 Kay, J. A., *The Truth about Markets*, London, 2003.
11 *Ibid*. The development of PCs is discussed in chapter 9.
12 Cited in Henderson, P. D., 'Two British Errors: Their Probable Size and Some Possible Reasons', in *Oxford Economic Papers*, vol. 29, issue 2, 1977.
13 Rauch, J., *Demosclerosis: The Silent Killer of American Government*, Times Books, 1994.
14 Kornai, J., 1992, *The Socialist System*, Oxford, 1992.
15 'Any observed statistical regularity will tend to collapse once pressure is placed upon it for control purposes'. Goodhart, C., *Monetary Theory and Practice: The UK Experience*, London, 1984.
16 Alan Greenspan quoted in Rand, A., *Capitalism: The Unknown Ideal*, New York, 1967.

2

The Ensuring State

Folke Schuppert

The aim of this chapter is to identify some of the general guidelines for public sector reform and renewal, rather than to discuss the reform of particular public services in detail. This analysis is set out in five stages. First, I will discuss the philosophy of public sector reform and outline some general guidelines for this by developing two key concepts: 'shared responsibility' and the 'ensuring state'. Second, the chapter will analyse public service renewal as an approach to structural reform by evaluating how we might break up decrepit structures and design new intelligent ones that foster progressive politics. Third, I look at the concept of the 'ensuring state' as it applies to theories of 'regulatory choice'. Fourth, the chapter discusses the general patterns for centre-left reform politics. Finally, I conclude by presenting my views on the challenges of the 21st century and the possible progressive responses to these.

The Philosophy of Progressive Politics

If we are to revitalise and renew progressive thinking there is no better way to start than by articulating a positive reform message and forging a distinctive agenda. Over the coming decade, centre-left politics must define itself positively and make clear what it stands for, not what it stands against. If this renewal is going to have electoral success, then the ideas and principles underpinning our programmes must be communicated to the electorate in a manner that captures both their hearts and minds. This message will only be successful if it strikes an emotional cord with the voters.

In Germany, the government has started down this road with the publication of Agenda 2010. In the UK, it is taken as given that public service reform is at the heart of New Labour's programme. In many developing nations across the world, progressive governments are getting to grips with building the kinds of institutions that will provide the most basic of social security for their citizens. There is, then, a broad consensus about the necessity of reform (especially of labour market policies, social insurance and the health system). Unfortunately, as yet, there does not seem to have been a message that strikes the necessary emotional chord. Citizens have yet to jump aboard the 'reform boat'. The charismatic Willy Brandt once won office under the slogan 'daring more democracy'. This slogan was effective because it meshed together two positive ideals: democracy and looking bravely to the future. It inspired people to believe we could move beyond the status quo toward a better world.

In 2003, as a substitute for Brandt's progressive slogan, I would propose the slogan 'shared responsibility for common values'. In contrast to the philosophy underpinning the 'minimalist state', this slogan presents a positive ideal and invites people to take part in a common endeavour – the search for greater social justice and the exercise of common responsibility for the common good. Two central concepts underpin the message this slogan presents: shared responsibility and the enabling state. Let me address each of these in turn.

Shared responsibility

As its starting point, shared responsibility presupposes that responsibility for the common good is not a responsibility wholly monopolised by the state. That is to say, in a liberal and pluralist society the responsibility for the common good is divisible, no one person or agency has a monopoly over this, and all must take part in setting the political agenda and implementing public policy.[1]

The idea of 'shared responsibility' requires that we develop criteria to determine how different sectors can share resources and design organisational and procedural structures for the division of labour in carrying out public objectives. A useful example that will help illustrate how this concept may be used in practice is shared responsibility for the protection of the environment. The actors and their respective responsibilities in this field could be summarised as follows:

- *The protection of the environment is the responsibility of every citizen*
  In Germany, for example, the general public on the whole feels obliged to sort their rubbish into different coloured waste containers for recycling, and takes this obligation very seriously.
- *The protection of the environment is the responsibility of the business community*
  Clearly, the manufacturers and retailers of environmentally harmful products have a particular responsibility to protect the environment, but more generally in this field organisational arrangements representing different combinations of responsibilities and actors have mushroomed. Various 'hybrid' institutions have emerged which transcend the traditional distinction between and border of the public and private sectors. One such example is the 'dual waste collection system', which mirrors the dual responsibility structure in the field of waste collection (cooperation between municipalities and private firms like glass or plastic-producers). A second example is the 'Ecological-Audit-System', also a good example of the regulatory approach dubbed 'regulated self-regulation', which I discuss below.
- *NGOs, such as Greenpeace or Oxfam, have a lobbying and watchdog responsibility*
- *The protection of the environment is the responsibility of the state*
  While the state clearly has a responsibility to regulate internally within the domestic space, given the transnational or global dimensions of many environmental concerns, the action of the state in this field is increasingly intergovernmental in this area. One could

argue that a new progressive agenda for state responsibility must be increasingly intergovernmental and multilateral, as exemplified by the Kyoto Treaty for example (see Rebecca Willis and James Wilsdon's, and David Held's chapters in this volume).

Other examples of how the principle of shared responsibility works in practice could include public private partnerships (PPPs) in the field of security, conflict and dispute solution models such as arbitration proceedings, and contemporary approaches to law making, in particular the increased importance of standard setting committees.

The ensuring state

The key concept that I want to propose for the appropriate role of the state is what can be called the 'ensuring state'. The concept develops, but is significantly different from, the idea of the 'enabling state' that has been central to much of the thinking that has guided state reform during the last two decades; in particular those reforms inspired by New Public Management theory. The 'ensuring state' emphasises the responsibility of the state in areas where non-state agents play a dominant role in the provision of public services. It argues that there exists a public responsibility 'after enabling' and that there are certain guarantees that the state has a moral and political responsibility to provide. Even if public goods or services are provided by private or third sector organisations and bodies, the state still has a major role in ensuring these goods, whether it is by audit, regulation or funding.

Periodic democratic elections do not cut the ties between government and citizen. Rather, in everyday life, where public goods are being delivered, that relationship is continual and ever present. Concepts such as 'shared responsibility' and the 'ensuring state' recognise this, and argue that the progressive left should carefully consider what structures, institutions and frameworks are both able and likely to deliver public goods in the complex and diverse societies of the 21st century.

Underpinning this idea of the appropriate role of the state is what Anthony Giddens has called 'publicisation' (see his introduction to this volume). Box 1 summarises the scale and range of the state's responsibilities.[2]

Box 1: The scale and range of state responsibilities

The state's performance responsibility

The state's standby responsibility

The state's ensuring responsibility

The state's performance responsibility refers to its responsibility to provide those public goals that it has sole responsibility for (nationalised public services via state-driven bureaucracies, for example). In general, these are services financed by public monies (taxes) or consumer fees.

The state's standby responsibility refers to the responsibility of the state to provide public services where the market fails.

In comparison to these two categories, the state's ensuring responsibility sits on the border between the public, private and third sector, and applies to situations where services are delivered via public private partnerships or not-for-profit companies. If the state is providing public services via private agents or PPPs it is still responsible for the performance of these services, and thus has a duty to monitor these policies.

The concept of the ensuring state:

- does not call for the 'retreat' of the state
- takes for granted a continuing state responsibility for the common good
- rejects the idea that changes in statehood reduce state responsibility

An ensuring state must recognise that changes in statehood actually imply changes in the modes, style and instruments of governance, not a rejection of responsibility. The ensuring state thesis argues that progressives should strengthen mechanisms of governance by working in partnership with society, and thereby encourage citizens to jump aboard the reform boat.

The Ensuring State

This concept is not merely a fashionable or stylish label, it is a concept with the potential to resonate with the changes our societies and states are currently experiencing. As Wolfgang Hoffmann-Riem asserts:

> The concept of the ensuring state does not claim a sudden change of statehood, but a gradual one. In important areas, the state remains responsible for the carrying out of public purposes. But the state reduces its own performance responsibility step-by-step, trying simultaneously to share the burden of performance by cooperation with private actors. The point is to balance out the different intense contributions of public and private actors, in brief: the responsibility sharing between state and non-state actors.[3]

However, the ensuring state not only mirrors processes of change in the appropriate role of the state, it is also a guiding principle that signals our intention to harness the self-regulatory powers of civil society. As Claudio Franzius asserts:

> [The] aim (of the ensuring state) is, to use private engagement for the common good. Public purposes are – as everyone knows – not necessarily state purposes. They could and should also be carried out by private actors. From this point of view a state is a modern state, if it is activating private capacities and is making possible the performance of public services by providing appropriate regulatory structures. The ensuring state wants to be the state of civil society.[4]

Perhaps one of the best illustrations of the usefulness of the idea of the ensuring state is its approach to the issue of privatisation. Here, two key questions are of utmost importance: First, how can one say with any precision what the limits of privatisation are? Second, how can one measure public sector performance without damaging professional autonomy?

The concept of the ensuring state is able to answer each of these questions because it approaches privatisation as a process, one in which the state is still at least partially responsible for the consequences of the act of privatisation itself. The ensuring state is responsible for the consequences of privatisation in at least three particular ways:

- the obligation to install a monitoring system for the performance of privatised public services
- the obligation to install, together with the non-state providers, a system of quality control and quality management
- the obligation to make sure that in the case of performance failure a return-option can effectively be successfully implemented

With these principles in mind, the question of the limits of privatisation are displaced, at least to the extent that this is no longer an issue of defining limits in the sense of clear cut boundaries. The privatisation of public services, or services of general interest, cannot be justified if it is impossible to install a regulatory regime (standards, proceedings etc.) or guarantee a performance compatible with the public good.

The second question, however, emphasises the need to reconcile professional autonomy and performance measurement. There exist many examples in the social and public services where both public authorities and third sector welfare organisations agree on standards and instruments of quality control. Progressives should learn from these.

The legal framework:
enabling, structuring, and limiting

Cooperative endeavours, in which a sense of shared responsibility for the achievement of public goods has been established, are still likely to require a regulatory framework that encompasses the organisational, procedural and financial aspects of this cooperation. This form of cooperation is unlikely to arise spontaneously, as if some 'invisible hand' were at work.

The necessary legal framework must have three elements: enabling, structuring and limiting. In each of these fields we are dealing with the creation of new forms of action, organisation and regulation. I will return to this below.

Progressive Politics as Structural Reform

The terms reform and restructuring have been in vogue for quite some time now, adorning the pages of almost every academic and political journal. Structural reforms are now commonly regarded as a precondition for effective and efficient public services. But what do we really mean by structural reform? In my opinion it is helpful to distinguish between two aspects of this phenomenon: the removal or breaking up of decrepit structures and the design of intelligent structures to put in their place.

Breaking up decrepit structures

If we are to create innovative solutions to social and political problems we have not only to design intelligent structures for progressive politics, but also to break up or remove decrepit structures that prevent the implementation of progressive governance. As Fritz Scharpf notes, often these structures do little more than protect 'the past gains of distributional coalitions against policy change'.[5] Such organisational responses are obviously closely related to one of the most important political questions progressives have to face: How should we deal with interest groups in the public sector that block change?

To approach this problem in a systematic way it might be useful to give some consideration to three organisational arrangements that are typically unsuitable for policy changes and innovative solutions. In federal political systems, such as the European Union, the importance of unanimity often leads to a continuation of earlier policy choices. Similarly, it is often noted that the composition of Reform Commissions can be crucial to the outcome of reform projects. Finally, the presence of corporatist structures in policy fields where clearly divergent and conflicting interests are present can pose particular problems. In the German health care system, for example, a set of strong and well-organised corporate actors is present. Any health care reform will, therefore, necessarily require the reform of those structures obstructing policy change.

Designing intelligent structures

If we are to emphasise in this brief outline the importance of 'structural design' we have to discuss the function of law in structural reform and the role of 'organisation' and 'law concerning administrative organisation and proceedings' as instruments of modern governance.[6]

In the ensuring as well as the enabling state, the function of law is not primarily as an instrument of command and control; it has to be a form of law that makes cooperative endeavours towards improving public welfare possible. In this sense, the law of the ensuring state is a facilitating law and has to be thought of as an important tool of intelligent governance.[7]

In addition to creating cooperative endeavours for the advancement of the public good a legal framework for the division of labour in the provision of public services has to serve as an instrument of coordination and control, and as a tool of structuring and limiting cooperative action. The best example of a legal framework serving both functions – facilitating on the one hand, and structuring and limiting on the other – is perhaps the task of regulating PPPs.

Where PPPs are concerned, we need a regulatory framework for the cooperative action of state and non-state actors consisting of four constituent elements: qualification and selection, guidance and control, evaluation and learning, and option for taking back. These principles are outlined in Box 2.

Box 2: A regulatory framework for PPPs

Qualification and Selection of the Private Partner
Evolution of a fair, transparent and competition-oriented selection procedure

Guidance and Control of Service-Performance
Development of methods and instruments for ensuring the agreed standards of quality. Design of proper contracts including rights of information and control for public officials.

Evaluation and Learning
Before cooperation starts all participants have to agree on the criteria for measuring service performance and to take part in periodic evaluations.

Effective Option for Taking Back Services by Administrative Agencies
In the case of unsatisfactory performance on the part of private providers, there should be an option to take the service in question back under the responsibility of a public agency.

The Ensuring State as a Regulatory State

At its heart, modern governance means the business of regulation –
simply because without installing an appropriate regulatory framework, the ensuring state will not function.

If the changing role of the state is to be described in terms of
categories of responsibility, ranging from performance to ensuring
responsibility, this move must be accompanied by a regulatory framework. We need a mechanism that allows a switch between the state's
performance responsibility and its ensuring responsibility. This new
form of responsibility changes the style and instruments of public
policy, but does not abandon the obligation public authorities have
to guarantee the effectiveness of privatised or partly privatised public
services.

Before we address the central tenets of a theory of regulatory choice,
I would like to discuss briefly the interrelation between different types
of states and different types of regulation.

Types of states and types of regulation

In their seminal text, James March and Johan Olsen[8] argue that a
correlation between different types of states and different types of
public administration exists. Indeed, if one examines this relationship
with regard to the so-called sovereign state, the 'supermarket' state,
and the 'corporate bargaining' state models, such a claim would
appear justified.

The sovereign state refers to those states in which Weber's classic
hierarchical bureaucracy is the most fitting characterisation of the
public administration. For the 'supermarket state model', the most
appropriate form of public administration is that driven by the spirit
of entrepreneurship. Here, public agencies act in competitive sur-
roundings: 'from an administrative culture to a service culture'.
Finally, in the corporate bargaining state, public agencies no longer
act in the political process as actors with a mandate to govern society,
but rather as mediators, brokers or managers: an *'état catalysateur'*
corresponds to an *'administration catalysatrice'*.

I propose to apply this way of thinking about the relationship between different types of states and their corresponding public administrations to our analysis of the form of law-making and regulation appropriate to the ensuring state. As an example, we shall look very briefly at the cooperative state – a type of state frequently discussed in the 1980s – and its cooperative structures of law-making and law implementation.

Cooperative law-making occurs mainly in two forms: as bargained laws (for example, the law relating to abandoning nuclear energy, which was adopted verbatim from a contract negotiated between the German Federal Government and the nuclear plant owners), and law drawn from voluntary agreements.

Putting such laws in concrete terms is a matter of cooperation. For example, in the case of the aforementioned agreement between the German Federal Government and the nuclear plant owners, the security standards to be observed are defined by standard-setting committees which consist of representatives of public authorities, the nuclear industry and scientists with experience in this field.

This form of law is also quite common as a method of resolving disputes. If state and non-state actors quarrel over the appropriate interpretation to attach to a vague legal term such as 'economically reasonable', working towards an agreement through discussion is often more effective than seeking the court's view, which could take five years or more to decide.

It is with this example in mind that the chapter will now assess the main political questions facing the ensuring state as a regulator. Here, three particular questions arise: What are the aims of regulation and who defines them? Who are the regulators? What are the appropriate instruments of regulation?

The first question here relates to the legitimacy of the goals of regulation. The aims of regulation can be varied, and different regulations may potentially conflict with one another. In most cases (as in the case of telecommunications) there are at least two aims: to ensure an infrastructure throughout the country at reasonable prices, and to promote competition and efficiency. As this example shows, regulation should not be understood as standing in simple opposition to markets and competition. On the contrary, regulation has to reconcile the demands of acting in competitive markets with the requirements of the public interest.

The second question relates to the relevance of particular actors. A choice, of course, has to be made between special watchdog regulatory agencies – as in telecommunications – or general regulatory agencies, such as the monopolies commission.

The third question relates to compliance with regulation. When regulating, a choice has to be made between different types that could be used – ranging from 'soft law' and incentive structures, to regulation of the command and control type (see below).

To answer all these questions we need to develop a theory of regulatory choice.

A theory of regulatory choice

It is quite common when discussing the appropriateness of different forms of regulation to judge these in terms of effectiveness or organisation fit.[9] However, when we discuss how we should regulate, only very rarely do we attempt to distinguish between different 'producers of law'. We must, therefore, add to our theories of instrumental and organisational choice a discussion of the evolution of a theory of regulatory choice. It is only by supplementing existing approaches with a sensitivity to the evolution of regulation that we will be able to evaluate the appropriate regulatory regime for any particular problem. Here, we can work with a very simple range of types, presented in Box 3.

Box 3: Types of regulation

Classical hierarchical regulation

Regulated self-regulation

Self-regulation

The most interesting type of regulation identified above is 'regulated self-regulation', as it represents the most appropriate form of regulating the complex relationship between the public, private and third sector in today's societies. The reform of public services should, for example, be accompanied by modernised law-making. According to the concept of 'legal pluralism', an approach that has evolved since the internationalisation and globalisation of the nation state, a theory of regulation has to give guidance in situations of 'regulatory choice'. New forms of regulatory regimes – like 'Co-Regulation' at the European level – might help this form of 'governance with society' to evolve.[10]

Risks, Responsibility Sharing, and the Enabling State

To discuss the problems of reforming all public services exhaustively in one chapter is an impossible task, not simply because the range of services is so broad, but also because the differences from country to country can be so vast. The problems of health care, for example, differ very much from country to country: while decentralisation of hospitals in response to the bureaucratic nature of the National Health Service is proposed in Britain, re-centralisation is the solution in an overly devolved French system.

It seems more sensible, then, to look for problems common to all countries, developed and developing, and to identify a specific, centre-left approach to resolving them. From this perspective, a crucial problem of all modern welfare states is how to deal with risks: risks to health, risk of unemployment, and so on. The classic answer of the welfare state has always been to establish a public insurance system. The ensuring state began life after 1890 as Bismarck's insuring state, the classic solution to the so-called 'social question', with the establishment of compulsory insurance. However, these insurance systems seem to be at breaking point, and so we are now forced to question whether the traditional burden-sharing needs to be replaced by a new package of rights and responsibilities.

As a guiding principle for unpacking this 'new deal', I will use the concept of shared responsibility to identify a progressive approach to three distinct areas: health risks, consumer protection, and unemployment.

Risks to health

Today, experts estimate that some 90 per cent of health risks could be controlled or reduced by individuals themselves.[11] One could say that everyone should be his or her own health minister: everyone decides alone, whether and to what extent he or she smokes, drinks alcohol, has unprotected sex, eats rich food, avoids exercise, etc.

For health care policy does this mean that the health care system has to encourage self-responsibility?

The answer to this question is, of course, yes. Public policy should thus be more active in communicating social and health risks to citizens through public awareness campaigns. This could be complemented by a system of incentives to promote healthy behaviour, including a fairer balance of insurance costs and benefits depending on one's own degree of personal responsibility. Recent developments in this direction include verbal contracts between patient and doctor.

Consumer protection

In the field of consumer protection, a widely discussed issue since the BSE crisis, progressives need to find a balance between the responsibilities of the consumer, the food producer and public agencies. A first step in consumer protection policy must be to encourage the responsibility of the consumer. On the one hand, consumers should have the responsibility to use consumer advice services. On the other, it is also important that the state enables consumers by giving them the right to claim information from the food producers themselves (possibly through a Consumer Information Act). If we take responsibility sharing seriously, the second step would be to oblige the food producers and food retailers to establish a compulsory standard and norm setting system (i.e. a system of regulated self-regulation). The task of the public agencies in this system would be to monitor the efficiency and effectiveness of this private system, and to give guidance to consumers on how to make use of their rights.

Folke Schuppert

Employment risks

A progressive approach to employment risks, as Tom Bentley and David Halpern address in their contribution to this volume, must identify a fair distribution of responsibilities between the social insurance system, the employer, and the individual in or seeking employment. How long should we pay unemployment benefits for? What is the appropriate contribution for the employer to pay? What kinds of jobs and types of work can individuals be obliged to accept? The boundaries between these spheres of responsibility – as these questions demonstrate – must be flexible and have to be redrawn anew. It is in the redrawing of these boundaries that the frontiers of the ensuring state will be determined.

In short, in whichever area it is applied, the principle of shared responsibility entails the search for a new balance of rights and responsibilities. Risk-sharing is not a question of 'either or', but a problem of drawing anew the 'borderlines' between the spheres of individual actors' responsibility in a specific policy field. In most cases a responsibility mix will already exist. The new balance will thus inevitably entail mixed organisational arrangements, whether in the form of a mix between private and public insurance, state regulation and self-control, etc.

The European Dimension of Governance

From a European perspective, any discussion about the appropriate regulatory framework for public services increasingly has to take into account that public services operate in a competitive surrounding – the Single European Market. The classic nation states are Europeanised states, belonging to a multilevel political system.

The Europeanisation of the nation state

Member states of the European Union are Europeanised states. To get a perspective on the degree of this Europeanisation one only has

68

to carry out two tests. Firstly, one can assess the degree to which Europe, or rather the European Union, is implicated in the formation of policy in a given area – ranging from the drafting of informal guidelines for employment, to much more prescriptive polices in agriculture, for example. The second test looks at the amount of European law present: nearly one third of all domestic laws, for example, are the result of European level directives. Reforming the public sector therefore has to take into account the European framework within which nation-state politics operates.

Services of general interest in Europe

A series of guidelines, issued by the European Commission, concerning 'Services of General Interest in Europe' form an integral part of this framework. These guidelines seriously limit the discretion of member states when it comes to the organisation of 'their' public services, especially for those countries orientated to the concept of 'public service' such as France, Italy, or Germany.

The message of these guidelines is clear, namely that the design and organisation of these public services have to appear to represent the principle of proportionality. The European Commission's Communication explicitly states that:

> [It] has to be ensured that any restrictions to the rules of the treaty, and in particular, restrictions of competition and limitations of the freedoms of the internal market do not exceed what is necessary to guarantee effective fulfilment of the mission. The viability of the service of general economic interest must be ensured and the entrusted undertakings must be able to carry the specific burden and the extra costs of the particular task assigned to them. The Commission exercises this control of proportionality, under the control of the Court of Justice, in a way that is reasonable and realistic. This is confirmed by its prudent use of the decision-making powers conferred to it by Article 86(3) for the application of Article 86.

It is, therefore, clear that progressives must define their own position, and embed public service renewal in a process that allows the appropriate balance between competition and the defined public interest to be maintained.

Progressive Responses to 21st-Century Challenges

The blurred boundaries between states and markets, public and private

If we are to successfully rise to the challenges the 21st century will present, it is only reasonable that we begin with an honest assessment of the principal characteristics of this century. Only then can we begin to think about the possible consequences of this changing order, and our own responses to them. In his contribution to this volume, John Kay claims that the following characteristics are the dominant features of 21st century society:

- Blurred borderlines between states and markets
- The presence of a variety of state and non-state actors (i.e. architectures of pluralism)
- An increasing role for intermediate institutions

For each of the dominant characteristics Kay identifies in the economic field, one can find an equivalent in the field of public administration and constitutional law. These are:

- Blurred borders between the public, private and third sector
- The presence of a variety of state and non-state deliverers of public services
- An increasing role for hybrid/intermediate institutions as halfway houses between the private and public sector

If we are to respond to these developments effectively, we must develop a new common language, vocabulary and concepts that help us to make sense of them. If we fail to develop this language, we will be unable to find adequate solutions to these challenges.

Challenges ahead

If blurred borderlines between state and market and the public and private sector are among the key features of 21st-century society, it would not be appropriate to think in terms of dichotomies of state and market, government and society, public and private sector, or state and non-state actors. What we need for dealing with the globalised new century are sector-crossing concepts. This is one of the central messages of this chapter and, I believe, John Kay's too. We should therefore investigate, if only briefly, what they offer in terms of crossing-cutting analytical tools and concepts. I propose that there are four potential concepts that could be used in this way: regulated self-regulation, public private partnerships, shared responsibilities, and the ensuring state. Each of these are summarised in Box 4.

Box 4: Sector-crossing concepts

Regulated Self-Regulation
In place of external public regulation, progressives need to promote internal regulation, and thus transfer the transaction costs of controlling and monitoring from the public to the private sector.

Public Private Partnerships
Progressives need to establish a framework for PPPs by offering a selection of organisational and procedural options or models.

Shared Responsibility
There are now a plurality of state and non-state actors who contribute in quite different ways to the delivery of public goods and services. To help define the share of responsibility and accountability that each should hold we need a script of 'shared responsibilities', what John Kay calls 'disciplined pluralism'.

The Ensuring State
Progressives need to stake out a new role for the state, one that goes beyond both the privatised 'minimal state' and the 'enabling state'.

The terms and concepts identified above should help provide the vocabulary for a renewed progressive approach to 21st-century challenges. It will be the task of politicians and experts alike to make sure

Folke Schuppert

that they are transferred successfully into their respective national settings.

Notes

1 Schuppert, G. F., ed., *Jenseits von Privatisierung und 'schlankem' Staat. Verantwortungsteilung als Schlüsselbegriff eines sich verändernden Verhältnisses von öffentlichem und privatem Sektor*, Nomos, Baden-Baden, 1999.
2 See Hoffmann-Riem, W., *Modernisierung von Recht und Justiz. Eine Herausforderung des Gewährleistungsstaates*, Frankfurt a. M., 2001.
3 See Hoffmann-Riem, W., *Modernisierung von Recht und Justiz. Eine Herausforderung des Gewährleistungsstaates*, Frankfurt a. M., 2001.
4 Franzius, C., *Der 'Gewährleistungsstaat' – ein neues Paradigma der Staatstheorie?*, unpublished, 2003.
5 Scharpf, F., *Decision Rules, Decision Styles and Policy Choices*, Max-Planck-Institut für Gesellschaftsforschung, Discussion Paper 3/88, 1988.
6 Schmidt-Aßmann, E., Hoffmann-Riem, W., eds, *Verwaltungsorganisationsrecht als Steuerungsressource*, Baden-Baden, 1977.
7 Franzius, C., *Gewährleistung im Recht. Vorüberlegungen zur rechtlichen Strukturierung privater Gemeinwohlbeiträge am Beispiel des Umweltschutzes*, European Centre for Comparative Government and Public Policy, Discussion Paper 36, 2002.
8 March, J. and Olsen, J., *Rediscovering Institutions: The Organisational Basis of Politics*, New York and London, 1989.
9 Hood, C., *The Tools of Government*, London and Basingstoke, 1983.
10 Kooimann, J., 'Social-Political Governance: Overview, Reflections and Design', in *Public Management*, 1999.
11 I am grateful to Jonas Store for bringing this fact to my attention.

3

21st-Century Citizenship

Tom Bentley and David Halpern

Introduction

The distribution of responsibility between state, individual and communities remains perhaps *the* key battleground between the left and right. It is of crucial importance that relations between citizen, community and state are structured in ways that will both sustain and advance the progressive movement. Western societies are characterised by social diversity, moral pluralism and organisational complexity. The challenge to the centre-left is to harness these qualities to the execution of progressive political strategies. To achieve this goal, we must reconsider the balance of rights and responsibilities between states, citizens and communities.

The distribution of rights and responsibilities is fundamental to two basic dimensions on which the progressive strategy rests: the reach, impact and legitimacy of *public intervention* by the state itself, and the extent to which citizens can expect to make claims on each other, especially in relation to questions of social equity, or the distribution of wealth and opportunity. This distribution tends to be *embedded* in institutions, social norms and constitutional traditions. Determining and creating the right combinations of the two is much more difficult than simply clarifying the principle and selecting a policy tool; it must also involve developing cultures and institutions which can sustain the combinations in complex circumstances over time. This aim requires a mix of long-term thinking, political narrative and strategy, democratic engagement, policy entrepreneurship and public-service leadership. All of these allow the very different energies of our societies to combine in ways which produce collective outcomes and cumulative progress. This chapter addresses how such strategies might be shaped around an emerging concept of 21st-century citizenship.

A coherent, progressive settlement of rights and responsibilities could help to provide:

- A language of ethical choices and limits which is recognisable and legitimate to citizens
- A framework for policy choices which helps to put goals and methods in a broader context and enables different elements of governance and policy to work in concert with each other and with informal norms and expectations. A connection between citizens' everyday experiences and the workings of democratic systems, so often criticised for being 'disconnected'
- A route for re-energising trust in politics and the legitimacy of political action

Too often, citizenship has been understood in terms of static and formal constitutional structures. Today, progressives must combine these traditional underpinnings with a new emphasis on culture and participation, on dynamic institutional adaptation, and on informal, self-organising social systems if they want to harness the power of citizens to produce lasting political solutions.

There is no shortage of challenges requiring collective solutions. The problem is that politics needs new tools with which to bring together disparate constituencies and persuade them to behave in ways which make collective solutions possible.

To do this, we have to go beyond traditional notions of citizenship. Progressives must draw on energies, commitments and knowledge that have become more widely dispersed and fragmented. But seeking only to satisfy personalised expectations, or to meet the demands of fragmented interest groups and shifting, media-based coalitions, can seriously limit what government or politics can achieve. Tackling deep-seated inequalities, reshaping communities or public service organisations, and addressing new global challenges all require sustained long term effort, and often call for serious changes in people's everyday behaviour. In this sense, the success of progressive policies relies even more on creating a sense of shared responsibility to motivate certain kinds of behaviour, and to generate causes and identities with which people are willing to engage.

If most citizens withdraw from political systems as a means of change, the capacity of politics to influence society drains away. The main losers from this process are those who are already disadvantaged, excluded or discriminated against. They are the least well-equipped to adapt successfully to change around them, and to compete in newly competitive marketplaces. They are also the most likely to be subjected to imposition or coercion by others, including the state.

Combined rights and responsibilities could be a potent set of tools with which to reshape the civic context in which individuals and governments operate. But to achieve this potential, they must be developed and implemented in novel ways. Learning how to do this, by building and revitalising institutions, influencing social and civic culture, and developing new practices for democratic deliberation and decision-making, is therefore fundamental.

The most important implication of this argument is that a progressive rights and responsibilities agenda over the next decade should focus less on determining the direct relationship between individual and state, and more on cultivating the conditions under which *relations between citizens*, often through intermediary institutions, can reflect the right combinations of entitlement, obligation and mutual respect. The role of the family and family policy is central to this set of issues, as Gøsta Esping-Andersen also emphasises in his contribution to this volume.

In policy terms, this means a very strong focus on creating choices for citizens which produce a combination of *private benefit and public good*; that is, which meet the increasingly personalised needs and demands of individuals, but in ways which actively renew the public goods on which individuals depend to thrive. This challenges the centre-left to get beyond the stale dichotomy between 'market' and 'collective' systems of public provision, and into a sharper and more nuanced set of policy choices and strategies.

We should be focused on how diverse, pluralised systems of service provision can be configured to encourage and reward norms of wider public value and fairness. Very often, this has to be achieved through interaction between the formal, institutionalised systems coordinated by governments and the informal, intangible systems of production and exchange which families, neighbourhoods and communities generate for themselves.

There are awkward questions to be addressed about diversification of public services; it is not automatic that an agenda focused on 'choice' will be capable of maintaining social equity or even of delivering better average service outcomes. But the left has to overcome its distrust of diversity and find new ways to generate tangible public value under current conditions if it is going to sustain credible political projects.

Connecting the rights and responsibilities agenda and the *renewal of democratic engagement* and governance *is the* overriding priority. At the core of both should be a conception of citizenship which is broad enough to encompass social and economic participation, and flexible enough to be meaningful under new and diverse socioeconomic conditions. In other words, giving practical meaning to citizenship and citizen responsibility in various settings may be central both to the effectiveness of progressive public policies, and to relegitimising collective action and progressive politics.

The rule of rights

Respect for rights depends as much on the informal behaviour of others in society as it does on enforcement by the state. In other words, rights are tied to the capacity and willingness of others to respect those rights, or to exercise responsibility.

But in social, political and constitutional terms, the last century (especially its second half) has seen rights used as the dominant tools of advancement for progressive causes, especially as they have been translated concretely into governance and institutions.

Box 1: Progressive values in a modern context: liberty, equality, solidarity

To offer a basic level of security and social fairness which equips each individual to develop and contribute his or her full potential.

To promote and enable forms of collective action which contribute to the overall vitality and fairness of society as a whole.

To create countervailing institutions which limit the power of the state, the majority and the market, and align the energies of capitalist wealth production with human need.

This has meant:

- Creating democratic and constitutional rights including the vote, freedom of information, and rights of free speech and association
- Creating and embedding workers' rights in labour law
- Ensuring social rights to minimum provision and insurance against risk: through the welfare state
- Guaranteeing civil rights against discrimination and unequal treatment, used especially as a tool of empowerment to release specific social groups from oppression or exclusion
- Ensuring personal rights to make choices over one's own life

Many of these rights are ancient, but it is only in the last half century that they have become genuinely universal, at least in law.

Perhaps most significant in this period, however, is the creation of a Human Rights framework. The Universal Declaration of Human Rights was a deliberate attempt to establish a body of values and expectations that was genuinely universal, and was part of a wider re-shaping of transnational governance: the Bretton Woods economic institutions, the UN, the new European Community (see David Held's chapter in this volume).

The Universal Declaration focused more explicitly on civil and political rights, while the Bretton Woods institutions emphasised social rights. But for now, the basic point is that the creation and enforcement of rights, through legislation and judicial protection,

77

has been the primary vehicle for institutionalising the progressive values discussed earlier.

Our legal and governance arrangements have not found ways to embed and enshrine responsibilities to others with the same degree of force. Concepts of 'duty' or 'obligation' have often been either associated with conservatism, or based on more organic and informal sources of authority; the left has relied on the family, occupational communities and broader social solidarity to provide the reciprocity and concern for others needed to make individual rights work in practice.

The modern welfare state was essential to the post-war progressive vision of how individual rights could combine with social cohesion and fairness. It relied essentially upon the bureaucratic management of collective life. It is striking that many of the post-war transnational institutions, from the European Commission to the UN, rely on the same kinds of governance structures to attempt coordination and policy coherence, although as institutions they have had to invent their own wider civic context, rather than operate in one which already exists.

The post-war social democratic settlements

All this matters because progressive politics depends both on the form of the state and on wider social culture to achieve outcomes that reflect its core values.

The social democratic settlements of the post-war period translated collective priorities into social reality by creating economic and social rights served by an expansive, vertically organised administrative state and institutionalised social partnership, legitimised by the machinery of 19th-century liberal democracy.

Key characteristics of these settlements included:

- A drive for high and stable levels of employment
- Income and wealth redistribution
- Welfare states based on universal basic entitlements and a range of services based on contributory financing
- Investment in tangible public goods and services: public transport and utilities, health services, schools, etc.

alongside:

- Party-based electoral competition
- Separation of constitutional powers
- Independent press and judiciary
- Permanent, non-partisan and professional public administration

The social roles and responsibilities of citizens were not a fixed or a guaranteed part of the settlement, and wider processes of change have helped to erode or unravel them.

The two great challenges to post-war institutions have come from the neo-liberal attack which used economics to challenge the moral basis of social equality; and from social change undermining the stability of social roles, and cohesion from which collective priorities emerged. In both cases, the attack has been partly fuelled by the success of earlier progressive settlements; bringing wealth and freedom to the majority, and encouraging liberation from traditional social and community hierarchies.

At the same time, the organs of international co-operation, the UN and other post-war transnational governance institutions, have helped to develop layers of global governance which enmesh both nation states and other organisations in rules and rights cutting across their borders. National governments, their executives and those acting under their authority, such as armies, can be challenged under law to respect individual rights, in cases ranging from discrimination at work to war crimes. But as many are painfully aware, these cross-cutting systems of rights and duties are only partially evolved, and the challenge for global governance is not just to extend the moral and legal coverage of these frameworks towards universality, but to build institutions and governance systems capable of making them work in practice.

Many on the left and beyond have made human rights the major focus of efforts to tackle discrimination, poverty and oppression. But the extent to which governance based on human rights has enhanced the capacity of societies to sustain progressive arrangements is very much open to debate. Critics argue that the interpretation and enforcement of human rights has become primarily an activity for lawyers and judges, often with negative side-effects and sometimes playing more into the hands of the powerful and privileged than the disadvantaged they were intended to protect.[1]

The result of these two sets of trends has been that, while the centrality of rights in governance has become entrenched, with many positive effects, the capacity of societies and governance systems to combine them effectively with rules and norms which sustain equivalent systems of responsibility has been diminished.

Challenges to the Progressive Settlement: Diversity, Complexity and Interdependence

A triad of powerful drivers – wealth, knowledge and diversity – are challenging traditional social forms, and with them many of the bonds and institutions which have sustained social fairness.

Wealth and the privatisation of consumption (economic individualism)

Over the last century, wealth in industrialised societies has roughly doubled with each generation. This affluence has freed most adults from direct dependence on others to meet material needs, and therefore from having to negotiate and cooperate with others in many domains of their lives.

The growth of affluence helps to explain the weakening of extended family ties and the traditional family, as husbands, wives and extended kin are no longer bound together by economic necessity. In most industrialised societies, family forms are far more diverse than a generation ago.

Rising wealth has released new aspirations and priorities, notably the emergence among younger generations in wealthier nations of 'post-materialist values', emphasising social objectives such as freedom of speech or personal expression alongside material comfort. This wealth-driven culture shift poses a direct challenge to the one-size fits all, top-down model of public services and our concept of rights and responsibilities.

Growing wealth has brought with it contradictions and tensions too. Privatised lifestyles increasingly come up against the 'social limits to growth', such as in transport, housing and the environment. The more we buy second homes, extra cars, and live in sprawling estates, the more we may be destroying the very goods we had hoped to acquire. Similarly, the more we use our affluence to escape from the 'inconveniences of others', the more we may risk cutting ourselves off from the positive satisfactions of the social world around us. Affluence poses challenges not only to the mass progressive settlements of the post-war era, but also to individuals as citizens and consumers.

Knowledge and communication: the growth of complexity

The post-war period has seen a spectacular growth in the volume and accessibility of information and knowledge. Information and communication technologies (ICTs), falling communications costs, and the cumulative impacts of increased educational participation have all led to a 'democratisation' of information.

One result is that the information needed to make decisions is more widely distributed. The presumption of privileged information held by government no longer holds – with 24-hour TV and worldwide media, the public often has access to much the same information as heads of government. Expert citizens and a powerful media pose challenges for traditional models of technocratic, top-down policy-making.

More subtly, our knowledge of causal processes is increasing constantly, and precipitates a myriad of difficult choices for both individuals and governments. We are increasingly able to predict who will live or die, who will have a high or low income, and who will be happy or miserable – and also what determines these outcomes.

A generation ago, an expectant parent would know little about their child-to-be. Today, they can know the child's sex, whether it has defects in its vital organs, and the probability that it will suffer from a wide variety of possible conditions. Similarly, we know about how diet, smoking and perhaps even stimulating the foetus will affect the child-to-be. Gradually, a whole series of choices – and therein responsibilities – have emerged for society and the parent-to-be. Growing knowledge – and our growing ability to measure, monitor and analyse – is sharpening our attributions of individual responsibility in health, the workplace, and civil society. Ignoring this knowledge is not an option, at least for progressives with concerns about social justice.

Sharpening attributions do not necessarily lead to attributions of higher personal responsibility. Insights from new knowledge sometimes show us that individuals are not causally responsible (e.g. crime was once said to be caused by organic degeneration) and sometimes that responsibility is real but collective (e.g. global warming). Greater knowledge rarely leads to simpler decision-making, and the trend towards individualism, perhaps paradoxically, reveals new forms of interdependence and shared responsibility as much as it personalises aspects of life that were previously collective.

The growth of knowledge and information itself adds to the complexity of the causal web, as human behaviour changes in response to new information and creates further interactions and feedback loops. Central authorities cannot fully predict or control the outcomes of their interventions. The range of possible outcomes and permutations of response is increased exponentially by the growing interconnections between populations through various kinds of networks.

Moral entrepreneurship and social diversity

Another defining feature of our societies, driven by the trends we have described, is social pluralism or diversity. Key features of this diversity include:

- The increasing ethnic diversity of modern societies
- The increasing fluidity and complexity of individuals' social identity and affiliation
- The association of social progress with 'liberation' of the individual
- And the steady decline of attachment to traditional institutions and collective identities

People are progressively less likely to behave according to homogeneous group identities, 'moral entrepreneurship' – the mixing and matching of different moral values by individuals – is increasing. In other words, it is no longer possible to easily predict an individual's stance on one issue from their values on another.

Politically, this shift also coincided with the emerging focus of political action in the 1960s and 1970s towards civil rights and equality expressed through anti-discrimination laws and 'empowerment' strategies. Social movements looked for political progress beyond the fixed ideological or institutional frameworks of formal politics, using them as vehicles for specific issues, but also using wider forms of mobilisation, campaigning and legal dispute as tools of emancipation.

One result of this complex social mix is that political mobilisation is increasingly difficult for the traditional institutions of party politics: more and more people eschew party identities, decline to vote and distance themselves from formal politics. Overall, people trust government less in general, and are less prepared to accept received authority in any institution.

The most dynamic forms of mobilisation are increasingly the preserve of network and protest based movements; whether campaigning against the effects of globalisation and corporate behaviour, or resisting the loss of traditional and protected ways of life.

Combined with rising inequality, this diversity has either eradicated or put under extreme pressure many of the institutions and informal norms on which social cohesion, insurance against social risk and civic obligation have relied.

Redistributing Responsibility

Progressive governments all begin by articulating policy goals which emphasise social equity, from the UK's policy of increasing low incomes, to Brazil's current creation of a food and anti-poverty programme. Some critics argue that the ambition of such objectives is too modest, but in the short term this is beside the point. The real challenge is to combine them with approaches which encourage active responsibility among citizens, in order to make the policies more successful in themselves and to strengthen the civic context in which further efforts might be undertaken.

The central insight is that security, in the social and the physical sense, has to be woven out of interdependence, rather than control. The challenge is to link it with a positive agenda for opportunity and well-being which is crafted from the increasingly diverse aspirations of citizens.

How can this be done? Several approaches can be distinguished, each with its advantages and limitations.

Codifying responsibilities: reasserting responsibility through state–citizen contract

One way is to make individual responsibilities more explicit; for example, making welfare benefits dependent on participation in re-skilling or job search programmes, making parents legally punishable for their children's non-attendance at school, or enforcing 'anti-social behaviour' orders on residents who infringe their neighbours' quality of life.

But this strengthening of the contract between individual and state does not solve the wider problem; it simply formalises and polices the negative boundaries of behaviour, and relies on the state's capacity to enforce individual cases in order to have any impact.

The idea that the state can clarify the limits of its own responsibilities, in part by formalising the personal responsibilities of citizens, is attractive for various reasons. It could lead to clearer and more legitimate principles for the rationing of scarce public resources, for example in health, education and welfare. But to do so it has to strengthen the capacity of citizens, communities and public institutions to reinforce positive forms of behaviour and share resources effectively, rather than simply allocating entitlements in formulaic ways.

Without this kind of capacity, simply adding more explicit conditions to the receipt of public resources, for example through 'behavioural contracts' in education and healthcare, is likely to have regressive effects, precisely because it will fall hardest on poor and disadvantaged people. Just as significant, the implication of the state becoming further involved in making 'micro-judgements' about individual behaviour creates its own problems of organisation and legitimacy.

Collective responsibility: investing in self-governance

Another approach is to recognise the limits to demanding individual responsibility in isolation from the wider social context, and concentrate instead on encouraging communities to generate their own solutions to shared problems. Under the collective responsibility approach, a central strategy of government becomes empowering communities – though not necessarily geographical ones – to govern themselves and shape the allocation of public goods and services.

This could mean, for example, devolving responsibility for service management and priority setting to local governance, and creating new subsidies and support for specific communities to develop their own health, education or crime reduction strategies. It could involve recognising the special claims of different ethnic or faith communities and giving them collective discretion over the ways in which services such as education or housing are delivered.

Such an approach recognises the extent to which factors like trust, social capital and informal community support influence social outcomes, and therefore the limited leverage which many individuals have over their own circumstances, without factoring in the wider social environment.

It would mean a shift in public policy priorities away from detailed intervention or service improvement strategies, and towards devolution of operational control to various kinds of community.

The problem, however, is that as a dominant principle it is as likely to exacerbate inequalities between communities as it is to reduce them. Policy-makers now recognise the huge influence of informal social factors in determining the outcomes of public interventions. But far less is known about how to build social capital through public strategy. Furthermore, better-off communities and neighbourhoods tend to have richer reserves of social capital as well, meaning that locating collective responsibility within different communities risks simply reinforcing structural inequalities. It is a sobering observation for progressive policy-makers that in the US the level of social trust in different states and communities can be correlated with historical differences in social capital among the societies from which migrants originally came. Thus Minnesota, with its high levels of Scandinavian ancestry, enjoys markedly higher trust and social capital than comparable areas. A simplistic strategy of 'letting go' without attention to wider, systemic issues, is inadequate.

Responsibilities across 'whole systems'

A much more positive, though more complex, challenge is to address the ways in which social, economic, spatial and cultural life holds itself together through partially self-organising systems. Part of the challenge to centre-left values from the neo-liberal right came from its claim that market competition represented a spontaneous, energetic and efficient way to create equilibria in organising social life. This was untrue – markets are institutions embedded in wider social norms and reliant on non-market goods, as John Kay's contribution to this volume illustrates. But the association of human spontaneity and creativity with selfish, rationalist individualism proved a deadly weapon against those arguing that human potential flourishes best under more egalitarian conditions, largely because they did not have an adequate response.

But more recently a wide range of analysis has brought to the fore the way systems of social order and collective organisation are underpinned by principles of self-organising adaptation, using networks as means to communicate, coordinate and hold together diverse populations in ways which enable them to meet their collective needs. Social capital studies, for example, show how informal social networks underpin health and quality of life for older people, opportunity and motivation for adolescents and guidance and mutual support for parents of young children.

Human systems, like natural ones, display their own self-organising tendencies. Large-scale organisations, whether public services, diaspora communities or multinational corporations, successfully maintain their core values and commitments while handling continuous adjustment and adaptation to change in their external circumstances; in fact, much of the adaptation is geared towards this preservation of the essentials. The key point for policy-makers to recognise is that in such systems the coordinated adaptation often takes place without central direction. In other words, the capabilities and resources of self-organising systems go well beyond what is captured by their formal organisational structures, budgets and lines of power and accountability.

These system-based accounts help to explain the resilience of many institutions and communities in the face of ongoing change, and also the difficulty of using central control to change the behaviour of organisations which are deeply embedded in complex sets of relationships. As Jake Chapman has recently argued, public services should be understood as 'complex adaptive systems'. A complex mix of competition and collaboration helps to hold in place a set of organisational priorities or routines which will eventually overcome temporary distortions or shifts in direction. This is unless the intervention is able to adjust the deeper relationships underpinning the integrity of the whole system, and acquire ownership and legitimacy among those responsible for implementing a solution.[2]

A practical example of the contrast between the systemic approach and those described above can be illustrated by policies that attempt to reduce school drop-out. A state–individual contract approach would involve ensuring that each young person had access to a good quality education, with tailored individual support and good information to help the young person to see the advantages of staying on in school. But if young people do drop out, the consequences of this life choice would fall on them, for good or for bad. This individual-focused approach may work well most of the time, at least as a general framework, but it has limitations. These limitations are illustrated by results from a recent study of 'under-aspirers' – young people who have the ability to stay on but indicate that they are intending to leave school. Under-aspirers were independently identified and then assigned to an intervention group, which received extra support and mentoring from the school. A second, control group remained anonymous. It was discovered that the individuals who were identified and given extra support actually did significantly worse in their subsequent exams! In other words, the place of the individual within a whole system of organisation, including informal norms and expectations is a crucial determinant of outcomes, whatever the specific resources or treatment directed towards them. But addressing this whole is one of the things for which progressive policy interventions often seem least equipped.

More than one study has found that when mentoring and support are provided to an entire class, and especially when this intervention starts from before the teenage years, staying-on rates and grades improve dramatically. For example, the US 'I have a dream' programme led to a doubling of staying-on rates, from around 35 to 70 per cent. The big difference between this and the unsuccessful individual-focused programmes is that they attempt to change the whole peer group at once, rather than inadvertently labelling an individual child as a success or failure.

Even in an era of moral pluralism, progressive strategies need an overarching moral narrative. Addressing the need for rights and responsibilities to be combined through the principle of reciprocity is a central dimension of this task. But given the complexity of the challenges we have described, politicians should be wary of trying to create simple and direct connections between the moral goal and single policy prescriptions.

This is where a new ideal of citizenship is relevant. A narrative of progress and shared aspiration has to find expression, not just in the high-level objectives of governments, but also in 'the creative power of the citizen'. But for civic identity to have a real impact on personal choices and collective outcomes, ordinary people have to be persuaded that the fact of living in a political or democratic community has some real moral value, even when its expression is increasingly diverse.

There are many candidates for the emphasis of these overarching narratives. One is responsibility towards future generations, through both the ways in which our societies care for their children and the challenges of environmental and cultural sustainability.

Another could be the 'universal' values expressed in the human rights framework; the ideal of treating all persons as having equal worth, recognising human dignity as a fundamental value, and seeking to develop and respond to people's existing capacity for empathy and mutual concern.

A third, related, focus, is the responsibility to protect people against random or illegitimate violence, and the insecurity created by violent conflict.

Running through all these abstract themes, all of which are central to current political debate, is the reality that achieving equal dignity, protection or respect for each individual relies on recognising the reality of human interdependence, and the need for institutions which make co-existence and mutual respect positive, practical realities. That, at root, is what politics is there to do.

Progressive political leadership needs broad narratives which root themselves in these values and fit loosely with the complex mix of policy and strategy needed to build new systems of pluralised, self-organising social support. In doing so, political leaders should be bold about the possibilities of radical transformation, but more humble about their ability to create such transformation without drawing on the energies and distributed intelligence of the societies they are elected to lead.

The narrative of human progress that begins to emerge, as a result, is one of human potential combined with respect for learning, and of cultures and institutions developed as far as possible towards openness and learning. In complex societies, the norm of reciprocity is not one in which every transaction must be based on generating a direct and immediate return, but where citizens need to be confident that if they make choices which reflect the needs of others, they will be rewarded in similar ways when they need support from others.

The final sections of this chapter address some of the concrete ways in which reform strategies can strengthen this kind of collective capability.

Children and families

Centre-left policies have traditionally focused on creating social and economic rights for parents, especially mothers, as their main tool of family policy. But the social fragmentation brought by value change, the erosion of the traditional nuclear family, declining birth rates and social exclusion all undermine the effectiveness of traditional welfare state solutions.

Tom Bentley and David Halpern

Children represent a classic example of interconnected responsibilities: they are physically, materially and emotionally dependent on others, and rely for their well-being on a much wider range of support, including the influence of positive role models, shared adult expectations, and physical safety and independent mobility in local communities and public spaces.

Post-war welfare strategies for children focused on providing health and education services and on generating employment to provide family income. Many countries, notably the Scandinavian social democracies, have used a combination of parental rights and universal early-years care to underpin high levels of support for children. Many others still rely heavily on the informal production of welfare within families, on the ability of labour markets and extended family structures to support the care of children.

Yet while it is widely acknowledged that the quality of care, parenting and emotional support is fundamental to children's long-term well-being, governments remain equivocal about the extent to which they can cross the boundary from public to private life. Parenting programmes are often a small part of the policy repertoire, and evidence on their impact is mixed.

Schooling has risen steadily up the political agenda in most countries, and is subject to intense competitive pressure from parents desperate to secure good places for their children. But recent analysis shows how much inequality in life chances is entrenched before the beginning of formal education, to the extent that schooling itself often exacerbates, rather than reduces, the difficulties. In this context, the wider distribution of rights and responsibilities is crucial to the prospect of influencing outcomes for most children. But there is no straightforward policy lever which can be used to produce different outcomes.

In fact, better outcomes for children require an approach which can deliberately address the fuzzy boundary between the public and private realms. In many western societies, child-rearing has become an increasingly privatised activity, with parents subject to growing expectations and cultural pressure to provide, but often separated from the sources of support on which they need to rely by the same processes of cultural and economic change. Thus working parents battle to find enough time to spend at home, competition for school

90

and childcare places is increasingly intense, and children themselves are prone to a new series of risks arising from material affluence and new social pressures; obesity and emotional disorders are increasing, there is more intense pressure to succeed from early on in education, and so forth.

A distributed responsibility approach to family policy would seek to provide universal public services in ways which also strengthen informal systems of mutual support and reciprocity, and to link wider information networks and efforts to encourage culture change with the basic, local services which virtually all children access.

For example, school choice policies are a priority in many systems, motivated by middle-class demand and by the search for ways of improving school systems. But simply introducing greater choice while keeping the supply of state school places fixed only benefits those families capable of climbing towards the top of a competitive ladder – only if the policy is combined with a number of others can it have the effect of increasing responsiveness and flexibility for disadvantaged families as well.

Likewise, parenting programmes do little to influence norms of behaviour if they concentrate solely on trying to correct the behaviour of individual parents, especially if they feel they are being stigmatised by the process. Programmes which succeed in generating positive, mutual relationships among networks of parents are likely to have a far more enduring effect. For example, the National Childbirth Trust, which is nominally about preparing couples for childbirth and postnatal care, serves the longer term purpose of creating mutually supportive groups of parents in close proximity.

The challenge is to develop the policies and spending allocations needed to make investments, to find ways of promoting shared values around the needs of children, and to develop local institutional systems capable of reinforcing them in everyday experience.

The policy mix for such an agenda might include:

- Progressive increases in financial support for children and family services
- Investment in universal early years infrastructure combining health, learning and play facilities

- New forms of single welfare account to act as a focus for public investment and the accumulation of assets
- Capacity building strategies to link informal, mutual networks of family support, information providers and so on
- A politically-led public debate on the influence of early child development and how it can best be supported
- Supports for family-friendly employment and flexibility for working parents
- Schooling linked more explicitly to social and emotional development, in tandem with wider community involvement for children and young people.

Governance as learning: reforming public institutions

For governments to be capable of shaping such multi-faceted strategies, the architecture of public administration itself needs to be reshaped. The central dimensions of the change are towards forms of governance capable of drawing more directly on diverse input and participation, of stimulating and transferring far higher levels of innovation across service providers at local level, and of promoting horizontal collaboration and joint production of outcomes among groups of producers and civic institutions across a given system or community.

The Australian State of Victoria has recently created a new Department of Victorian Communities, whose formal remit combines strategic investment in 'community capacity', for example, through local organisations working to promote civic participation, with development of policy in tandem with other departments in key areas where service provision can be combined with more direct community participation, such as extended community schooling, housing and social care.

More widely, many different countries are experimenting with new strategic and learning functions in government, making more intensive use of research-based evidence to inform policy development, and of 'knowledge networks' to promote better feedback between policy design and implementation process. The starting point varies according to the prevailing constitutional design: in highly decentralised and federal systems, the challenge is often generating greater strategic coherence across different layers of governance, as for example in

Sweden and the Netherlands, while in more centralised states like Britain and France better use of learning will often involve wider distribution of executive power, along with a new emphasis on building horizontal partnership or network structures at local level.

Overall, progressive reformers must find ways of convincing public servants to participate in the process of making governance structures more open and porous, even while they continue with the struggle to maintain clear priorities and improve basic levels of service.

Mobilising user and practitioner innovation: public service networks

Another set of opportunities for progressive governance lies in the potential of networked and collaborative forms of organisation to provide services and opportunities at citizen level. The traditional organisational forms taken by public and social service delivery agents like schools and hospitals create barriers to the extent to which they can draw citizens directly into their activities, beyond defined participation as pupils, patients, and so on. In most societies, the self-organising energies of citizens and user groups are creating networks of information exchange, mutual support and informal provision across the range of traditional public service functions. In most systems, however, the actual deliverers of services are constrained from playing a role in contributing to or making use of these networks.

But innovation in organisation form and the effort to create collaborative networks across the familiar institutional boundaries holds out the promise of radical improvements in organisational performance combined with the capacity to provide far more diversified and personalised pathways through learning, health improvement and clinical treatment, or social care.

The creation of collaborative networks can operate on a very large scale, such as the Cochrane Collaboration, a health project based in the US which aims to make research evidence and guidance about effective clinical practice freely accessible to health practitioners in the developing world.

More locally rooted are growing efforts to promote collaborative learning and resource sharing between networks of partly autonomous schools, such as the Networked Learning Communities programme developed by the English National College for School Leadership, which provides part-funding and facilitation to facilitate new reciprocal ties between schools dedicated to innovation in teaching and learning.

Conclusion: The Need for Local Democratic Innovation

Using public policy to generate more complex strategies for behavioural change, and embedding public rules in informal systems and cultures which cover non-state institutions, raise new challenges for democratic legitimacy.

The implication of our argument is that people will only be persuaded to enact their individual rights in responsible ways if they are offered membership of organisations whose routines and priorities are actively responsive to their own changing identities, needs and patterns of engagement.

This requires organisational innovation, to create systems of provision that can be responsive enough to growing social diversity. But it also needs new means of deliberation, leadership and legitimation, which cannot necessarily be met with the institutions currently at our disposal. For parliaments, local councils and political parties, the response to fragmentation and disengagement too often looks like defence or defiance – the attempt to preserve forms of decision-making with which democratic legitimacy is equated. In their study of 'empowered participatory governance', Fung and Olin Wright[3] identify the common principles of a set of concrete experiments in democratic governance which have engaged citizens in new ways to generate public solutions. They are:

• Addressing a specific area of public concern
• Empowering the involvement of ordinary citizens and officials in the field
• Attempting to solve the problems through processes of reasoned, shared deliberation

- Devolving decision and implementation power to local action units
- Ensuring that local action units are not autonomuous, but connected to each other and to other levels of the state in order to share resources, solve common problems and diffuse innovations and learning
- Colonising and transforming existing groups
- Creating a rough equality of power, for deliberative purposes, between participants.

One striking example of this approach is the way in which the city of Porto Allegre, in Brazil, has created a 'participatory budgeting' process, creating forums in which neighbourhood representatives can participate directly in the setting of budget priorities and allocations through a series of regional plenary meetings intertwined with smaller technical and neighbourhood-focused meetings to focus on more detailed allocation issues. Over two decades the numbers of participants in the process have rapidly increased to numbers approaching 20,000. One lesson is that building new structures and deliberative processes is intertwined with civil society efforts to generate 'shared conversation' about the issues covered by the formal governance arrangements.

Similar lessons can be learned from the success of police and schooling reform in Chicago. Diverse coalitions of reformers, civic and residents groups, businesses and others succeeded in overcoming the resistance of entrenched public-service unions and centralised authorities to create new decentralised governance structures which created more direct accountability to local communities and specific performance goals. At the same time they also created much greater flexibility and autonomy for schools and police units to be proactive and creative in addressing specific aspects of community need, often working directly in partnership with community groups and residents to improve outcomes.

Recognition of the fundamental importance of local governance as the level at which different services and community interests 'join up' is a basic lesson for progressive strategies, which some national cultures will find harder to accept than others. But equally important is the recognition that locally devolved public institutions are effective only when they remain interdependent with wider systems of communication and provision.

The question, therefore, is whether collective responsibilities can be articulated by politics in ways which individuals are prepared to recognise and act on. This is why trust in government and in politicians is so important to the prospect of strengthening responsibility across whole communities and societies.

The crucial point of recognition is not that progressive leaders must carefully choose both the ethical roots and the practical focus of their priority issues, though this is true, but that that political strategy must be mediated through people's *everyday experience of institutions* if it is to regenerate the public support on which it ultimately rests.

This is where the greatest gap currently exists between the aspirations of progressive political leadership and the possibility of lasting change. In almost every area of political conflict, from public service reform to international violence, poverty reduction to intercultural understanding, the source of disconnection lies in the inability of both political vision and abstract institutional values to translate into tangible, collective experience which can reproduce itself at an everyday level.

These challenges and methods go against the grain of entrenched public institutions, and the expectations of formal accountability systems. But they offer precisely the synthesis of differentiation and solidarity which 21st-century citizenship will need to embody.

Notes

1 See for example the Canadian experience, Chrétien, J., 'Immigration and Multiculturalism: Lessons from Canada', *Progressive Politics*, vol. 2.2, July 2003.
2 Chapman, J., *System Failure: why governments must learn to think differently*. Demos: London, 2002.
3 Archon Fung and Erik Olin Wright, 'Thinking about Empowered Participatory Governance', in Archon Fung and Erik Olin Wright (eds), *Deepening Democracy: institutional innovations in empowered participatory governance*. London: Verso, 2003.

4

Against Social Inheritance

Gøsta Esping-Andersen

Today's welfare states – with the notable exception of the Scandinavian – have changed little since the great reforms of the post-war years. They basically mirror the kind of employment, family and risk profiles that existed in the epoch of our fathers and grandfathers. Many advocates of the welfare state will view this positively as irrefutable confirmation of its powerful and lasting legitimacy. Others see such resistance to change as cause for major concern, pointing to a deepening gap between emerging new needs and risks, on one side, and an increasingly archaic social protection system, on the other hand. Among the concerned, some champion more markets and less state; others call for a recast welfare model. I belong to the latter group, and in this chapter I argue that the first and most important step towards a positive new welfare equilibrium entails major investments in our children. Most welfare states aim the bulk of redistribution at pensioners, but invest little in children and youth. Most steadfastly assume that families must remain responsible for their own caring needs and thus there is very little service provision to families. But whether we are revolutionaries, conservatives or reformers, we need to confront the social changes underway in order to design a viable strategy for the future.

The Backdrop: What Has Changed?

Six major social changes merit special attention since they powerfully affect the distribution of social risks and needs.

The life course

In the Golden Age of the traditional welfare state the transition to adulthood occurred early and was typically smooth, orderly and, above all, predictable. Adulthood coincided with men's first stable employment and marriage. Most women ceased to work at first birth, and only a minority would later return. When we examine the biographies among older age groups, we are immediately struck by the degree of homogeneity in behaviour. First employment and family formation occurred early and, for most citizens, the active phase of the life course was quite standardised and linear: a long working career, with few interruptions, for men; a life of housewifery for women. When men retired, however, they would enjoy few years of 'leisure', simply because their life expectancy was 67–69. Poverty in old age was widespread, not least because few women had individual pension entitlements.

The transition to adulthood today is both delayed and prolonged. It is now common in Southern Europe that youth remain in the parental home until age 25–30. Longer education delays its onset and often formidable obstacles in labour and housing markets help prolong it. It also appears more disorderly inasmuch as youth (especially women) need to juggle many priorities at once before they begin forming families. In all countries, first births occur when women, on average, are 28–29 years old. Marital and employment instability combine to produce much less linear biographies and complex household reconfigurations. It is increasingly common for a child to have eight or even twelve grandparents, all depending on the frequency of partnership change.

Families and households

The standard, post-war family is in rapid decline, being superseded by a plurality of new household forms. In part, we see a rise in one person, or one-parent, households (usually 10–15 per cent of all now). In part, we see the consolidation of the two-earner norm. We also see far more instability and fragility, with informal partnerships, separations and divorces in steady growth. The majority of newborn Americans will not experience a full childhood with both parents. The proliferation of 'atypical' households and more conditional partnerships implies new vulnerabilities but also new strengths. Lone parents face substantial poverty risks, and the sole breadwinner family is losing ground – especially if headed by a low-skilled earner. Marital selection means that households may be polarising. We see, at once, a sizable share of 'work-poor' households, often very distanced from any solid employment relationship, and also a growing number of 'work-rich' households. The welfare gap between the two is likely to widen because less educated women are least likely to work. If they do, we shall most likely see a polarisation between too low and too high wages.

An alarming welfare gap is evident in latter-day birth rates. Citizens are simply not capable of forming families according to their preferences. It is well-documented that fertility falls far short of what people express as their desired number of children, namely about 2.4 in just about all countries.[1] In some European countries, the birth rate has fallen to 1.2 and less; in some regions, to 0.8. Forming independent families is, and obviously remains, the bedrock of most citizens' life experience as well as of society itself. Many nations are in the grip of a low fertility equilibrium, and this must be interpreted as evidence of serious welfare deficits.

The new employment dilemmas

In the future we must rely entirely on services for job growth and this poses a new set of dilemmas, some of which are serious. First, many services compete with the household's own ability to self-service.[2] Hence, the dynamics of the service economy depend very much on households' (and firms') ability to externalise service demand and this, in turn, depends on affordability and need. The eclipse of the housewife implies that the need for services grows, but this alone may not translate into fact if they are unaffordable. Since it is difficult to raise productivity in many services, in particular in personal and social services, they easily face constant cost pressures. The affordability problem is more than evident to families seeking to place their toddler in private day care, or their frail elderly relative in residential care.

The second obstacle to a dynamic service economy lies in wage setting practice. Wage compression, the minimum wage and high fixed labour costs all pose obstacles to private sector service employment, especially in low-productivity services. As Scharpf and Schmidt argue,[3] those welfare states (like Germany or Italy) that principally rely on employment-based contributions are especially prone to job stagnation, both because fixed labour costs are steep and because the revenue base is narrow.

The dynamics of services destined to households depend on overcoming the affordability problem. A large low-wage economy, as in the US, may provide affordable services to the well-to-do families and, hence, the share of personal services is about twice the typical European.[4] To cite an example, Americans do ten times as much laundry as Danes or Swedes. Low-wage employment, however, provokes more poverty and also huge differences in servicing quality. The latter may not matter much in the laundry or restaurant sector, but it can be highly problematic in motor, education, or health services. If we want to ensure affordability in such services the only realistic option is to promote public subsidies or provision. This, the Scandinavian strategy, results in a highly social service-biased employment profile, and it necessitates a very strong tax base. Failing either a low-wage economy, or public subsidies, we will most likely face sluggish service growth. This is precisely the situation in which most EU countries find themselves.

The low-wage problem poses a particularly difficult welfare issue in the long run, to the extent that workers may find themselves locked into persistently poor quality employment. Since low-end services very rarely offer training and the opportunity to improve skills, the likelihood of being trapped in this career is very real. From a life-chance perspective, the challenge is how to ensure the opportunity for social mobility and this, effectively, means ensuring that youth have adequate skills to begin with.

The rising ante

There is nothing new in the fact that skills are crucial for life chances. The knowledge economy, however, is raising the 'ante', i.e. the basic requirements for securing a good job and income. In the Golden Age, low-skilled workers could normally count on stable and decently paid jobs. This is no longer the case. The skill-ante may be rising, but marketable skill requirements are simultaneously becoming more diversified. Life-long learning presupposes an adequate cognitive base to begin with, and there is a clear widening of the gulf in terms of the returns to human capital. In the knowledge economy it is quite probable that low education and insufficient cognitive skills will lock citizens into life-long precariousness, low wages, and high unemployment risks. This, in turn, will raise the likelihood of poverty in old age. We see here a potent source of a coming welfare abyss between the post-industrial winners and losers.

An exaggerated focus on knowledge production needs to be corrected. Even if the service economy is strongly biased in favour of skilled jobs, the social, distributive and personal services will, inevitably, produce a substantial share of routine and low-skilled jobs.[5] This is equally true in a Nordic-type model, heavily biased towards social service, as in an American-style low-wage scenario. True, the former will minimise the welfare problems associated with such employment, the latter will not. Still, the key question may not be whether an economy is replete with bad jobs – an inevitable outcome of any truly dynamic service economy – but whether citizens can be assured of realistic mobility chances. Data from the US and also the UK suggests that de-regulated labour markets do not sponsor greater mobility chances; indeed, to the contrary. In other words, if our goal is to equalise life chances we need to accompany any conceivable employment promotion policy with measures to sponsor upward mobility. This means investing in skills from the day children are born. Remedial programs, later in life, are costly and ineffective.

Intensifying income inequalities

The Golden Age was 'golden' in large part because it diminished inequalities. This was mainly because less skilled workers experienced major improvements in their relative wages. Since the 1970s we see a great u-turn with rising market inequalities in just about all OECD countries. The Gini coefficient for pre-tax/pre-transfer household incomes has risen by 10–25 per cent as the top deciles have pushed ahead and, in some countries, as the bottom has lost ground. The increase in post-tax/post-transfer inequalities has been more modest, mainly because welfare states have succeeded – so far – to stem the tide of inequality.[6] But the driving forces behind the new inequalities are part and parcel of the emerging new social economy and, hence, they are likely to intensify. The challenge is to attack the roots of such inequalities and this implies, primarily, a two-pronged strategy biased towards high-risk households with the aim of equalising the acquisition of human capital.

A looming generational clash

The Golden Age was premised on an implicit generational contract that enjoyed considerable legitimacy, simply because it was considered equitable and fair. The pensioner bias of welfare policy was unproblematic because full employment and rising real wages established a strong revenue base for spending growth while steadily improving the living standards of the working-age population. In addition, the aged population was small. This generational contract is under pressure, not only because of population aging but also because contemporary retirees generally enjoy high living standards while young households encounter rising welfare risks. It is additionally under pressure because the median voter (now about 50 in Europe) is aging, and because it is increasingly evident that we need to invest more in children and youth. This is the real essence of the sustainability challenge.

The new risk structure is not, as many believe, the inevitable outcome of sinister forces like globalization. If this were the case, one would expect that unusually open economies, like the Dutch, Danish or Swedish, would be topping contemporary poverty, unemployment and inequality rankings. Instead, we see that these same countries perform best on most available welfare and employment indicators. The thrust comes from endogenous forces, in particular from changes in employment structure, demography, and from the ripple effects associated with the new status of women. These are long-term, structural forces, unlikely to go away. The challenge to social policy, therefore, is to realign our welfare edifice. The flagship policy in such a programme must be an active family policy that invests in children.

A New Family Policy

Most European welfare states define family policy narrowly, limiting social support to abject family failures. This residual approach was perhaps not especially problematic in an epoch when most marriages were stable, when women provided unpaid care, and when the male breadwinner could provide adequately for his family. The post-war baby-boom was, undoubtedly, the by-product of the kind of security that then prevailed. Contemporary statistics tell us that none of these conditions remain valid, in part because citizens' preferences have changed; in part because an array of novel obstacles and risks has emerged.

We confront three overriding challenges: the first related to forming families in the first place; the second to the reconciliation of family and working life; and the third to the increasingly serious consequences of income and welfare problems in childhood. The design of an effective new family policy must begin with the realisation that the male breadwinner family is demonstrably counter-productive for the post-industrial order. To achieve a positive welfare equilibrium, we need to invest far more in children, and strengthening the role of women is sine qua non.

A note of caution is, however, in order. We only face a genuine policy challenge to the extent that observed 'dysfunctions' or welfare problems are unwanted. No doubt, as the theory of the second demographic transition suggests, many of the changes we see are the fruits of individuals' desires and are not social pathologies caused by environmental constraints. Youth prefer more education and, hence, delay independence and family formation. Women control their fertility and hence can opt for a timing and quantity of births that suit their wishes. Adults are now at liberty to terminate unsatisfying partnerships. Family policy is needed in order to facilitate, not limit individual choice. It is needed if families are not autonomously able to secure sufficient resources so as to secure the welfare of their members.

Having children

The low fertility rates we observe throughout Europe cannot be ascribed to citizens' preference sets. Rather, the problem is that the cost of children has risen, both to women and to society. Most welfare states assume that families internalise the entire cost. This was less problematic once, when women had little education and saw themselves primarily pursuing lifelong housewifery. The 'child penalty' is rising with female educational attainment and improved earnings power – while less skilled and young males experience wage deterioration. For society, the child penalty takes the form of two competing evils: either sub-optimal employment levels, if mothers are forced to abandon work, or sub-optimal fertility rates, if women forgo motherhood. Our aging societies can ill afford either and, consequently, the cost of children needs to be redistributed.

Affordable and adequate childcare, in particular for the ages one to three, is a necessary precondition for compatibility.[7] The affordability issue is important to understand correctly. Prevailing market prices for quality care are everywhere beyond the reach of most working mothers. Full-time, full-year care for one or two toddlers will easily eat up 30 or even 50 per cent of an average woman's wage. The cost of day care is not just a tax on mothers' employment but is, in fact, a hugely regressive tax. This has perverse results since it is among less educated women – and lower income households – that additional female labour reserves exist. We hardly need to be reminded that the goal of raising overall female activity rates can only be attained by mobilising less educated women.

One solution is to ease access to care via subsidies. This is the policy pursued in Scandinavia, with the result that coverage for the under-threes is now virtually universal – as is, of course, female labour supply. Failing public subsidies, the alternative is either market purchase or familialism; both are demonstrably inadequate. The market option means that access and quality of care will mirror parents' purchasing power. The familial solution will, likewise, reproduce prevailing socio-economic and educational differences and will, additionally, pose obstacles to women's employability. In contrast, universal quality care may, at least potentially, equalise the kind of cultural and cognitive stimulus that children receive. If we are committed to equal opportunities, we must accept the need for publicly guaranteed quality care for all children.

Families with children

Recent data show that families with children fare very poorly.[8] In most countries, the relative disposable income of young families has deteriorated and poverty has risen, in some cases at alarming rates. The menace stems from more fragile partnerships, the rise of lone parenthood, and also from greater employment precariousness and eroding earnings among younger workers. With few exceptions, Europe's high and stubborn unemployment rolls are mainly inhabited by youth. Likewise, where unstable, temporary work contracts proliferate (now a third of all Spanish employment) it is predominantly young workers who are affected. If we add to this the prevalence of marital selection in terms of education, we should expect more polarisation between households. Unemployment and precariousness, just like wealth, tend to bundle within the same families.

We have here a double-whammy: the very same trends that make family formation difficult also affect negatively the welfare of those young adults who do manage to form a family. The emerging post-industrial society, unlike its industrial forebear, is not kind to youth.

Table 1 Poverty rates and trends in families with children

Country	Poverty rates in child families, mid-1990s	Trend in child poverty, 1980s–mid-1990s	Trend in extreme poverty in child families**	Lone mother poverty, mid-1990s Mother works	Lone mother poverty, mid-1990s Mother inactive
Denmark	6.9	+2.6	+2.6	10	34
Sweden	2.2	–1.3	–1.3	4	24
France	7.0	–0.4	–0.4	13	45
Germany	14.1	+10.0	+10.0	33	62
Italy	18.6	0	0	25	79
U.K.	14.3	+7.4	+7.4	26	69
U.S.A.	21.4	+3.8	+3.8	39	73

* Poverty is measured as <50 per cent of median equivalent disposable income (using new OECD equivalence scale).
** Extreme poverty is <33 per cent of median equivalent disposable income.
Source: LIS databases

This means that families with children face often severe welfare risks. Table 1 presents a summary overview of income poverty in today's child families.

The intensity of child poverty depends very much on whether mothers are employed. Where this is the case, the risk of poverty drops sharply and in two-parent families to almost negligible levels. Scandinavia's enviable performance is actually less due to generous social transfers than to the mere fact that virtually all mothers work (lone mother activity rates in Denmark and Sweden are around 80 per cent). In the UK and the US, lone mother employment is low and this is a primary reason why poverty rates are extremely high.[9] The risk of child poverty in a typical OECD country increases by a factor of three to four (in two-parent households) and five to seven (in lone mother households) when mothers are inactive.[10]

We should interpret poverty statistics with care. Few will experience lasting harm from a brief spell of want if, indeed, it is brief. The mere existence of bad jobs, low wages, or sub-optimal housing is not nearly as worrisome as is the possibility that these become persistent, a seemingly inescapable fate in people's lives. When citizens find themselves trapped in a world of poverty and insecurity, this is when the downward spiral is most likely to set in. The good news is that a large majority everywhere experience economic hardship intermittently and for relatively brief periods. The bad news is that there remains a minority of truly entrapped citizens and families. The size of that minority is almost perfectly correlated with a nation's overall profile of inequalities. Where economic inequalities are high, as in the US and in Britain, poverty entrapment is far more common than in egalitarian societies. If our primary goal is to ensure good life chances, policy will need to establish guarantees against long-term entrapment.

There exist compelling reasons why governments should guarantee adequate incomes to families with children. For one, poverty in childhood can have very negative long-term consequences for children's life chances and, hence, also for society. Still, we must remember that the single most powerful antidote to child poverty lies not in social transfers but in the earnings potential of working mothers. Scandinavia's exemplary performance in terms of child poverty is mainly the result of its heavy investment in childcare and paid parental leave.

In other words, resolving women's incompatibility problem with employment is arguably the cornerstone of any future welfare equilibrium in so far as it supports citizens' desires for children. It helps diminish child poverty and helps ensure that our societies will evolve towards a superior demographic equilibrium in terms of supporting tomorrow's ageing population.

All this will seem very supportive of a make-work-pay strategy. But, it is of utmost importance that we do not throw the baby out with the bathwater. Mothers' employment may very well be the decisive solution, but no government so far invented is effectively capable of guaranteeing such. Depending on country, lone mothers account for up to 10 or 15 per cent of all child families and their earning power is usually modest to begin with. Mothers of small children are most likely to be in part-time employment and/or very likely in precarious jobs and/or unemployed – all depending on nationality. Hence, income guarantees remain vital and, if we are concerned about social justice, there are very good reasons for why we should redistribute income from the childless to child families. Children are now a scarce social good and anyone facing retirement in the coming decades will have a personal interest in not only the quantity but also the quality of today's children and tomorrow's workers.

There are, in other words, two issues at stake here: supporting working mothers and pursuing a policy that will minimise economic hardship in child families. The two issues, moreover, condense into one overriding policy because, in large measure, investing in our children is synonymous with reconciling employment and motherhood.

The argument in favour of investment in families comes from evidence concerning the long-term consequences of childhood deprivation. Research shows that poverty – especially in early childhood – is associated with substantially less schooling, sharply reduced earnings prospects as an adult, and substantially higher risks of becoming a poor (and possibly welfare dependent) parent.[11] Research by Mayer[12] shows that poor American children will have, on average, two years' less education and though European estimates are somewhat less dramatic, they are nonetheless worrying. Put differently, the individual and social returns to economic security in families are potentially very high.

The Need to Diminish Social Inheritance

Over the past half century, social democracy's promise of equality underwent major redefinitions. Once a question of class inequalities, the egalitarian ideal eventually came to mean a more individualised notion of equal opportunities. In any case, most post-war welfare states promised that life chances would no longer depend on inherited privilege. This promise seems of late to have been forgotten, or at least shelved. There are probably several reasons involved. Decades of welfare state building helped shift attention towards the more immediate policy challenges, such as broadening social entitlements and attacking poverty. Moreover, the terrain of social injustice became increasingly colonised by categorical inequities (like gender equality), or by victimisation claims. Finally, most post-war egalitarians became convinced that educational expansion and reform were the way to bring about equal opportunities for all. There is now mounting evidence that educational reforms do little to weaken social inheritance but, alas, this seems to have provoked political paralysis rather than serious reconsideration of public policy.

The evolving knowledge economy raises the prerequisites for good life chances, punishing those with inadequate skills and rewarding those with. Which skills are central is rather less clear. Formal educational credentials continue, no doubt, to exert a powerful role. OECD[13] studies show that, everywhere, the risk of unemployment doubles among those with less than secondary level education, and a huge literature shows that the returns to education are rising.[14] Yet, there is evidence that different human capital dimensions are gaining in importance, especially less identifiable traits such as social skills, leadership abilities, 'emotional intelligence', cultural and social capital. Of these, cognitive skills stand out as being the single most crucial. The argument is that a person's ability to understand, interpret and productively utilise information is sine qua non in knowledge economies where technologies and skill requirements are apt to change rapidly. A brave new world of lifelong learning assumes that people are able to learn and re-learn quickly and effectively, and this is where cognitive abilities are central. To the extent that formal

109

credentials remain crucial we know that children's cognitive skills are one precondition for successful schooling. As so much evaluation research has concluded, remedial programs later on in life are quite ineffectual unless a person possesses adequate cognitive skills to begin with. These are developed very early in a child's life – in large part *prior to* school age.

All this is to say that life chances are powerfully overdetermined by what happens in children's life prior to their first encounter with the school system. It is this that explains why a century of educational reform has failed to diminish the impact of social inheritance; why parents' social status continues unabated to dictate children's educational attainment, income or occupational destination.

For both welfare and efficiency reasons this impact must be weakened. For citizens, a strong cognitive base is a precondition for educational attainment, subsequent earnings potential and career chances. For society, it is vital that future generations will be resourceful and productive, simply because they will be numerically few, destined to shoulder huge dependent populations. We can ill afford a future working population in which maybe 20 or 30 per cent are functionally illiterate and/or have failed to attain even secondary-level education.[15]

The question, then, is how to combat social inheritance. Past policy was focused on reforming education, pursuing four objectives in particular: avoiding early tracking, sponsoring comprehensive schools, minimising private schools, and affirmative action for underprivileged children. The first two are, in practice, part and parcel of the same problem, namely to reduce class differences in attrition by keeping kids together in school as long as possible.[16] The third, it is well known, is doubly important, in part to ensure adequate funding for, and broad involvement in, high quality public education and, in part, to avoid segregation by class, race or ethnicity. The fourth dimension is probably the single best documented, certainly in the case of the US's Head Start programme. Head Start evaluations systematically report substantial gains in terms of school attendance and performance.[17]

The bad news, as far as educational reform is concerned, is that the real mechanisms of social inheritance lie mostly elsewhere. The prevailing view is that school and neighbourhood effects are decidedly less important than are factors related to the family milieu.[18]

What precisely are the attributes of families that help perpetuate inherited life chances and can these be influenced via policy? Contemporary research converges around two principal causal mechanisms, 'money' and 'culture'. The 'money' argument derives from human capital theory and focuses on parents' ability to invest in their children's future.[19] A large literature demonstrates that offsprings' income is strongly correlated with parents', but one of the surprising findings is that the social origins effect is far stronger in countries like the UK and US than in Canada, Scandinavia or Germany.[20] This implies that social inheritance is far stronger in less egalitarian societies.

Another literature shows that economic deprivation and insecurity have very serious negative effects on children's educational attainment, subsequent earnings capacity and, perhaps most alarmingly, on the probability that – once adults – they will also become poor parents.[21] Long spells of poverty are especially damaging and, as Abel and Elwood[22] note, it is therefore of vital importance that society provides ladders out of poverty. Again, comparative evidence shows that mobility out of poverty is related to overall inequality: unequal societies, like the US, are far more likely to exhibit persistent poverty than are more egalitarian societies.[23]

All this suggests that a frontal attack on poverty in families with children would be an effective tool in the pursuit of more equal opportunities. This is also what emerges from international comparisons of inter-generational mobility. The two most authoritative such studies, namely Eriksson and Goldthorpe's *Constant Flux*,[24] and Shavit and Blossfeld's *Persistent Inequality*,[25] come to a similar conclusion – namely that there has been no real decline in social inheritance over the past half century, be it in terms of occupational or educational attainment. Yet both studies identify Sweden as an exception to the rule and hypothesise that this may be one of the notable effects of its unusually egalitarian welfare state. Indeed, in Sweden, like in neighbouring Denmark and Norway, child poverty is close to non-existent.

Prolonged economic hardship and insecurity should probably be regarded as fundamental, but perhaps not sufficient, causes of disadvantaged life chances. They are fundamental because poor parents

Table 2 Money and culture. OLS regressions of cognitive performance among children in seven countries (Beta coefficients)[1]

	Germany	France	Denmark	Sweden	Canada	U.K.	U.S.A.
Cultural capital	.296***	.307***	.297***	.255***	.272***	.317***	.259***
Father's education	.118***	.003	.157***	.002	.080***	.023	.047 *
Socioeconomic status	.178***	.213***	.126***	.190***	.145***	.212***	.172***
Household 'wealth'	.020	.033*	-.031*	-.011	-.001	.042***	.057***
R2	.213	.198	.177	.131	.142	.193	.163
N	4,164	3,774	3,572	3,970	26,735	7,752	2,732

[1] Dependent variable is the mean test-score performance on three tests of reading ability, comprehension and interpretation. Its distribution is almost perfectly normal.
Source: OECD's PISA micro-data set

simply lack the resources needed to plan and invest in their children's future. They form an insufficient explanation because there is mounting evidence that 'cultural' factors are also decisive, in particular for the cognitive and motivational development of children.[26] This is illustrated in Table 2, which compares the effect of father's education, parents' income status, and cultural level on their children's cognitive performance (at age 15).

Since we here compare standardised coefficients, the table shows us the relative weight of each of the factors. It is evident that families' 'cultural capital' exerts a very powerful influence. It is important to note that 'culture' and 'money' are weakly correlated.[27] This is tantamount to saying that a strategy based exclusively on income redistribution may be necessary, but not sufficient. An effective policy would have to also attack inequalities in cultural resources *if*, that is, cognitive skills are becoming ever more crucial for life chances.

We know that cognitive abilities are key to a child's educational performance; they are a precondition for successful adult retraining and activation. We also know that the returns to education are rising. To furnish one example, the probability of making the transition into upper secondary education typically doubles or triples for those who score higher on cognitive tests, even when controlling for such factors as immigrant status or parental education.

The situation we face is that parental origins influence both cognitive development and educational attainment. That is, the social inheritance effect is, in a way, double-barrelled. The key lies in identifying policy that may reduce the influence of unequal cultural and cognitive resources in the family of origin. This is no easy task, but one very suggestive clue comes from international comparisons of the impact of parental social status on children's educational achievement across cohorts. The important information lies in comparisons over time: has a country been able to reduce the parental inheritance effect? Statistical estimations (not shown here) demonstrate that, in most countries, there has been no decline in social inheritance at all. The US, Germany and basically also the UK, conform to the *constant flux* scenario. In contrast, all three Nordic countries exhibit substantial reductions, Denmark in particular. Indeed, the impact of father's education on child's secondary school attainment has disappeared altogether in the youngest Danish cohort! What previous research identified as Swedish exceptionalism is now, in reality, a common Scandinavian feature.

How do we explain this? No doubt, the egalitarian achievements of the Nordic welfare states in terms of minimising child poverty are crucial. But there is a second – and not rival – explanation, namely that these same countries – Denmark as the vanguard, Norway as the laggard – have now for decades furnished near-universal day care for pre-school children. With female employment approaching saturation levels across all educational levels, children from economically and/or culturally weaker homes have come to benefit from pedagogical standards and cognitive impulses that are basically the same as for children from privileged backgrounds.[28] Hence, irrespective of origins, children arrive at the first day in school much more homogenously prepared. And it is this which experts stress as important: the single most important phase of cognitive development occurs *prior* to school age. Children with inferior cognitive resources are likely to fall gradually behind in their educational careers because schools are ill-equipped to remedy initial handicaps.[29]

In conclusion, if we agree that greater equality of opportunities is important not just for ethical or equity reasons, but also for the well-functioning of tomorrow's society, clearly we cannot tolerate a continuation of the *constant flux*. More equality of opportunity can be achieved through welfare policy and, as my argument goes, this entails a double-barrelled strategy: an effective guarantee against poverty in childhood coupled to measures that equalise the cognitive stimulus that pre-school-age children receive. The lessons we can draw from Scandinavia suggest that such equalisation is far from utopian. Indeed, a strategy that calls for universal and high quality day care is a double winner. It will help equalise life chances while also helping promote women's employment. The costs of investing in such are undoubtedly substantial but failure to undertake the investment will incur far greater costs to our future society.

In fact, the financial costs involved in the proposed strategy are, in practice, modest. Beginning with income guarantees to families with children, if we were to peg the guarantee to 50 per cent of median household income, the additional cost to the exchequer would not exceed 0.2 per cent of GDP.[30] If most mothers were employed, this outlay would not in any case be less pressing. Ensuring that mothers can remain employed is, by far, the single best 'ladder' out of poverty. Hence, the crux lies in investments in childcare. Establishing a comprehensive system of high quality day care is undoubtedly costly, but here we need to establish a relevant accounting system. If mothers have access to day care, their employment interruptions will be far shorter and this translates into far superior life-long earnings records. Calculations based on the Danish system suggest that working mothers actually reimburse the initial cost of day care provision because their life-time earnings (and, hence, tax contributions) will be far greater.[31]

The main argument against such a formula is that mothers' (and parents') employment intensity may have adverse effects on their children's development and school performance. Even if mothers' employment may be positive because it reduces poverty, this should be weighed against the possibility that the quality parent–child interaction may suffer. Existing research on this question fails to produce straightforward answers. Overview studies, such as Duncan and Brooks-Gunn[32] and Haveman and Wolfe,[33] suggest that maternal employment is generally positive, or at least neutral, but that harmful effects occur when employment is combined with stress or fatigue. Ermisch and Francesconi,[34] in a study using British data, come to more pessimistic results and conclude that mothers' full-time employment is decidedly negative for children's learning performance. The effect of part-time work is less clear. The interpretation of their findings is made difficult by the fact that negative effects of fathers' employment are also evident. From my own comparative analyses of the PISA data, there is partial support for Ermisch and Francesconi's results. Mothers' full-time employment tends to be a negative factor for children's cognitive performance in several countries. However, I still find almost uniform positive effects of part-time work.

The impact of parental employment is doubly important to sort out. One, it undoubtedly depends on *when* in the child's development it occurs. Negative effects are arguably concentrated in the youngest ages, zero to five, as Ermisch and Francesconi insist. Additionally, harmful effects are probably related to the nature of mothers' jobs more than employment *per se*. Two, we should probably expect a priori that the impact of mothers' employment will vary across nations – producing more problematic effects where non-family care of children is of low or uneven quality, and less problems where care is of high quality. Returning to my analyses of the PISA data, there are clear national discrepancies: in the Nordic countries, mothers' employment, either on a part- or full-time basis, seems to have no effects whatsoever.

In the final analysis, we must simply accept that mothers' employment is becoming universal across all advanced countries. The challenge, therefore, is to design policy that prevents this *fait accompli* from producing adverse secondary effects. This brings us back, once again, to the broader package of family policy. If the negative effects on children of parents' work are particularly acute in early childhood, policy must obviously combine liberal and flexible parental leave provisions while children are small. Here Ermisch and Francesconi's finding that both fathers' and mothers' work may be problematic suggests important substitution effects between fathers and mothers. It probably matters less who stays with the children than that someone does. In other words, here is additional ammunition in favour of parental leave schemes that encourage take-up among both parents.

This also brings us back again to the childcare question. If childcare policy were nothing more than a response to women's demands for greater compatibility, there would a priori be no reason why the welfare state should assure uniform high quality standards. After all, the US seems to present a degree of compatibility commensurate to, say, the Nordic countries, considering its high fertility and female employment levels. But the distribution of American pre-school care is a mirror image of parents' ability to pay. A minority enjoy high quality care; the rest must make do with informal care (by the lady down the street) or even no supervision at all.[35] Hence, American children arrive at school already hugely stratified and, hence, the United States exhibits unusually strong correlations between social origins and destinations.

The key point is that a policy of universal access to high quality day care for the zero to six-year-olds kills two birds with one stone.

Against Social Inheritance

It obviously helps resolve the incompatibility problem that working mothers face, and it is arguably an effective tool in the war against social inheritance as well. Put differently, it is not only a 'win-win' policy but it is also a productive investment in children's life chances and in society's future productivity.

Notes

1   Bien, W. 2000. 'Changing Values among the Future Parents of Europe'. Paper presented at the European Observatory on Family Matters, Seville, 15–16 September. Hank, K. and Kohler, K. 'Gender Preferences for Children in Europe', *Demographic Research*, 2, 2000.
2   Gershuny, J., *After Industrial Society*, London, 1979.
3   Scharpf, F. and Schmidt, V., *Welfare and Work in Open Economies*, Oxford, 2000.
4   Esping-Andersen, G., *Social Foundations of Postindustrial Economies*, Oxford, 1999.
5   OECD, 2000. *Employment Outlook*, Paris, 2000; Esping-Andersen, G., *Social Foundations of Postindustrial Economies*, Oxford, 1999.
6   Esping-Andersen, G., *Why We Need a New Welfare State*, Oxford, 2002.
7   For a general overview, see Waldvogel, J., 2002, 'Child Care, Women's Employment, and Child Outcomes', in *Journal of Population Economics*, 15: 527–48; Esping-Andersen, G., *Why We Need a New Welfare State*, Oxford, 2002.
8   Bradbury, B., Jenkins, S. and Micklewright, J., *The Dynamics of Child Poverty in Industrialized Countries*. Cambridge, 2001; Vleminckx, K. and Smeeding, T., *Child Well-being, Child Poverty And Child Policy in Modern Nations*, Bristol, 2001.
9   UK child poverty drops to 3 per cent in families where both the mother and father work.
10 Esping-Andersen, G., *Why We Need a New Welfare State*, Oxford, 2002.
11 Haveman, R. and Wolfe, B., *Succeeding Generations. On the Effects of Investments in Children*, New York, 1995; Duncan, G. and Brooks-Gunn, J., *Consequences of Growing up Poor*, New York, 1997; Mayer, S., *What Money Can't Buy*, Harvard, 1997.
12 Mayer, S., *What Money Can't Buy*, Harvard, 1997.
13 OECD, 2001, *Employment Outlook*, Paris, 2001.

14 Card, D., 'The Causal Effect of Education on Earnings', in O. Ashenfelter and D. Card, eds, *Handbook of Labor Economics*, vol. 3. New York, 1999; Bowles, S., Gintis, H. and Osborne, M., 'The Determinants of Earnings: A Behavioural Approach', in *Journal of Economic Literature*, XXXIX, 2001.

15 More than 20 per cent of young (16–25) Americans fall in the bottom, 'dysfunctional' cognitive level. In several European countries, up to 30 per cent of present youth fails to attain the equivalent of secondary education.

16 Eriksson and Jonsson suggest that the Swedish reforms since the 1960s probably did help reduce the class bias of traditional tracking. Erikson, R. and Jonsson, J., *Can Education be Equalized? The Swedish Case in Comparative Perspective*, Boulder, Col., 1996.

17 Heckman, J., 'Doing it Right: Job Training and Education', in *The Public Interest*, 1999.

18 Shavit, Y. and Blossfeld, H. P., *Persistent Inequality*, Boulder, Col., 1993; Erikson, R. and Goldthorpe, J., *The Constant Flux*, Oxford, 1992; OECD, 2001, *Employment Outlook*, Paris, 2001.

19 For an overview, see Haveman, R. and Wolfe, B., *Succeeding Generations: On the Effects of Investments in Children*, New York, 1995; Solon, G., 'Intergenerational Mobility in the Labor Market', in O. Ashenfelter and D. Card, eds, *Handbook of Labor Economics*, vol. 3A. New York, 1999. Note that also much sociological mobility research implicitly emphasises monetary resources. The socio-economic status indices used for cross-generational correlations represent weighted combinations of occupational status and income.

20 Solon, G., 'Intergenerational Mobility in the Labor Market', in O. Ashenfelter and D. Card, eds, *Handbook of Labor Economics*, vol. 3A, New York, 1999.

21 Haveman, R. and Wolfe, B., *Succeeding Generations: On the Effects of Investments in Children*, New York, 1995; Duncan, G. and Brooks-Gunn, J., *Consequences of Growing up Poor*, New York, 1997; Mayer, S., *What Money Can't Buy*, Harvard, 1997.

22 Aber, L. and Elwood, D., 'Thinking about Children in Time', in B. Bradbury et al., eds, *The Dynamics of Child Poverty in Industrialized Countries*, Cambridge, 2001.

23 Bradbury, B., Jenkins, S. and Micklewright, J., *The Dynamics of Child Poverty in Industrialised Countries*, Cambridge, 2001; Vleminckx, K. and Smeeding, T., *Child Well-being, Child Poverty And Child Policy in Modern Nations*, Bristol, 2001.

24 Erikson, R. and Goldthorpe, J., *The Constant Flux*, Oxford, 1992.

25 Shavit, Y. and Blossfeld, H. P., *Persistent Inequality*, Boulder, Col., 1993.

26 Jencks et al., *Inequality: A Reassessment of Family and Schooling in America*, New York, 1972; DeGraaf, P., 'Parents' Financial and Cultural Resources, Grades, and Transitions to Secondary School', in *European Sociological Review*, 4: 209–21, 1998.

27 The 'cognitive' returns to cultural capital are substantial when we consider that a one-level jump in the 5-level cultural capital variable implies an added 35 points (or an 8 per cent improvement) on children's cognitive score (estimates taken from US model, but the cultural capital effect is quite similar across countries).

28 Most telling is the extraordinary high level of employment among lone mothers (approximately 75–80 per cent in Denmark and Sweden). Additionally, day care is practically free of charge for single mothers.

29 OECD, 2002, *Employment Outlook*, Paris, 2002.

30 Esping-Andersen, G., *Why We Need a New Welfare State*, Oxford, 2002.

31 *Ibid.*

32 Duncan, G. and Brooks-Gunn, J., *Consequences of Growing up Poor*, New York, 1997.

33 Haveman, R. and Wolfe, B., *Succeeding Generations. On the Effects of Investments in Children,* New York, 1995.

34 Ermisch, J. and Francesconi, M., 'Intergenerational Mobility in Britain: New Evidence from the BHPS', in M. Corak, ed., *The Dynamics of Intergenerational Mobility*, Cambridge, forthcoming.

35 Waldvogel, J. 2002. 'Child Care, Women's Employment, and Child Outcomes', in *Journal of Population Economics*, 15.

5

Managed Diversity

Nicola Rossi

Immigration is here to stay. It represents a demographic and economic need for host states and a safety valve for source countries. It also symbolises hope for many individuals looking to improve their lives. However, host states seem to be caught in a vicious circle. Restrictive policies have led to an undesirable mix of legal and illegal migrant inflows; this has an adverse affect on the labour market performance of migrants. The more hostile the attitude of natives towards immigrants, the greater the fear of losing national identity, and thus the more restrictive and discriminating the policies become. In addition, the deeper the social resentment, the more acute the fears of losing national identities become. To break the vicious circle, zero migration policies that often violate the fundamental rights of migrants and natives alike should give way to progressive policies geared to opening up channels of legal immigration. The goals underlying this is are at least threefold.

First, to improve the skill composition of migrants and their labour market performance. Second, to promote managed economic migration and restrain immigration channels unrelated to labour market needs. Third, to mix carefully permanent and temporary immigration as well as to balance present and future social contributions and costs of migrants to the host country. New duties and rights should characterise the lives of permanent migrants as citizens of industrialised societies and provide the basis for the process of social integration. Host governments should also recognise that migration and successful social integration require significant innovation in public policy, and are dependent on the active participation of citizens in a new social contract. In the international sphere, new rights and responsibilities between migrant destinations and countries of origin must be specified. This would help strengthen cooperation in managing legal and illegal migration flows. Finally, though it would be overly optimistic to speak about a common EU immigration policy, progressives should realise that the reasons for defining a common set of rules for admitting non-EU country nationals are now greater than ever.

Migrants, Refugees, Dependants and Natives[1]

During the last decade, gross legal migration flows of non-EU nationals into the EU totalled 1.2 million per annum, and around 500,000 per annum for illegal immigration. Corresponding figures for the United States averaged 1 million legal immigrants per annum and about 300,000 illegal immigrants. Thus since 1990, total gross immigration in the EU-15 has been about 1.7 million per annum, approximately one-third higher than the US (whose total population is, however, approximately one-third lower). Today, over 5 per cent of the EU-15 population are not nationals of their country of residence (with the largest proportions of non EU-15 nationals being recorded in Austria and Germany) while in the US, the percentage of those born outside that country is roughly 10 per cent.

Migration flows – while still reflecting geographical proximity and historical ties – have significantly changed with regard to origin, destination and composition. For example, Iraqis and US citizens increasingly travel along new migration routes leading to European countries, while Indians and Chinese immigrants are increasingly represented in immigration flows into the US. Moreover, while up to the mid-1990s migration into the EU was, to a large extent, a German phenomenon (with negative net migration still prevalent in a few member states) net positive inflows are now general to all EU member states. Immigration for family reasons continues to be the predominant motive for migration, accounting for as much as 70 per cent of the inflow into the EU and over 80 per cent in the US. In the EU the number of asylum seekers and refugees rose substantially by the end of the 1990s, owing to regional conflicts and a tightening of entry and acceptance conditions, to about 350,000 applicants (well below the 1992 peak of 670,000). The corresponding figure for the US was slightly more than 50,000 (less than one third of the 1995 peak). It is interesting that rejection rates tend to be extremely high and signal political unrest to be only one of the determinants of asylum claims. Between 1999 and 2000, permanent and especially temporary employment-related migration also increased substantially to meet a growing demand for skilled and highly skilled labour. Finally, since 1990 a higher rate of female immigration has been observed.

Migration flows have been taking place in an ageing European Union. Since 1990, the EU population grew by about 12 million to total over 377 million in 2001 and is projected to reach 388 million in 2020 before reverting to current levels by 2050. As fertility rates dropped substantially, net migration accounted for about two-thirds of the total population increase in the last decade (as opposed to 40 per cent in the US) and three-quarters of the increase in most recent years when four of the current member states would have experienced a slight population decrease in the absence of migration. In all likelihood, migration flows will continue to be the largest component of population change in the EU over the next two decades, only marginally mitigating demographic trends in European countries. Actually, to maintain a stable share of the working age population within the EU, an average net migration of around 1.4 million people a year would be needed until the year 2050. Moreover, in the future, the net share of the population most likely to migrate (the 20–35 age cohort) will tend to shrink in most of the main source countries.

Both push and pull factors are likely to account for the immigration into the EU and the US, and these are not likely to disappear in the medium term. Migration flows will continue in both regions. The slow speed of convergence in Central and Eastern European countries will also contribute to migration flows during the next decade. Non-economic (psychological and cultural) factors may mitigate the impact of relative income discrepancies. However, the social and economic costs may be reduced through the presence of existing migrant networks in the host countries.

Despite the heated debate international migration still remains – by all historical standards – the missing link of the current era of globalization. The dawning of the 20th century witnessed, for example, massive international movements in labour, along with capital and goods. This fostered price and income convergence between countries with different factor endowments. From 1900 to 1917, for example, over 14 million immigrants entered the US, whose population at that time was 76 million. Similarly, during the 1950s and the 1960s, migration played a crucial role in shaping the process of European economic integration. In the aftermath of the Second World War around 12 million Germans left Eastern Europe, two thirds of them migrating into West Germany. In the 1910s and 1920s as well as in the 1950s, absolute and relative orders of magnitude tended to be significantly larger than those we are witnessing today.

While the majority of Americans – even those who support more restrictive policies – tend to recognise the economic and cultural benefits of immigration and rightly recall its role in building the US, Europeans appear prejudiced and hostile. In fact, migration is more likely to challenge the European cultural model than it is to challenge their social and economic system. Immigration will remain the subject of an irrational fear. It has accurately been noted that European institutions 'have grown up around a culture of immobility and have been designed not only to support but also to defend it . . . against outsiders'.[2] The ethnic hostility and racism visible on the walls of European cities, the resentment so explicit in the eyes of Amsterdamers and Venetians, Londoners and Parisians, are not related to the economic consequences of migration but to what these Europeans perceive as threats to their traditional cultural roots and, more generally to the national way of life. This culture of immobility is testified to by the fact that more than 98 per cent of EU citizens reside in their country of birth. It may also be triggered by economic and security fears after the September 11th terrorist attacks after which the US also introduced a tough new visa policy.

As one commentator remarked, by allowing the Statue of Liberty to turn her back on potential immigrants, America might be throwing away its 'secret weapon: bringing people there to see what America is like'.[3] On both sides of the Atlantic, international migration tests political values. It is not just an issue of carefully designed policies: it requires a change in people's emotions and asks that progressives articulate a language of truth and reassurance.

Legends, Myths and Fears

Even countries that have a long history of generous immigration policies are experiencing growing tensions between new arrivals and the native population. These concerns and tensions are what the far right thrive on, but they mostly originate from an ill-founded perception that immigration is out of control.

When asked, 50 to 60 per cent of Europeans and more than 40 per cent of US citizens point to migration as the cause of domestic problems and consider the presence of immigrants as a threat to their jobs and salaries. Furthermore, 50 per cent of Europeans and Americans alike take it for granted that migrants rely more heavily on welfare than natives. On the basis of the available empirical evidence, both beliefs are likely to be inaccurate.

Consider first the impact of foreign workers on natives' wages. Depending on the approach and the country in question, EU estimates suggest that a 10 per cent increase of foreign workers is likely to cause at most a 1 per cent wage loss (if not a gain) to natives. Similarly, as far as the US is concerned, there is ample evidence to show that immigration can generate a negligible pressure on wages (with the possible exception of wages at the bottom of the distribution). Much the same could be said for the idea that immigrants might displace native workers. EU citizens' chances of finding a job or becoming unemployed are unaffected by immigration, while the data for the US suggests that migration flows trigger native population flows.

If migrants do not steal our jobs, do they abuse our welfare? Again, the answer is not necessarily, and if so, only to a very limited extent. If characteristics of migrants are taken into account (their lower education, average age and higher fertility) they are no more likely to depend on welfare than do natives. However, in relative terms, humanitarian migrants tend to rely on welfare due to their average age and generally lower level of entry into the labour force. In turn this distorts the composition of migrants towards those with lower earning capacity.

If immigrants do not abuse our welfare systems they cannot be expected to save it. True, their lower average age may certainly ease the financing of the pension system for some period, but it would be unrealistic to rely entirely on migration inflows to solve the ageing population problem. Estimates for the US actually suggest that the aggregate net fiscal impact of immigration is likely to be low in the long run. The main factor determining the overall impact of immigration on the welfare state is the use of educational services not standard welfare programs. This provides a clue as to why substantial political conflicts characterise the immigration policy debate. The issue is almost entirely one of social distribution, with rather clearly identified winners and losers.

Nannies, Waiters, Seasonal Workers and Cleaners

Institutional arrangements have been far from neutral in the evolution of migration. In Europe, for example, the migratory balance was positive since the early 1960s. Since then labour migration, mostly from Southern European countries and North Africa, induced by wage differentials and an open-door policy stance, grew for almost a decade. It came to an end with the first oil shock in 1973 when most Western European countries, in the face of rising unemployment levels, embraced zero immigration policies. Policies of restrained migration resulted in a different composition of migrant inflows: since 1973, legal migrants only have entered the EU on grounds of family reunification.

This did not significantly change with the application of the single market. But later, a renewed inflow of migration in Europe was driven by a gap in per capita income levels estimated at around 50 per cent.

To a very large extent, this pattern is not likely to change with the enlargement process.

An immigrant population where the frequency of relatives, refugees and illegal migrants is substantial, ends up showing some noteworthy socio-economic characteristics. Usually immigrant populations tend to contain a larger percentage of young males than the native population. However, when the most important channel for legal immigration is family reunification, the network effect operates fully, and the migrant population ends up concentrating in urban areas and tight immigrant communities, increasing, in the medium term, the social costs associated with social tensions and lower social integration. When relatives and asylum seekers make up a substantial share of the migrant population, their average skill level may end up lower than that of natives.

Family dependants of manual workers, refugees from politically unstable regions and workers in grey sectors of the economy all embody relatively lower levels of human capital. The comparison with the labour-market performance of relatively high-skilled intra-EU migrants could not be more illuminating.

French and Italians, Austrians and Germans alike may well be happy with their non-EU nannies, waiters, nurses and window cleaners. After all, migrants take up jobs that locals drawing social welfare would refuse. US employers may be happy with their unskilled workers and onion pickers, but theirs is still an expensive choice. There we have, in fact, come full circle. The migrants' composition with respect to education and skills as well as legal or illegal channels of entry is to a significant extent endogenous, and determined by present regulatory policies combining high formal barriers to labour immigration and relatively low barriers to family reunification and humanitarian immigration. The more restrictive the policies, the more problems are likely in terms of labour market performance and dependence on welfare. The worse migrants' labour market performance is, the more hostile the native attitude towards immigrants. In turn, electorates demand preferential treatment for EU or US citizens. The deeper the social resentment, the more restrictive and discriminating the policies. So an endless spiral is set in place.

Barriers and Amnesties, Quotas and Points

To break the vicious circle, a radical overhaul of the European – and to some degree the American – approach to migration is called for. The European zero migration policy of the past 20 years led to the normalisation of illegal immigration (about 500,000 persons per annum). A large inflow of asylum seekers and dependants has led to a growing shortage of skilled labour. Similarly, the US mix of a preference-based system with a ceiling and ineffective border enforcement has ended up encouraging illegal immigrants with lower levels of educational attainment. Since the Second World War, tight border controls have often paved the way for repeated amnesties both in the EU (four in Spain, three in Portugal and two in France, for example, and as many as five in Italy where the latest amnesty is estimated to have provided a channel of legal entry to some 800,000 illegal migrants) and in the US (in 1986 legal residence was granted to over 2.5 million individuals). Illegal inflows may be expected to come down in the near future, as border controls become more effective, although the incentive for illegal immigration may still be rather high in southern European countries where the underground economy is still a major factor. However, immigrants' dependants and refugees will, in all likelihood, continue to put pressure on the EU and US to provide for a continuous inflow of low-skilled workers.

As noted earlier, today's zero-migration policies should give way to tomorrow's progressive policies. If it ever truly was, *laissez-faire* is not an option anymore. Evidence suggests that a strict regulatory attitude is not an option either. A managed economic migration policy based on a careful mix of permanent and temporary immigration, one that balances present and future social contributions and costs is a viable progressive option. A balanced approach to migration would not entirely stop attempts at unauthorised entry but, when coupled with sustained cooperation with source countries, it would certainly contain illegal inflows more effectively than current restrictive policies.

Legal economic migrants pay social contributions and taxes, thereby contributing to the long-term sustainability of the European welfare

Nicola Rossi

system. Moreover, if low-skilled, they tend to complement the existing factor endowment in many host countries and take up job positions which would otherwise remain vacant. At the same time, migrants benefit from the welfare system and more generally, make use of the public goods generously supplied in many host countries, above all the education system. If so, low-skilled migrants tend to perform unsatisfactorily in the labour market and depend excessively on welfare. Herein lie the reasons for a balanced, open-door, but managed, immigration policy designed to reverse the vicious circle of recent European and American immigration policies: an unhealthy sequence of barriers and loopholes, resentment and amnesties.

In Europe, postponing free movement of workers from Central and Eastern European countries will not significantly alter migration patterns. Over time, however, it may change it enough to extend further overall social uncertainty linked to the enlargement process. In principle, quota arrangements and safeguard clauses could reduce such uncertainty, and smooth out migration pressures from Central and Eastern European countries after the transition period. However, the actual working of quota systems in Europe forcefully suggests caution: today's Italian quota system, being possibly the best, or should we say the worst, example at hand. Moreover, it has to be recognized that radically shifting the orientation of immigration programmes is far from easy in many host countries: the recent experience of Australia and Canada goes a long way in suggesting that shifting the policy focus in favour of skilled migrants may actually be a long-term goal.

Nevertheless, ensuring some degree of correlation between labour demand and migrants' skill mix remains an important social objective. Carefully matching economic migrants with the needs of today's labour market may actually help support family cohesion among migrants and ensure full social support for dependants in the future. Qualifying criteria such as non-dependence on public funds for tied movers, or waiting periods for new arrivals, can contribute to controlling the inflow of migrants' dependants and the implied burden for the host countries' social expenditure. In changing the eligibility criteria, host countries should carefully weigh the costs and benefits, and avoid accumulating lower levels of human capital between second-generation immigrants. A successful migration policy is the one which, from its inception, maintains family reunification as a priority.

The social contribution and the social costs attached to an inflow of permanent economic migrants may be affected by time factors. Both economic and social cycles may require additional flexibility in the number of migrants and their skill mix. In fact, European countries have been employing temporary foreign workers both on a seasonal basis (mostly in the agricultural sector) and on a fixed-term basis (for highly skilled individuals). Contracted temporary migration can prove a useful tool in a balanced immigration strategy if the benefits and disadvantages of an inflow of temporary workers are carefully accounted for. Local firms should balance the need to invest additional training costs; lower incentives to invest in human capital, and the provision of social services such as housing against the easier access local firms gain to unskilled and skilled migrant labour. In addition, there are further economic benefits from differences in wage and nonwage labour conditions embodied in temporary contracts. Authorities should weigh both the positive and negative impact of temporary migration on illegal flows. Illegal migrants who enter for long or short periods of time are able to find temporary work. The ability to effectively enforce a policy of contracted temporary migration is key.

Duties and Rights

Whatever the future of the European migration policy, current migration flows that are bound to challenge everyday life require a significant redefinition of the rights that form the basis of personal and collective relationships in host countries, as well as between countries of destination and countries of origin. Steps in this direction have already been taken, making a clear break with the previous policy of equality between natives and legal immigrants.

Rights and responsibilities should identify permanent migrants as citizens of Western societies and provide the basis for the process of social integration. Duties such as compulsory language courses should be seen as key to social integration, and stronger rights should be linked to migrants' employment status, such as wage and labour conditions. The same approach can be applied to the political status of migrants, by extending the right to vote in local elections. A migration policy that is responsive to labour market needs should also require local employers to carry a large share of the burden in the fight against illegal immigrants. Large fines for hiring illegal immigrants and random, unannounced inspections of worksites should become the norm, not the exception.

A progressive migration policy should also ask citizens to play an active role in public policy, recognising that effective migration policy requires significant innovation. Resentment by parents of native children where local classrooms are dominated by immigrants should not be directed towards the children of migrants (whose parents may happen to be employed by the natives' parents). Efforts should be directed to provision of an education policy that provides preparatory language courses. As immigrants acquire language skills and improve their understanding of labour market institutions and training, greater convergence between immigrant and native unemployment rates will occur.

Language skills, in particular, are the single most important factor limiting labour market integration. Language training for immigrants, their children and spouses should now be a top priority. We should learn from the Dutch experience of the late 1990s, when a significant shift in the public's view of migrants occurred. Migrants were no longer regarded as passive recipients of welfare, but as individuals who had both social and economic potential. Integration is a process, not an event, and it can take more than a generation to achieve. Nevertheless, social integration is the key to multiculturalism, and is critical to public support for future migration policy. Strengthening policies that aim at both the social and economic integration of migrants should be high on the public agenda as it is also likely to reassure natives that immigration is being carefully managed.

A new balance of rights and responsibilities should also characterise the relationship between host and source countries. The outflow of labour, in particular of highly skilled labour, may significantly change the economic perspectives of source countries and regions. Admittedly, remittances from emigrants represent an important source of finance for sending countries. As of 1998, workers' remittances were close to the net level of official foreign aid from OECD countries. However, falling behind, instead of catching up, is the likely result of the 'brain drain' of skilled workers. Instead of establishing barriers and thus increasing the probability of an increase in illegal immigration, host countries should feel obliged to minimise welfare reduction in source countries. Contracted temporary migration – which might imply reciprocal obligations for host and source countries – goes some way in this direction. Returnees from international migration usually possess positive economic externalities, embodied in the human capital acquired abroad, which in turn may contribute to significantly improving the economic prospects of sending regions.

An explicit compensatory policy should be envisaged in the case of permanent migrant flows. From a European perspective, the European Union's structural and cohesion funds could be the compensatory instruments for Central and Eastern European countries, but in the case of other non-EU (or non-US) source countries specific measures – such as scholarships for foreign students or 'brain drain' taxes *à la* Bhagwati – would be needed in order to sustain the process of human capital accumulation in sending regions. Source countries would, at the same time, be made responsible for refugee flows and their compensatory measures reduced by, for example, levying fines related to illegal flows and violations of domestic human rights.

All this entails a sustained cooperation between host and source countries in the active management of both legal (and illegal) migration flows. A policy of 'co-development',[4] intended to regulate without halting the circulation of immigrants, would allow host countries to focus on the problematic consequences of migration and social integration. Actually, the potential for re-emigration is much larger than usually expected and the US experience suggests that as many as 25 per cent of immigrants eventually return to their country of origin. A sizeable fraction of migrants wish to maintain active ties to their homeland and here cooperation between host and source countries can be crucial. A progressive policy could provide seasonal migrants with renewable visas allowing them to work in the host countries for a certain period of time and for several consecutive years provided they return home after each working season (and if not, lose the right to return). Host countries should also consider ensuring the pension rights of immigrant retirees wanting to return to their country of origin after years of work in the host countries, and grant re-emigrating individuals the right to return to the host countries to visit friends or get medical care. In addition, a progressive policy would envisage permanent visas for highly skilled individuals so as to enhance the likelihood of them maintaining relations with their country of origin.

Local Problems, Global Governance

European immigration policy, with regard to the admission of non-EU workers, is still a largely national affair (as, interestingly, US immigration policy is increasingly becoming a state rather than a federal issue). Non-EU foreigners cannot move freely in the Union area and national regulations control their residence and work permits as well as their access to welfare benefits. True, the Tampere European Council, in October 1999, and more recently the Seville European Council should have brought changes in European migration policy toward the opening up of European labour markets. Yet the recent terrorist attacks on September 11th have significantly altered the political environment and strengthened security concerns. While, as previously mentioned, it would be overly optimistic to speak about a common EU immigration policy (in the light, for example, of the EU-specific nature of the Schengen Accord), the reasons for defining a common set of rules for the admission of non-EU country nationals remain valid.

In this respect, the recent lessons from the US should not be dismissed. Changes in the welfare funding structure introduced a new distributive dimension into the immigration debate: local versus federal. The former had been the main provider of public goods related to immigration. However, legislative reforms reduced the federal government's ability to coordinate and, hence, reduced the strength of the national policy in general.

The EU needs a common European asylum and refugee policy, as the European Convention has finally recognised. The Geneva Con-

132

vention on refugees, asylum and refugee policies is the reference point for a whole set of national regulations controlling (sometimes in rather different ways) rules of admissions as well as procedures to deal with non-accepted asylum seekers. In recent years, regulations have been tightened by some member states, limiting entries and shortening the duration of stays. Evidence suggests that in response to these developments refugee flows simply changed direction as applications increased in other member states. Avoiding a 'race to the bottom' should be high on the EU agenda as the Tampere Summit recognised when it called for a common EU policy on 'asylum and migration'. However, in the face of sometimes substantial differences in national regulations, a common set of rules for admitting asylum seekers and refugees into the EU (and as near as possible to the region of origin) might be out of reach. It would be wiser and more realistic to adopt a more flexible approach whereby EU-wide minimum standards of acceptance and support, financed at the European level, could go hand in hand with national policies leaving member states free to admit further non-financed humanitarian migrants. After all, our attitudes towards asylum seekers and refugees play a key role in defining the soul of our communities.

The case for a common EU policy is not limited to asylum seekers and refugees. It should be openly recognised that free movement within the EU calls for a common set of immigration and naturalisation policies, if negative consequences are to be reduced. In the absence of a common framework, lax countries that are likely to be a port of call are unlikely to increase incentives to control immigration and, somewhat paradoxically, could even be tempted to grant citizenship to immigrants in order to see them move elsewhere. For example, immigrants, when choosing their country of destination, may well look at incentives provided by the different national settings as far as the admission of dependants is concerned. Here, again, EU member countries might consider setting a common baseline designed to define what Europeans might regard as acceptable immigration, associated with an open-door but managed economic immigration policy supplemented by common enforcement of external borders. In much the same way, it would be wise to harmonise the position of migrants vis-à-vis national social security systems.

133

Nicola Rossi

Pushing hard for better European cooperation and for common European guidelines on migration issues should not be seen as an excuse for avoiding national and local actions. After all, citizens' perception of the social and economic consequences of immigration are to a very large extent formed at the local level. Asserting Europe's need for immigrants, improving their skill composition, acting against illegal immigration, tackling the widespread feeling of insecurity and promoting integration are even more necessary if, as in present times, progress toward a harmonised European migration policy turns out in practice to be very difficult and unilateral action is still the order of the day. Migrants tend to congregate in disadvantaged areas with lower than average human capital and above average unemployment rates. Such deprived areas usually have difficulties in meeting a growing demand for public services (from education and health care to low cost housing) and easily give way to entrenched and concentrated pockets of poverty whose social cost falls on the shoulders of the immigrants and native population alike. Adequate financing of public infrastructure and appropriate social planning are, in this respect, key elements of a balanced immigration policy designed to respond positively to the local communities' fears and concerns as well as the needs of migrants. In short, global governance is just one of the very important ingredients of the recipe, the other being a change in national and local policy.

A Challenge for the Progressive Left

Global issues – such as migration – require and expect global solutions. The European level is, today, the only one in which it is possible to define a new social contract capable of providing positive responses to the needs of different sectors of society.

It is now possible to begin to define the essential ingredients of this agreement. Our idea of globalization and our relations with a large part of the rest of the world – and, in particular, with source countries – requires first of all the reform of the Common Agricultural Policy. European progressives must encourage the liberalisation of trade in agricultural products and, simultaneously, continue the gradual but definitive replacement of support for producers with support for consumers, as well as broader rural policies (i.e. the protection of the environment and the preservation of the rural landscape). More generally, trade policies in industrial countries – especially in sectors such as textiles and clothing, where source countries have a comparative advantage – are not a substitute for migration policies but rather a much needed complement. Restrictive trade policies tend to provide incentives for additional migration flows by discouraging labour demand in labour intensive sectors in the sending regions and fostering it in the destination countries.

Our answer to the challenge of global competitiveness necessarily involves a policy of research (and to a large extent of secondary education) on a European scale. European reformism must give the world of post-secondary education, research and technological innovation the central position that other sectors have had (and still have) in the budget of the European Union. A rather important part of this strategy could be contracted temporary migration of the highly skilled, if properly channelled into a revised set of relationships between host and source countries.

Finally, our capacity to reassure many Europeans requires that we define the body of rights and obligations of each European citizen. Here too, progressives must acknowledge the supranational nature of issues like immigration and population ageing by transferring decisions whose consequences affect the entire continent to a high level. However, they must also simultaneously promote the gradual convergence of important elements of product and labour market legislation and social security systems. Market institutions and policies that provide the right framework in which migrants and natives can find work can only enhance the potential benefits of migration.

Here is a starting point for the progressive movement. The process of the transfer of sovereign power, much opposed today, must be linked to a process of a different nature and direction: the definitive acquisition of a European citizenship. This is the way to define the terms of a new social contract that combines the need to be competitive with the progressive goals of the European social model.

Notes

1   Given the nature of the main data sources, caution should be exercised when discussing the scale and characteristics of immigration phenomena and, to an even greater extent, when attempting international comparisons. International organisations – such as the United Nations (*Recommendations on Statistics of International Migration Revision 1*, New York, 1998) or the OECD (*Trends in International Migration*, Paris, various editions) – have been recently involved in the collection of data based on a common approach as well as in the comparative analysis of international migration trends. A thoughtful and comprehensive collection of comparative essays on migration is: Boeri, T., Hanson, G., and McCormick, B., *Immigration Policy and the Welfare System*, Oxford, 2002. The report and references therein provide a basic road map for a growing literature.

2   Burda, M., in Boeri, T., Hanson, G., and McCormick, B., *Immigration Policy and the Welfare System*, Oxford, 2002.

3   Bill Reinsch, *The Financial Times*, 29 January 2003.

4   The term is taken from Patrick Weil, 'Towards a Coherent Policy of Co-Development', in *International Migration*, 40: 1, 2002.

6

Global Social Democracy[1]

David Held

The term 'globalization' denotes the expanding scale, growing magnitude, speeding up and deepening impact of transcontinental flows and patterns of social interaction. It refers to a shift in the scale of human organisation that links distant communities and expands the reach of power relations across the world's regions and continents. However, it should not be mistaken for prefiguring the emergence of an harmonious world society or a process of global social integration. For not only does the awareness of growing interconnectedness create new animosities and conflicts, it can fuel reactionary politics and deep-seated xenophobia. Since a substantial proportion of the world's population is largely excluded from the benefits of globalization today, it can be a deeply divisive and contested process. The unevenness of globalization ensures it is far from a universal process experienced uniformly across the planet.

Globalization is a highly contested notion. In academic discourse, whether it be in economics, political science or law, globalization is an intensely disputed subject and researchers do not agree about aspects of its underlying processes. Globalization is fought over both in academia and, more broadly, in the streets from Seattle to Geneva, Rio to Tokyo. One of the reasons for the highly contested nature of globalization lies in poignant aspects of its past. Peoples in different cultures, countries and regions have different historical experiences of globalization and different historical memories. It needs to be emphasized that there is nothing new about globalization *per se*. There have been many phases of globalization over the last two millennia including the development of world religions, the Age of Discovery, and the spread of empires. As European countries exploded onto the world over 500 years ago, linking parts of it together which had previously been isolated, they brought with them not just new technologies and economic techniques, but also new forms of political oppression and exploitation. These early forms of globalization generated experiences and memories of not just the opportunities posed by a growing interconnected world, but of the dangers and threats. In many parts of the world this legacy continues and still conditions how contemporary forms of globalization are understood and shaped.

In order to cut through the many controversies that surround the great globalization debate, it is useful to begin by dispensing with some of the most profound myths about globalization. Following this, the chapter will turn to global economic issues and global politics since the recent war in Iraq. The chapter will conclude by setting out the basis of a new global covenant, which has the possibility of linking the economic processes of globalization, on the one hand, with the core concerns about social integration and social justice, on the other.

Countering Myths about Globalization

While many researchers do not agree about how to characterize the main substantive processes of globalization and their impacts, there is some measure of agreement, in the light of recent research, about what globalization does not entail. Some of these positions are set out below.

Globalization does not mean Americanization

Globalization cannot be taken as a synonym for Americanization or for Western imperialism. While it may certainly be the case that the discourse of globalization, and aspects of it, serve the interests of powerful economic and social forces in the West, globalization is an expression of deeper structural changes in the scale of modern social organization. Such changes are evident in, among other developments, the growth of modern communication systems, the emergence of a world trading system, the development of international law, and global environmental transformations.

There has been no simple race to the bottom in welfare, labour and environmental standards

A cursory survey of European countries over the last 20 years reveals that, despite experiencing many common processes of global economic change, their welfare regimes remain diverse. European welfare institutions have not converged on one single model. This diversity is testimony to the endurance of national state formations, national political traditions, and the importance of particular cultural and local conditions. The absence of a race to the bottom highlights the continuing significance of political institutions. Political institutions matter, and can broker different kinds of agreements between leading economic and social actors. While developing countries are in general much more vulnerable to global economic change, and can afford much less social protection, the diversity of welfare regimes in these countries clearly indicates the significance of political institutions and sound public policy in the determination of welfare and labour outcomes. Politics clearly matters in relation to the environment as well. The last few decades have seen a growing array of new environmental standards, promulgated locally, nationally, regionally and globally. Yet, it is clear that many pressing environmental problems, such as global warming, will continue unabated unless the economic processes of globalization are better managed and regulated. This is a political and ethical issue as much as one about economic globalization *per se*.

Globalization is not associated with the end of the nation-state

Many have argued, or asserted, that globalization involves, or will involve, the end of the nation-state. In the first instance, the number of internationally recognised states has more than doubled between

1945 and the late-1990s to over 190 today. The high point of the modern nation-state system seems to have been reached at the end of the 20th century. In many aspects of political and military affairs, states remain the primary actors – and world order is still shaped decisively by powerful states. None of this is to say that globalization has not altered the nature and form of political power – it certainly has. But it has not simply eroded or undermined the power of states; rather, it has reshaped and reconfigured it. Political power is diffused 'below', 'alongside' and 'above' the state, as fast growing cities, subnational regions, supranational regions and global networks and organisations all create new forms of political dynamics. Political power has become multilayered and multilevel. This leads to a much more complex political picture than the view that globalization engenders the death of the modern state.

Globalization does not simply compound global inequities

While the average incomes in the wealthiest and poorest countries are now further apart than they have ever been – due to the continuing growth of OECD countries in comparison to the stagnating economies of many countries in Sub-Saharan Africa – the proportion of those who live in the very poorest conditions has declined across the world. In addition, the distribution of incomes within some countries has improved.[2] Yet, the distributional picture in many places remains complex.[3] For example, while China and India have enjoyed rapid economic growth for several years, rural areas have not grown rapidly and have often suffered prolonged periods of economic stagnation relative to the growth of many urban and coastal areas. This poses serious policy challenges at both the national and global levels, but they cannot be reduced to questions about globalization alone.

Developing countries as a whole are not losing out in world trade

Over the past decade, developing countries have consistently outperformed developed countries in terms of export growth – enjoying an average increase of almost 10 per cent a year, compared to 5 per cent for the industrialized countries.[4] Moreover, trade among developing countries has been growing more rapidly than trade with the industrialised North. Even after September 11th, developing countries' export performance measured in terms of trade growth has been stronger than that recorded by the industrialised economies. Despite an overall decline in trade growth across the world in 2001/2, East Asia and Eastern Europe increased their trade growth. Against this, African trade continued to decline. Clearly, some developing countries are doing much better than others. The country-specific and regional disparities in trade growth and economic development need to be understood.

The simple removal of all barriers to free trade and capital movements is not the best route for all countries to economic prosperity and growth

Many of the poorest countries cannot easily find a successful entry point into the highly competitive world economic order. Integrating into trade and financial markets has different consequences for countries at different stages of development. There appears to be a minimum threshold of development for benefiting in general from globalization, and most low-income countries (measured by World Bank criteria) have not yet reached that threshold.[5] The experience of China and India – along with Japan, South Korea and Taiwan in earlier times – shows that countries do not have to adopt, first and foremost, liberal trade and capital policies in order to enhance trade, to grow faster and to develop an industrial infrastructure able to produce an increasing proportion of national consumption.[6] While economic protectionism must be resisted as a general strategy, there is much evidence to suggest that a country's *internal* economic integration – the development of its human capital, of its economic infrastructure, of robust national market institutions, and the replacement of imports with national production where feasible – needs to be stimulated by state-led economic and industrial policy. Higher internal economic integration can help generate the conditions from which a country can benefit from higher *external* integration.

141

David Held

Economic globalization and the current structure of international governmental organisations do not merely undermine the 'voice' and leverage of developing countries

For example, development issues are now on the WTO's agenda. The rule-making and dispute mechanisms of the WTO allow small countries to challenge the power of larger countries. Costa Rica defeated the US under the rule of international law at the WTO. While there are huge asymmetries of power and authority at the global level in relation to both international governmental organisations and the distribution of economic resources, politics at the global level cannot simply be understood as the outcome of the preferences of the most powerful. If this were the case, it would not be possible to comprehend the shifting nature of agendas in the leading institutions of global governance.

The challenges posed by the contemporary nature and form of globalization will be of enduring significance. The deep drivers of these processes are likely to be operative for the foreseeable future; irrespective of the exact political form globalization takes. Among these drivers are:

- The changing infrastructure of global communications linked to the IT revolution
- The end of the Cold War and the diffusion of democratic values across many of the world's regions (alongside some marked reactions to this)
- The development of global markets in goods and services, linked to the new worldwide distribution of information
- The reconfiguration of political power and the development of multilayered and multilevel politics
- The emergence of a new type and form of global civil society, with the crystallization for the first time of elements of a global public opinion
- The growth of migration and the movement of peoples, linked to fundamental shifts in demography and the growth of populations

---

Box 1: Twenty global issues

Sharing our planet: issues involving the global commons
Global warming
Biodiversity and ecosystem losses
Fisheries depletion
Deforestation
Water deficits
Maritime safety and pollution

Sharing our humanity: issues requiring a global commitment
Massive step up in the fight against poverty
Peacekeeping, conflict prevention, combating terrorism
Education for all
Global infectious diseases
Digital divide
Natural disaster prevention and mitigation

Sharing our rulebook: issues needing a global regulatory approach
Reinventing taxation for the twenty-first century
Biotechnology rules
Global financial architecture
Illegal drugs
Trade, investment and competition rules
Intellectual property rights
e-commerce rules
International labour and migration rules

Source: Rischard, J.F., *High Noon*, New York, 2002.

These deeply structured processes can be linked to a number of urgent political and regulatory problems which one writer has referred to as the 'high noon' of our global age.[7] While there are many ways of conceiving and categorising these issues, Rischard usefully thinks of them as forming three core sets of problems: those concerned with sharing our planet, our humanity and our rulebook. He lists 20 core challenges under these headings (see Box 1). In our increasingly interconnected world, these global problems cannot be solved by any one nation-state acting alone. They call for collective and collaborative action – something that the nations of the world have not been good at in the past, and which they need to be better at if these pressing issues are to be adequately addressed.

David Held

Globalization and Social Democracy

Before developing the main arguments of this chapter, a few clarifying points can usefully be made about globalization and social democracy. Traditionally, social democrats have sought to mould national institutions to a particular political project: a compromise between the power of capital, labour and the state which seeks to encourage the development of market institutions, private property and the pursuit of profit within a regulatory framework that guarantees not just the civil and political liberties of citizens, but also the social conditions necessary for people to enjoy their formal rights. In the post-Second World War period, in particular, many capitalist countries sought to reconcile the efficiency of markets with the values of social community which markets themselves presuppose, in order to develop and grow. The nature of the balance struck took different forms in different countries, reflecting different national political traditions: the New Deal in the US, and social democracy or the social market economy in Europe. Yet, the underlying idea was similar: 'a grand social bargain whereby all sectors of society agree to open markets . . . but also to contain and share the social adjustment costs that open markets inevitably produce'.[8] Governments had a key role to play in enacting and managing this compromise: moderating the volatility of transaction flows, managing demand levels, and providing social investments, safety nets and adjustment assistance.

The contemporary constellation of global forces and networks puts considerable pressure on these conditions. As Ruggie has explained, 'for the industrialised countries, it is the fact that [this grand bargain] . . . presupposed the existence of *national* economies, engaged in *external* transactions, conducted at *arms length*, which governments could mediate at the *border* by tariff and exchange rates, among other tools'.[9] While for three decades after the Second World War it seemed that a satisfactory balance could be achieved in the long run between self-government, social solidarity and international economic openness – at least for the majority of Western countries, and for the majority of their citizens – it now appears that this balance is much harder to sustain. The mobility of capital, goods, people, ideas and pollutants increasingly puts pressure on the capacity of individual governments to sustain their own social and political compromises within delimited borders.[10] Globalization, as noted earlier, does not lead to the end of state diversity, but the regulative capacity of states increasingly has to be matched by the development of collaborative mechanisms of governance at supranational regional and global levels. New challenges are posed by the increasing divergence between the extensive spatial reach of economic and social activity, on the one hand, and the traditional state-based mechanisms of political control, on the other.

The values of social democracy (from its earliest days to the third way) – the rule of law, political equality, democratic politics, social justice, social solidarity and community, economic efficiency and effectiveness – are of enduring significance. But the key challenge today is to elaborate their meaning, and to re-examine the conditions of their entrenchment, against the background of the changing global constellation of politics and economics. In the current era, social democracy must be defended and elaborated not just at the level of the nation-state, but at regional and global levels as well. With this in mind, the project of global social democracy, as I call it, can be conceived as a basis for promoting the rule of law at the international level; greater transparency, accountability and democracy in global governance; a deeper commitment to social justice in the pursuit of a more equitable distribution of life chances; the protection and reinvention of community at diverse levels (from the local to the global); and the regulation of the global economy through the public management of global financial and trade flows, the provision of global public goods and the engagement of leading stakeholders in corporate governance. These guiding orientations set the politics of global social democracy apart from the pursuit of the Washington consensus, neo-liberalism, and the aims of those pitched against globalization in all its forms.

A number of social democratic tests can be devised to help demarcate a range of policies and politics for which social democrats can strive. These allow fundamental questions to be asked about competing policies and politics at all levels, including the global. Accordingly, competing prescriptions and policy programmes at the global level can be assessed insofar as they:

- Promote the rule of law and its impartial application
- Enhance political equality and its core social conditions
- Develop democratic politics through a cluster of rules and institutions permitting the broadest possible participation of citizens in decisions affecting their lives
- Promote social justice by ameliorating the radical asymmetries of life-chances which pervade the world today, and by addressing the severe harm inflicted on many people against their will and without their consent
- Enhance social solidarity and social integration insofar as they depend on a set of common values and human rights, which all human beings can, in principle, enjoy irrespective of the particular culture or religion in which they are born and raised
- Pursue economic efficiency and economic effectiveness as far as possible within the constraints of the other tests set out above, and as far as they are compatible with stewardship of the world's environmental resources

These tests generate a useful filter mechanism for thinking about the nature of contemporary political and economic processes, and the extent to which their form, dynamic and trajectory are compatible with social democracy. To the extent that they are not, and there are good reasons for being concerned about such a disjuncture, a useful point of orientation is provided to help steer policy choice in a more social democratic direction.

The Regulation of Economic Globalization: A New Policy Mix

There is no uncontentious way through the mire of issues which form the debate about economic globalization, global economic governance and the regulation of the world trade and financial systems.

Global Social Democracy

However, it is possible to distinguish broadly between a narrow economic agenda and a social democratic vision of the reform of global economic processes. The narrow agenda is focused typically on free trade, capital market liberalization, floating exchange rates, the deregulation of all markets, the transfer of assets from the public to the private sector, balanced budgets and the protection of intellectual property rights. It has been the dominant orthodoxy over the last 20 years in leading OECD countries, and in the international financial institutions. Although elements of this orthodoxy rightly retain a place in a social democratic framework, the latter is distinguished by being tough in pursuit of free markets while insisting on a framework of shared values and common institutional practices, i.e. balancing open markets, strong governance, social protection and distributive justice at the global level. A progressive economic agenda needs to calibrate the freeing of markets with poverty reduction programmes and the immediate protection of the vulnerable – north, south, east and west.

If globalization is to mean not just global market integration but also global social integration and a commitment to social justice, then a social democratic agenda needs to be concerned with the promotion of those core values and principles which affirm that each and every person is treated, in principle, with equal concern and respect. This involves the promotion of a set of internationalist or cosmopolitan values, from the sanctity of life to a diversity of human rights, that attach to every human being, irrespective of where he or she was born or brought up. It involves the promotion of these values and principles in regional and global governance. In case it be thought that these values and principles are for another world – for future times and not the present – it needs to be remembered that they are at the core of the 1948 UN Declaration of Human Rights and subsequent 1966 Covenants of Rights which raised cosmopolitan aspirations to a universal reference point: the requirement that all individuals be treated with equal concern and respect, irrespective of the state in which they were born or brought up. It is the central pillar of the human rights world-view, and of a wide range of international treaties that have been agreed under UN auspices.[11] Anchored in this postwar legacy, global social democracy aims to combine a universal

147

focus with policies that address the most pressing cases of harm and need. This can be thought of as *targeted egalitarianism*,[12] addressing the marginal and excluded while seeking to ensure that globalization works for all.

Economic growth can provide a powerful impetus to the achievement of human development targets. But it does not necessarily achieve these targets; unregulated economic development, which simply follows existing rules and entrenched interests, falls short of managed economic change geared to the prosperity of all. Economic development needs to be conceived as a means to an end, not an end in itself. Understood accordingly, it should be recognised that while international trade has huge potential for helping the least well-off people and countries to lift themselves out of poverty, and for enhancing the welfare and well-being of all nation-states, the current rules of global trade are heavily structured to protect the interests of the well-off and are heavily stacked against the interests of the poorest countries.[13]

According to the World Bank, abolishing all trade barriers could boost global income by $2.8 trillion and lift 320 million people out of poverty by 2015.[14] In principle, this could cut global poverty by a quarter, which represents the equivalent of lifting out of poverty the very poorest in sub-Saharan Africa. If the WTO's Doha round, which was started in January 2002, achieves even half of this objective, it would be a major step forward. However, while free trade is an admirable objective for progressives in principle, it cannot be pursued without attention to the poorest in the least well-off countries who are extremely vulnerable to the initial phasing in of free trade and capital market liberalisation, and who have few resources, if any, to fall back on during times of economic transformation.[15] The same is true, of course, for many people in wealthier societies. If they lose their jobs or have to settle for lower wages, they are also vulnerable in times of major economic shifts.

It is, thus, crucial to any social democratic agenda for free markets that it addresses simultaneously the needs of the most vulnerable wherever they are. This will mean the provision in developed countries of, among other things, generous safety nets alongside sustained investment in life-long learning and skills acquisition. For the poorest countries this will mean that development policies must be directed to ensure the sequencing of global market integration (especially of portfolio capital markets), long-term investment in health care, human capital and physical infrastructure, and the development of transparent, accountable political institutions. What follows here is complex and challenging. But what is striking is that this range of policies have all too often not been pursued. This seems more a matter of psychology and political will, and less a matter related to any fundamental obstacles in the nature of the economic organisation of human affairs.

A more detailed social democratic agenda for economic globalization and global economic governance follows. Each element would make a significant contribution to the creation of a level playing field in the global economy; together, they would help shape an economic system that was both free and fair. The agenda is set out under a number of core headings:

Trade

- The pursuit of impartial, rule-based free trade through the current round of trade negotiations is urgent. The trade round begun at Doha needs to be a successful development round – one that brings real benefits to poor countries.
- Access to developed markets for developing countries needs to be improved, involving, at a minimum, the removal of quotas on textiles and clothing by the agreed deadline of 2005, and the tighter application of the rules governing anti-dumping measures.
- Agricultural subsidies in all OECD countries need to be phased out. This includes the fundamental reform of the CAP, leading to the eventual abolition of domestic and export subsidies for EU agricultural products. Tariff-escalating mechanisms which discriminate against developing countries adding value to farmed products, among other goods, need to be removed.
- The reform, if not outright abolition, of the Trade-Related Aspects of Intellectual-Property Rights Agreement (TRIPs) is critical.[16] At the minimum, there should be an end to the universal application of the WTO intellectual-property blueprint with developing countries enjoying the right to maintain short-term and

more flexible systems of intellectual property protection; there must be a clear and continuing commitment to put public health priorities before the claims of patent holders, building on commitments made at the Doha ministerial conference in 2001; and there must be a prohibition on patent protection for genetic resources for food and agriculture, along with stronger rights for poor countries to develop more appropriate forms of plant-related protection, and to protect farmers rights to save, sell and exchange seeds. In addition, the option should be removed to enforce TRIPs by imposing trade sanctions.[17]

- Strengthening the capacity of developing countries to participate more effectively in international trade negotiations, including at the WTO, is an important additional step. Many of the poorest countries have no permanent representation at the WTO headquarters in Geneva, and programmes which enhance their representative capacity are urgent. Initiatives like the WTO legal advisory centre need to be built upon.

- The promotion of good governance at all levels of economic activity – i.e. the establishment of transparent public services, the protection of commercial activity from corruption, the rule of law and the maintenance of relevant property rights, alongside accountable and replaceable politicians – all need to be nurtured further to ensure that markets work without political, bureaucratic and corrupt impediment.

- There needs to be an improvement in the transport and support infrastructures of developing countries in order that they can export more. Transport costs, for example, can often be a serious barrier to trade, and better transport infrastructure can help in the expansion of trade.

- The possible establishment of a social chapter or social clause in the core provisions of the WTO should be explored. This could provide the means to help ban forced and child labour, to enforce trade union freedom, collective bargaining and the right to strike, and should involve the elimination of all forms of discrimination. The point of such a social clause would not be to erode the competitive advantages of developing and transitional economies on a comparative cost basis but, rather, to build into the free trade system the necessary requirements for free trade to be fair, that is, respecting minimum social and trade union conditions.

Aid

- All developed countries must adopt legally binding minimum levels of overseas development assistance if there is to be adequate investment in the internal integration of the poorest countries. All developed countries should be called upon to set a clear timetable for reaching the UN 0.7 per cent GNP/overseas aid target. In addition, aid should be refocused on poverty reduction in particularly low income countries. At present, too much of global aid is spent on middle income countries at the expense of the poorest nations. More aid resources should be linked to supporting directly developing countries own Poverty Reduction Strategy Papers.

- Governments should agree to untie their aid budgets so that developing countries can strengthen their own procurements systems and purchase goods and services from the most cost-effective source.

- A radical reduction in the international debt burden borne by the Heavily Indebted Poor Countries is also necessary to ensure that debt levels are brought down to sustainable levels. Despite numerous debt relief initiatives by the World Bank, the IMF and other agencies, debt remains a burden preventing poorer countries from generating consistent economic growth. Every dollar the West gives in aid to developing countries is met by several dollars returning in the form of debt servicing.[18]

- A reduction in debt levels and debt servicing could be linked to a system that encourages families to send their children to school by compensating them directly for the loss of a child's income.[19] For example, it has been estimated that the cost of getting four million children back to school for one year in Brazil is equivalent to just over 1 per cent of that country's 1998 debt servicing repayments. Extending such a programme to 10 million children between the ages of 6 and 10 would cost just over 3 per cent of debt servicing payments. In other words, a direct link could be

151

made between the reduction of debt servicing commitments, of debt overall, and the funding of children in schools.

- An international poverty line needs to be established that has a clearly defined threshold of income (including the value of income in kind). Such a line should be subject to demonstrable scientific consensus, and linked to future aid programmes directly. The UN and other principal international agencies need to establish a clear monitoring system for measuring the success or failure of anti-poverty policies in meeting this standard.

New financial resource capacities

- The creation of an International Finance Facility is indispensable to help meet internationally agreed poverty reduction targets and, in the first instance, the agreed Millennium Development Goals (see Box 2). A model for such a facility has been set out by the UK Treasury, in association with the UK Department for International Development.[20] The aims of such a facility are inspired by the world's commitment to tackling illiteracy, disease, poverty and under-development in the world's poorest countries. The founding principle of the facility is long-term funding guaranteed to the poorest countries by the richest as a supplement to national aid development programmes. The funding would be conditional on efforts to fight corruption, improve public financial management, encourage investment and develop further country-owned poverty reduction strategies.
- In the longer run, a new transfer system has to be established within and across national communities to allow resources to be generated to alleviate the most pressing cases of avoidable economic suffering and harm. Whilst such a system can be partially built on the model of the finance facility suggested above, it has to have a more durable foundation in the long term. Just as national governance requires a national taxation system to ensure adequate resources for public goods, so a similar fund-raising and distributive system is required at the global level to ensure the means exist to alleviate systematically the conditions of the least well off. What is needed are new instruments creating new forms

of regional and global taxation – for instance, a consumption tax on energy use, or a tax on carbon emissions, or a global tax on the extraction of resources within national territories, or a tax on the GNP of countries above a certain level of development, or a transaction tax on the volume of financial turnover in foreign exchange markets. The ultimate purpose of such measures is the creation of independent (non-national) funds that could be established to meet the most extreme cases of need. Sustained social framework investments in the conditions of every human being's development (sanitation, health, housing, education and so on) could then follow on a routine and regular basis.

Box 2: UN millennium development goals, 1999–2015

Eradicate extreme poverty and hunger
Halve the proportion of people with less than one dollar a day and who suffer from hunger

Achieve universal primary education
Ensure that boys and girls alike complete primary schooling

Promote gender equality and empower women
Eliminate gender disparity at all levels of education

Reduce child mortality
Reduce by two-thirds the under-five mortality rate

Improve maternal health
Reduce the maternal mortality ratio

Combat HIV/AIDS, malaria and other diseases
Reverse the spread of HIV/AIDS

Ensure environmental sustainability
Integrate sustainable development into country policies and reverse loss of environment resources, halve the proportion of people without access to portable water, and significantly improve the lives of at least 100 million slum dwellers

Develop a global partnership for development
Raise official development assistance, expand market access, and encourage debt sustainability

---

David Held

Financial governance arrangements

• Just as the phased opening of markets to global trade is essential to the successful integration of a country into the world economic system, so is the phased opening of financial markets. This is especially true in relation to portfolio capital investment. In addition to sound frameworks of macroeconomic management, the development of a country's capacity for governance with respect to domestic financial markets is an important element of its overall economic strategy in the long run. The enhancement of financial transparency, the control of corruption, the maintenance of the rule of law and the development of financial supervisory capacity are all important for a country to pursue if it is to integrate itself successfully into the global financial infrastructure. In many cases, this will require that developing countries are given both technical and financial assistance to create the necessary institutions.

• Developing countries require greater access to, and an enhanced participatory role in, the core institutions of global financial governance. The arguments against giving developing countries such access are weak. The World Bank and the IMF are much less reliant now on wealthy country contributions than they were when they were initially founded. As repayments of existing loans constitute a significant proportion of the World Bank's income, the case for developed countries' dominance of the World Bank Board and other institutions of global financial governance have weakened.[21] A range of institutional innovations are, accordingly, essential, from altering the ways in which leaders are selected for the World Bank and the IMF to increasing the voting shares of developing countries in their Boards. Developing countries are under-represented in international financial institutions. It is also essential to expand significantly the participation of developing countries in the Bank for International Settlements. Important progress has been made in this regard in the 1990s, but a great deal more remains to be achieved.

• Developing countries, in addition, need to be included in the crucial financial fora from which they are currently excluded, including the Financial Stability Forum (FSF). At the present time, developing

154

countries have no voice in some key international financial organisations, and this despite the fact that decisions are taken in them that affect them significantly. One proposal in this regard suggests that developing countries could be included in the FSF and Basel Committees on a rotational basis, without significantly increasing the size of these groups and, therefore, not risking their effective working practices. An example of this might be two representatives per developing country region (Latin America, Asia and Africa) who might be nominated for two years and then rotated.[22]

- Attention must be focused on improving co-operation among international financial institutions and other international donors, thus consolidating the policy-making efforts of the international community with regard to financial governance within the UN system. At the moment, institutional arrangements and divisions too often lead to initiatives which conflict or undermine each other. For example, mandates vary, jurisdictions conflict, responsibilities overlap, and even the geographic location of some of the core international financial organisations are based on Cold War considerations that are now out-of-date.

- The world's current financial institutions were created more than 50 years ago in an economic context that has drastically changed. These institutions are no longer self-evidently equipped to deal with the challenges that many countries face today and, accordingly, their mandates and briefs should be reassessed. There should be a substantial review of the functioning of the Bretton Woods institutions. Such a review should include a re-examination of the framework for structural adjustment programmes with a different range of conditionality, linking the latter to wider social justice considerations; a change in the capital quotas in the IMF and World Bank with a view to their more equitable distribution; new or reinforced regional financial institutions with a mandate to serve more local needs.

Multinational corporations (MNCs)

- The corporate coverage of the Global Compact (GC) should be extended and deepened, with a view to the engagement of companies in the promotion of core UN principles (see Box 3). The overall objective should be to encourage companies to move towards 'good practices' as defined through the maintenance of these principles and multi-stakeholder dialogue and partnership about their implementation.

- The creation of a code of conduct for MNCs, which would be voluntary in the first instance, and would build on the principles and regulatory rules laid down in the GC.
- In the long term, governments should aim to create a legally binding international protocol, based on the GC Principles, to govern the production, trade and consumption of all resources.[23]
- The development of a global anti-trust mechanism is a final element that needs to be stressed. In light of the concentration of corporate power in the global economy today, it is necessary to extend the principles of anti-monopoly legislation found within national borders to the wider global economy.

Box 3: Core UN principles

The core principles are:

Support and respect for the protection of internationally proclaimed human rights

Non-complicity in human rights abuses

Freedom of association and the effective recognition of the right to collective bargaining

The elimination of all forms of forced and compulsory labour

The effective abolition of child labour

The elimination of discrimination in respect of employment and occupation

A precautionary approach to environmental challenges

Greater environmental responsibility

The encouragement of the development and diffusion of environmentally friendly technologies

---

The policy objectives set out above, and the underlying reasons for them, provide a rationale for a politics of intervention in economic life – not to control and regulate markets for their own sake, but to provide the basis for a free, fair and just world economy, and to ensure that the values of efficient and effective global economic processes are compatible with the agenda of social democratic values. The roots of such necessary intervention lie in the indeterminacy of the market system itself.[24] Market economies can only function in a manner commensurate with self-determination, democracy, human rights and environmental sustainability if this indeterminacy is addressed systematically and if the conditions of the possibility of social democratic governance are met, in the short and long term.

Recasting Security and International Law Enforcement

As with geo-economics and the politics of global economic governance, there is, of course, no single way forward in global politics post September 11th and Iraq that would command general assent. But it is possible, here again, to distinguish broadly between a narrow security agenda and a social democratic programme focused on security, law and social justice. The difference can be articulated by recalling Tony Blair's famous slogan on crime: 'tough on crime, tough on the causes of crime'. In global political terms, this means being tough on security threats and tough on the conditions that breed them.

If one takes a narrow security agenda and ignores the social and political causes of sympathy for terrorism, then it will be harder than ever to win over the many millions who, across many countries in the Middle East and elsewhere, hold a romantic conception of the role of the September 11th terrorists. This is not to say that Al Qaeda or the Saddam Husseins of the world are the Robin Hoods of our age – not in the least. But many perceive them in that way, and this is related to the geopolitical and social stagnation of some of the world's most vulnerable areas. It is the result of the disenchantment felt about the chances of successfully establishing peaceful ways of addressing long-held grievances. In general terms, what is required, if the tests of

David Held

global social democracy are to be met in the sphere of security, is movement toward the application and extension of the rule of law in international affairs and conflict situations, and the fostering of collaboration between communities in place of violence and terror.[25] This requires three things of governments and international institutions.

First, there must be a commitment to the rule of law and the development of multilateral institutions – not the prosecution of war *per se*. Civilians of all faiths and nationalities need protection, wherever they live. Terrorists and all those who systematically violate the sanctity of life and human rights must be brought before an international criminal court that commands cross-national support. This does not preclude internationally sanctioned military action to arrest suspects, dismantle terrorist networks and deal with aggressive rogue states – far from it. But such action should always be understood as a robust form of international law enforcement, above all as a way of protecting civilians and bringing suspects to trial. Moreover, this type of action must scrupulously preserve both the laws of war and human rights law. In short, if justice is to be dispensed impartially, no power can act as judge, jury and executioner. What is needed is momentum toward global, not American, Russian, Chinese or French or British justice.

Second, a sustained effort has to be undertaken to generate new forms of global political legitimacy for international institutions involved in security and peace-making. This must include the condemnation of systematic human rights violations wherever they occur, and establishing new forms of political accountability. This cannot be equated with an occasional or one-off effort to create a new momentum for peace and the protection of human rights. Many parts of the world will need convincing that the UN's – not to mention the Western-based coalition's – interest in security and human rights for all peoples and regions is not just a product of short-term geopolitical or geo-economic interests.

Finally, there must be a head-on acknowledgement that the ethical and justice issues posed by the global polarisation of wealth, income and power, and with them the huge asymmetries of life chances, cannot be left to markets to resolve alone. Those who are poorest and most vulnerable, linked into geopolitical situations which have

158

neglected their economic and political claims for generations, may provide fertile ground for terrorist organisations looking for new recruits. The project of economic globalization has to be connected to manifest principles of social justice; the latter need to frame global market activity.

Today, the attempt to develop international law, to enhance the capacity of international institutions for peace-keeping and peace-making, and to build bridges between economic globalization and the priorities of social justice, are threatened not just by the dangers posed by extensive terrorist networks, but also by some deeply mis-guided responses to them. These have been given particular shape by the new security agenda of the American neo-conservatives and the National Security doctrine of the current American administration (published in September 2002), with its emphasis on necessary unipolarity and the unilateral and pre-emptive use of force. This doc-trine, which arrogates to the United States the global role of setting standards, weighing risks, assessing threats and meting out justice, breaks with the fundamental premises of the post-1945 world order with its commitment to deterrence, stable relations among major powers and the development of multilateral institutions to address common problems.[26] It regards formerly held strategic views and diplomatic positions as, in general, obsolete.

The new doctrine of American pre-eminence has many serious im-plications.[27] Among these are a return to an old realist understanding of international relations as, in the last analysis, a 'war of all against all', in which states rightly pursue their national interest unencumbered by attempts to establish internationally recognised limits (self-defence, collective security) on their ambitions. But if this 'freedom' is (dan-gerously) granted to the USA, why not also to Russia, China, India, Pakistan, North Korea and so on? It cannot be consistently argued that all states bar one should accept limits on their self-defined goals. The flaws of international law and the UN Charter can either be addressed, or taken as an excuse for further weakening international institutions and legal arrangements. In sum, there is a serious risk at present of the triumph of a narrowly focused security agenda.

Of course, terrorist crimes of the kind witnessed on September 11th and on many occasions since (in Chechnya, Saudi Arabia,

David Held

Pakistan, Morocco and elsewhere) may often be the work of the simply deranged and the fanatical and so there can be no guarantee that a more just and institutionally stable world will be a more peaceful one in all respects. But if we turn our back on this project, there is no hope of ameliorating the social basis of disadvantage often experienced in the poorest and most dislocated countries. Gross injustices, linked to a sense of hopelessness born of generations of neglect, feed anger and hostility. Popular support against terrorism depends upon convincing people that there is a legal and peaceful way of addressing their grievances. Without this sense of confidence in public institutions and processes, the defeat of terrorism becomes a hugely difficult task, if it can be achieved at all.

A number of clear steps could be taken to help put these issues at the heart of global discussion. These include:

- Re-linking the security and human rights aspects of international law – the two sides of international humanitarian law which, together, specify grave and systematic abuse of human security and well-being, and the minimum conditions required for the development of human agency.
- Reforming UN Security Council procedures to improve the specification and legitimacy of credible reasons, thresholds and promises in relation to armed intervention in the affairs of a state. The objective being to link these directly to a set of conditions which would constitute a severe threat to peace, and/or a threat to the minimum conditions for the well-being of human agency, sufficient to justify the use of force.
- Recognising the necessity to dislodge and amend the now outmoded 1945 geopolitical settlement as the basis of the decision-making in the Security Council, and to extend representation to all regions on a fair and equal footing.
- Expanding the remit of the Security Council, or creating a parallel Social and Economic Security Council, to examine and, where necessary, intervene in the full gamut of human crises – physical, social, biological, environmental – which can threaten human agency.

- Building global networks and institutions, focused on poverty and welfare, to act as counter-weights and countervailing powers to the market-driving IGOs (the WTO, IMF and World Bank).
- Founding a World Environmental Organisation to promote the implementation of existing environmental agreements and treaties, and whose main mission would be to ensure that the development of world trading and financial systems is compatible with the sustainable use of the world's resources.
- Adapting the principles and mechanisms of global public goods theory, as the UNDP has suggested, to help reform the wider UN system by:
  - developing criteria for fair negotiations at the global level
  - strengthening the negotiating capacity of developing countries
  - developing rules for interactions between state and non-state actors
  - creating advisory scientific panels for all major global issues, following the example of the Intergovernmental Panel on Climate Change
  - creating negotiating arenas for new priority issues (such as the right of access to water for all people) together with appropriate grievance panels (such as a world water court)
  - creating demand-driven review and response facilities to promote flexible implementation of policy regimes, such as a trade and development review council within the World Trade Organisation.[28]
- Finally, building UN peace-making, and not just peace-keeping, capacity.

In order to reconnect the security and human rights agenda and to bring them together into a coherent framework of law, it would be important to hold an international or global legal convention. Rather than set out a blueprint of what the results of such a convention should be, it is necessary to stress the significance of a legitimate process that reviews the security and human rights sides of international law and seeks to reconnect them in a global legal framework. One demonstrable result of such an initiative could be new procedures at the UN to specify the set of conditions that would constitute a threat to the peace and the well-being of humankind sufficient to justify the use of force.

In a recent paper, Anne-Marie Slaughter[29] has argued that the proper specification of such conditions depends on weighing the balance between three factors: (1) the continuing possession of weapons of mass destruction or clear and convincing evidence of attempts to gain such weapons; (2) grave and systematic human rights abuses (ethnic cleansing or genocide) sufficient to demonstrate the absence of any internal constraints on government behaviour; and (3) evidence of aggressive intent with regard to other nations. How one weighs the balance of these factors, establishes a framework that can be applied to each country (and not just those who are perceived as a threat to leading interests in the West), and creates a new threshold for the legitimate use of force, needs to be tested against the views and judgement of people who are representative of the world's regions and nations. A solution to this problem needs to be found that is not imposed by the select few from above, but rather from a legitimate process that has a reasonable chance of winning global political legitimacy. Only such a process, in the long run, can stipulate a new balance between international law and coercive power. Clearly, there would be much to gain from such a project – for it would take account not only of the security concerns at the heart of the recent war against Iraq, but also the fundamental human rights concerns which left many people unconvinced about the justification, nature and extent of the intervention in Iraq.

Linked to such a settlement in the long run would need to be new institutional mechanisms to assess breaches of security and human rights law. At issue would be the creation of new global organisations that could weigh evidence in a manner that peoples around the world could find compelling and acceptable – ways which were independent of the particular interests and concerns of any one nation-state, however powerful or humble. Under consideration in such a settlement would need to be the establishment of new forms of submission to the International Criminal Court and the International Court of Justice jurisdiction, the creation of a new international

162

human rights court, the further development of regional human rights organisations, and the development of new procedures to test claims to breaches of any new conceptions of security in the UN Security Council itself. The outcome could be the specification of acceptable or credible reasons for armed intervention in the affairs of another state, acceptable threshold tests for the justification of such intervention, and clear, credible sets of promises by any occupying power as to how it proposed to transform a country in order to meet the standards of international political legitimacy and international law.[30]

But the Security Council at the centre of such deliberations could not be the same Security Council that prevails today; for it is (as noted earlier) constituted by the geopolitical settlement of 1945. The international power structure as it was understood then was built into the UN Charter. One of the most obvious manifestations of this is the special veto power accorded to the Permanent Members of the UN Security Council. Against the backdrop of the reconfiguration of political power today, and shifting patterns of power across the world's regions, this 1945 veto power system is anachronistic. It is not just that Britain and France would not be considered major powers today deserving of such status, or that India, Japan and Brazil might be candidates for permanent inclusion, it is that the whole voting system needs to be recast to reflect better an equitable and legitimate balance of voices from across the world's regions and nations.[31]

Global Social Democracy:
Towards A New Global Covenant

The contemporary phase of globalization is transforming the foundations of world order, leading to a shift from a purely state-centric politics to a new and more complex form of multilayered global politics and governance. At the beginning of the 21st century there are good reasons for believing that the traditional international order of states cannot be restored and that the deep drivers of globalization are unlikely to be halted. Accordingly, a change in political orientation is unavoidable. Changes of outlook are clearly delineated in the

David Held

contest between the principal variants in the politics of globalization. The perspectives sitting at opposite ends of the political spectrum of globalization – neo-liberalism and the anti-globalization movement – are both deeply problematic. Whereas neo-liberalism simply perpetuates existing economic and political systems and offers no real solutions to the problems of market failure, the radical anti-globalist position appears deeply naive about the potential for locally-based action to resolve, or engage with, the governance agenda generated by the forces of globalization. How can such a politics cope with the challenges posed by overlapping communities of fate?

The alternative position is global social democracy. It seeks to nurture some of the most important values of social democracy while applying them to the new global constellation of economics and politics. National social bargains, as noted previously, are insufficient to ensure an effective trade-off between the efficiencies of markets, the values of social community and the politics of democracy. The challenge today, as Kofi Annan has written,[32] is to devise a similar bargain or project to underpin the new global economy. The project of global social democracy addresses this call. It is a basis for promoting the rule of international law; greater transparency, accountability and democracy in global governance; a deeper commitment to social justice; the protection and reinvention of community at diverse levels; and the transformation of the global economy into a free and fair rule-based economic order. The politics of global social democracy contains clear possibilities of dialogue between different segments of the 'proglobalization/anti-globalization' political spectrum, although it will, of course, be contested by opinion at the extreme ends of the spectrum.

Box 4 summarizes the project of global social democracy. It does not present an all-or-nothing choice, but rather lays down a direction of change with clear points of orientation. In so doing, it draws together some of the main threads of this chapter. One of the principal political questions of our times is how such a programme can best be developed, and how global public goods can best be provided. Global social democracy provides a framework for further thought and action, offering a framework of ideas that might help shape progressive opinion.

Box 4: Manifesto for a new global covenant: towards global social democracy

Guiding ethical principles/core values	Rule of law, global social justice, universal human rights, social solidarity and community, economic efficiency, environmental sustainability.
Priority measures	*Economy*

- Regulating global markets: ensuring the success of the Doha trade negotiating round; removal of EU and US subsidies of agriculture and textiles; reforming TRIPS; expansion of the terms of reference of the Global Compact; global anti-trust authority.
- Promoting development: phasing in trade and financial global market integration (particularly of portfolio capital markets); expanding the negotiating capacity of developing countries at the WTO; enhancing developing country participation in international financial institutions; abolition of debt for highly indebted poor countries (HIPCs); linking debt cancellation to the funding of children's education; meeting UN aid targets of 0.7 per cent GNP; establishing a new international finance facility to aid investment in poorest countries; and, in the longer term, the development of a new international tax mechanism.

Security

- Enhancing monitoring capacity of the risks of, and developments concerning, humanitarian crises; implementation of existing global poverty reduction and human development commitments and policies; creation of permanent peace-making and peace-keeping forces.

Law

- Convene an international convention to begin the process of reconnecting the security and human rights agendas through the consolidation of international humanitarian law; establishment of an international human rights court with a strong supporting network of regional courts.

Governance

- Reform of global governance: developing UN Security Council procedures in relation to the use of armed force

(Continued)

> in the affairs of another state; establishing a representa-
> tive Security Council; establishment of an Economic and
> Social Security Council to co-ordinate poverty reduction
> and global development policies; creation of an environ-
> mental IGO; strengthening the negotiating capacity of
> developing countries; developing criteria for fair negotia-
> tions among states and nonstate actors; improving
> co-operation among IGOs; and enhanced parliamentary
> scrutiny of regional and international bodies.

The story of our increasingly global order is not, as this chapter
indicates, a singular one. Globalization is not, and has never been,
a one-dimensional phenomenon. While there has been a massive
expansion of global markets that has altered the political terrain,
the story of globalization is far from simply economic. Since 1945
there has been a reconnection of international law and morality, as
sovereignty is no longer cast merely as effective power but increasingly as legitimate authority defined in terms of the maintenance of
human rights and democratic values; a significant entrenchment of
cosmopolitan values concerning the equal dignity and worth of all
human beings in international rules and regulations; the establishment of complex governance systems, regional and global; and the
growing recognition that the public good – whether conceived as
financial stability, environmental protection, or global egalitarianism – requires co-ordinated multilateral action if it is to be achieved
in the long term. These developments need to be and can be built
upon.

A coalition of political groupings could emerge to push these
achievements further, comprising: European countries with strong
liberal and social democratic traditions; liberal groups in the US polity which support multilateralism and the rule of law in international
affairs; developing countries struggling for freer and fairer trade rules
in the world economic order; non-governmental organizations, from
Amnesty International to Oxfam, campaigning for a more just, democratic and equitable world order; transnational social movements
contesting the nature and form of contemporary globalization; and

those economic forces that desire a more stable and managed global economic order.

A complex set of parties and commitments would be needed to make a compelling coalition for global social democracy. But while it would be complex, it is not impossible to envisage. In fact, some of its core ingredients could be stipulated as follows:

- Leading European powers need to commit to the creation of a multilateral order, and not a multi-polar one in which they simply pursue their own state interests above all else.
- The EU must address its weak geopolitical and strategic capacity via the development of a rapid reaction force and the creation of a common European armed force.
- The US needs to acknowledge that its long-term strategic, economic and environmental interests can only be achieved collaboratively, and it must, as a matter of principle, accept the opportunities and constraints afforded by multilateral institutions and international regimes.
- Developing countries, seeking major aid and overseas investments (public and private), need to accept the establishment of transparent and good governance as part of the requirements to attract investment in the infrastructure of their economies and societies.
- INGOs need to understand that, while their voices in global affairs are important, they represent particular interests which need to be articulated with, and harnessed within, wider frameworks of accountability and justice.
- IGOs utilising and advocating greater public funding have to recognise that they are part of an international civil service delivering core public goods – and not outposts of particular nation-states. The confusing and conflicting mandates and jurisdictions of IGOs need to be streamlined and clarified.
- Regional governance structures, while enhancing and expanding the developmental opportunities of their member states, must commit to keeping regions open for economic and diplomatic engagement with others. In short, they need to nurture open forms of regionalism.

167

David Held

- National governments must recognise that they are stakeholders in global problems and that ownership of these is a crucial first stage in their resolution – national and regional parliaments need to enhance their communication, understanding of and engagement with supranational governance.

Europe could have a special role in advancing the cause of global social democracy.[33] As the home of both social democracy and a historic experiment in governance beyond the state, Europe has direct experience in considering the appropriate designs for more effective and accountable supra-state governance. It offers novel ways of thinking about governance beyond the state, which encourage a (relatively) more democratic – as opposed to more neo-liberal – vision of global governance. Of course, this is not to suggest that the EU should lead an anti-US coalition of transnational and international forces. On the contrary, it is crucial to recognise the complexity of US domestic politics and the existence of progressive social, political and economic forces seeking to advance a rather different kind of world order from that championed by the current neo-conservatives.

Although some of the interests of those who might coalesce around a movement for global social democracy would inevitably diverge on a wide range of issues, there is potentially an important overlapping sphere of concern among them for the strengthening of multilateralism, building new institutions for providing global public goods, regulating global markets, deepening accountability, protecting the environment and urgently ameliorating social injustices that kill thousands of men, women and children daily.

Conclusion

Over the last 100 years political power has been reshaped and reconfigured. It has been diffused below, above and alongside the nation-state. Globalization has brought large swathes of the world's population 'closer together' in overlapping communities of fate. Yet, there are, obviously enough, many reasons for pessimism. There are storm clouds ahead. Globalization has not just integrated peoples and nations, but created new forms of antagonism. The globalization of communications does not just make it easier to establish mutual understanding, but often highlights what it is that people do not have in common and how and why differences matter. The dominant political game in the 'transnational town' remains geopolitics. Ethnic self-centredness, right-wing nationalism and unilateralist politics are once again on the rise, and not just in the West. However, the circumstances and nature of politics have changed. Like national culture and state traditions, internationalism and global social democracy are a cultural and political project, but with one difference: they are better adapted and suited to our regional and global age. Unfortunately, the arguments in support of them have yet to be articulated in the public sphere in many parts of the world; and we fail here at our peril.

It is important to add a reflection on September 11th and the war in Iraq, and to say what they mean in this context. One cannot accept the burden of putting accountability and justice right in one realm of life – physical security and political co-operation among defence establishments – without at the same time seeking to put it right elsewhere. If the political and the security, the social and the economic dimensions of accountability and justice are separated in the long term – as is the tendency in the global order today – the prospects of a peaceful and civil society will be bleak indeed. Popular support against terrorism, as well as against political violence and exclusionary politics of all kinds, depends upon convincing people that there is a legal, responsive and specific way of addressing their grievances. For this reason, globalization without global social democracy could fail.

Against the background of September 11th, the current unilateralist stance of the US, the desperate cycle of violence in the Middle East and elsewhere, the advocacy of global social democracy may appear like an attempt to defy gravity or to walk on water! Indeed, if it was a case of having to adopt global social democracy all at once, or not at all, this would be true. But it is no more the case than was the pursuit of the modern state at the time of its founders. Over the last several decades the growth of multilateralism and the development of international law has created social democratic anchors for the world. These are the basis for the further consolidation of social democratic

169

principles and institutions. Moreover, a coalition of political group-ings could emerge, as indicated above, to push these achievements further. Of course, how far such forces can unite around these objec-tives – and can overcome fierce opposition from well-entrenched geopolitical and geo-economic interests – remains to be seen. The stakes are high, but so too are the potential gains for human security and development if the aspirations for global social democracy can be realised.

Notes

1 Many people have provided invaluable criticism of earlier drafts of this chapter. I would like to thank, in particular, Anthony Giddens, Anthony McGrew, Matt Browne, Jean-François Rischard, Zaki Laïdi, Phillipe Legrain, David Mepham and Stephany Griffith-Jones. Phillipe Legrain and David Mepham have been particularly helpful on trade and aid reform; and Stephany Griffith-Jones provided much useful guidance on the reform of international finance institutions. This chapter is a con-siderably shortened version of the original which contains a much fuller account of the issues, including extensive empirical material and argu-ment. The full version is to be published by the author shortly.
2 Held, D., McGrew, A., eds, *The Global Transformations Reader*, 2nd edition, Cambridge, 2003.
3 *Making Sense of Globalisation*, Centre for Economic Policy Research, London, 2002.
4 Moore, M., *A World Without Walls*, Cambridge, 2003.
5 Garrett, G., *The Distributive Consequences of Globalisation*, unpub-lished paper available at http://www.international.ucla.edu/profile/ggarrett/papers.asp, 2001.
6 Wade, R., 'The Disturbing Rise in Poverty and Inequality', in D. Held and M. Koenig-Archibugi, eds, *Taming Globalization*, Cambridge, 2003.
7 Rischard, J. F., *High Noon*, New York, 2002.
8 Ruggie, J., 'Taking Embedded Liberalism Global: the Corporate Connection', in Held, D. and Koenig-Archibugi, M., eds, *Taming Globalization*, Cambridge, 2003.
9 Ibid.
10 Held, D., McGrew, A. G., Goldblatt, D. and Perraton, J., *Global Trans-formations*, Cambridge, 1999.

11 Held, D., 'Law of States, Law of Peoples', in *Legal Theory*, 8(1).
12 Kelly, P., 'Ideas and Policy Agenda in Contemporary Politics', in P. Dunleavy, et al., eds, *Developments in British Politics 7*, London, 2002.
13 Oxfam, *Rigged Rules and Double Standards*, Oxford, 2002; Moore, M., *A World Without Walls*, Cambridge, 2003.
14 World Bank, *Global Economic Prospects 2002*, Washington DC, 2001.
15 Garrett, G., *The Distributive Consequences of Globalisation*, Unpublished paper available at http://www.international.ucla.edu/profile/ggarrett/papers.asp, 2001; Legrain, P., *The Open World*, London, 2002.
16 TRIPs raises the price of all know-how and technology, especially in poor countries: patented rice that poor farmers plant, copyrighted textbooks that poor students need, patented software that poor businessmen use – are all examples of the ways in which TRIPs currently works to increase the price of knowledge related goods for development purposes. I am indebted to Phillipe Legrain for clarifying these issues.
17 Oxfam, *Rigged Rules and Double Standards*, Oxford, 2002.
18 Hertz, N., *IOU*, London, 2004.
19 Roy, S., 'What do Anti-global Protestors Want Exactly?', *Global Agenda*, 2003.
20 HM Treasury, *International Finance Facility*, London, 2003.
21 Griffith-Jones, S., 'International Financial Stability and Market Efficiency as a Global Public Good', in I. Kaul et al., eds, *Providing Global Public Goods*, Oxford, 2003.
22 Ibid.
23 Oxfam, *Rigged Rules and Double Standards*, Oxford, 2002.
24 Sen, A., 'The Moral Standing of the Market', in *Social Philosophy and Policy*, 2(2), 1985.
25 Held, D. and Kaldor, M., *What Hope for the Future?*, at http://www.lse.ac.uk/depts/global/maryheld.htm, 2001.
26 Ikenberry, J., 'America's Imperial Ambition', in *Foreign Affairs*, Sept.–Oct., 2002.
27 Hoffmann, S., 'America Goes Backward', in *New York Review of Books*, 12 June 2003.
28 Kaul, I. et al., eds, *Providing Global Public Goods*, Oxford, 2003.
29 Slaughter, A.-M., 'A Chance to Reshape the UN', *Washington Post*, 13 April 2003.
30 Keohane, R., 'The War Against Iraq and the Failure of Accountability', *Financial Times*, 31 March 2003.
31 Held, D., *Democracy and the Global Order*, Cambridge, 1995.

32 Annan, K., *A Compact for a New Century*, 31 Jan. (UN, SG/SM/6881), 1999.
33 McGrew, A., 'Between Two Worlds: Europe in a Globalising Era', in *Government and Opposition* 37(3), 2002.

7

Global Terrorism[1]

Mary Kaldor

Nowadays, it is increasingly difficult to distinguish between external and internal threats. In his Chicago speech of 1999, Tony Blair argued that we 'cannot turn back on our conflicts and the violation of human rights in other countries if we still want to be secure'.[2] Global terrorism could be said to epitomise this blurring of internal and external. The neo-conservatives in the United States make the argument that we have to address authoritarianism and conflict in the Middle East if we want to tackle global terrorism. It is very important for those who oppose many of the policies of the Bush administration, especially the concept of pre-emptive attack, to take these arguments seriously and to elaborate progressive policies for dealing with global terrorism.

Terrorism is a technique, which is increasingly used by extreme religious and/or nationalist political movements. It has to be understood as part of an array of forms of violence that are mainly directed against civilians; these various forms of violence include armed conflict, genocide, or communal riots in which many more people have been killed than in terrorist incidents. In this discussion, I will try to describe the broad phenomenon – the rise of extreme nationalist and religious groups that use violence, although I will focus on terrorism. In particular, I am interested in groups that are exclusive, i.e. groups that want to exclude people from a different religion or nationality, and/or fundamentalist, i.e. groups that are inflexible about their doctrines and try to impose these doctrines on others.

It is sometimes argued in Europe that, unlike the United States, Europeans are experienced at dealing with terrorism, and the examples of the IRA or ETA are often cited. Yet what happened on September 11 was qualitatively different from anything that has been experienced in Europe and, in this chapter. I will try to draw attention to the new features of global terrorism. I will start with some general considerations about the relationship of these groups to globalisation and I will then describe their ideologies, their methods and their forms of organisation and how these are different from earlier forms of terrorism. Before concluding I will say something in particular about Al Qaeda. Finally, I will set out some ideas about policy towards dealing with this dangerous phenomenon.

Globalisation and the Rise of New Religious and Nationalist Militant Groups

Table 1 on pages 176–7 provides a selective account of the growth of nationalist and religious groups. It is not possible to provide a comprehensive list; the aim of the table is to provide an indication of the kind of groups described here. Most of the groups shown in the table were formed after 1970, although many had their origins in earlier organisations, many of which were formed in the 1920s and 1930s. Thus the Hindu nationalist family of organisations trace their origins to the founding of the Rastryiya Swayemsevak Sangh (RSS) founded in 1925. The Muslim Brotherhood, founded in Egypt in 1928, is often considered the source of most contemporary Islamic groups. And the nationalist parties in Central Europe and the Balkans often reproduce the symbols and language of the pre-war nationalist parties. But these groups seem to have been quiescent during the immediate post-Second World War period. In the last two decades, we have seen an increased political presence of these groups both in electoral terms[3] and through their involvement in violent episodes.

Although most public attention is focused on Islamic groups, this trend towards extremist political mobilisation, often involving violence, can be found in all major world religions (Christian, Jewish, Hindu, Sikh and Buddhist) and also among many national groups.

Indeed, it is sometimes difficult to distinguish between religious and nationalist groups since national identity is often equated with religion, e.g. Catholics and Protestants in Ireland or Hindu and Sikh nationalists.

Table 2 on pages 178–9 shows the scale of casualties in major episodes of violence – wars, communal clashes, and so on. It is difficult to argue that terrorist incidents or major episodes of violence have actually increased in the last two decades. But it does seem to be the case that both the actors and the character of the violence have changed. In recent decades, it has become more difficult to distinguish between state and non-state actors. More and more violence spills over borders. And there has been a shift from ideological causes to religious and nationalist causes. In Europe, for example, 'red terrorism' has almost disappeared. Nowadays, the overwhelming majority of terrorist or other violent episodes are perpetrated by nationalist and/or religious groups. Moreover, more and more violence is directed against civilians as opposed to enemy forces.

What are the factors that have contributed to the rise of religious and nationalist militancy over the last two decades? It is not possible to provide a comprehensive causal explanation but it is possible to point to some common trends. First, and perhaps most important, is the decline in secular left ideologies, particularly socialism and postcolonial nationalism. For millions of people, disillusion set in long before the end of the Cold War because of authoritarianism, corruption and the failure to deliver on promises of development. The new militancy developed in response both 'from above' and 'from below.' Political leaders use nationalist and religious appeals when other tools of political mobilisation have failed. Often it was secular leaders who opened the space for these ideologies. Thus the Congress Party in India began to use Hindu rhetoric long before the rise of the BJP. In the former Yugoslavia and Soviet Union, nationalism grew within the administrative confines of the centrally planned system because other forms of ideological competition were excluded. In Africa, patrimonial leaders used tribal networks as a way of rationing out scarce governmental resources. And in the Middle East, the failures of Arab nationalism led many leaders to emphasise a religious identity and the conflict with Israel.

Table 1 Selected religious and nationalist militant groups

Name/ organisation	Type	Primary area(s) of operation	Leader	Goals	Strategy	Members/ supporters	Founded in	Global links	Web page
Africa									
Groupe Islamique Armé, GIA	AG	Algeria	Abdel Rahman al-Zaytouni	Algerian Islamic state	Terrorism	200	1992	Al Qaeda	www.aum-shinrikyo.org/
Interahamwe	AG	Rwanda		Hutu State	Genocide; guerilla tactics	Several thousand	1988	Support from Congo	
Lords Resistance Army, LRA	AG	Uganda (North)	Joseph Kony	Millennarianism	Extreme violence	7,000		Support from Sudan	
Sudan People's Liberation Army, SPLA	AG	Sudan	John Garang	Autonomy for Southern Sudan	Armed struggle	Ten thousands	1983	US support via Uganda	
Asia									
Aleph (formerly Aum Shinrikyo)	S	Japan		Apocalypse	Education; terrorism	1,500–2,000	1987		www.aum-shinrikyo.org/
Jamaat-e-Islami Party	N	India, Pakistan, Bangladesh		Muslim unity	Support Islamic groups	2.2 million	1941		www.jamaat.org
Jemaah Islamiya, JI	AN	Indonesia, Malaysia, Philippines, Singapore	Abu Bakar Ba'asyir; Abdullah Sungkar	Islamic Asian state	Terrorism	Few hundred	1995	Alleged links to Al Qaeda	http://jemaahislamiah.newstrove.com/
Liberation Tigers of Tamil Eelam, LTTE	AG	Sri Lanka	Velupillai Prabhakaran	Tamil homeland	Ethnic violence	8,000–10,000	1972	Tamil Diaspora	www.eelam.com & www.eelamweb.com
Patani United Liberation Organisation, PULO	AG	Thailand (South)	Tunku Bilor Kortor Nilor	Islamic autonomous state	Ethnic/ religious violence		1968		www.pulo.org/
Rashtryia Swayamsevak Sangh, RSS	SM	India		Hindu nationalism	Violence; grass-roots mobilisation		1925		www.rss.org

			leadership			supporters			
Askatasuna, ETA Real IRA, RIRA	AG	Ireland, UK (Northern Ireland + mainland)	Changing leadership	Basque state Union with Ireland	Terrorism	100–200	1998		
Serbian Radical Party	PP	Serbia	Vojislav Seselj, facing charges in The Hague	Greater Serbia	Win votes; violence	840,000 votes	1991		www.srs.org.yu
Middle East									
Gush Emunin	SM	Israel	Rabbi Moshe Levinger	Biblical Israel	Settlements; paramilitary	20,000?	1973	Jewish Diaspora	
Hamas	AN	Palestine; Jordan	Sheik Ahmed Yassin	Islamic Palestine state	Terrorism; social services; grass-roots mobilisation	Unknown members; 10,000s sympathisers	1987	Palestinian Diaspora, Saudi Arabia	
Hizbollah	AN	Lebanon		Islamic Lebanon	Paramilitary; social services; win votes	1982		Worldwide network; support from Syria and Iran Iran	www.hizbollah.org/
Islamic Jihad	AG	Palestine	Mohammed Abdel-Salam Faraq	Pan-Islam	Terrorism	Several hundred	1970s	Iran	
al-Jamaa al-Islamiyya	AN	Egypt	Sheikh Omar Abdel-Rahman		Terror; social services	Members 1,000s; sympathisers 1,000s	Late 1970s	Part of Al Qaeda	www.ummah.org.uk/ikhwan/index.html
Kurdish Freedom and Democracy Congress, KADEK, formerly Kurdistan Workers Party, PKK	AG	Turkey	Group leadership under direction of Abdullah Ocalan	Kurdish nationalism	Renounced armed struggle	4,000–5,000	1974	Kurdish Diaspora	www.pkk.org/
Al Qaeda	AN	International	Osama Bin Laden	Muslim caliphate	Terrorism	Several thousand	Late 1980s	Worldwide network	

Abbreviations of types: AG: armed group; AN: armed network; SM: social movement: S: sect
Source: Global Civil Society Programme database. For comments and suggestions, e-mail: kaldor_muro@postmaster.co.uk

Table 2 Major episodes of political violence (MEPVs) 1990–1999 and terrorist incidents 1991–2001

	1990	1991	1992	1993	1994	1995	1996	1997	1998	1999	2000	2001
Africa												
MEPVs	11	16	14	15	16	15	14	15	10	11		
Deaths	115,000	122,000	118,000	136,000	632,000	127,000	152,000	154,000	148,000	148,000		
Terrorist incidents		5	12	7	25	10	11	24	21	53	55	33
Deaths and injuries		3	29	1,013	55	8	80	35	5,379	185	102	150
Asia												
MEPVs	13	13	9	8	8	9	10	9	10	10		
Deaths	29,000	22,000	13,000	12,000	12,000	16,000	16,000	15,000	16,000	16,000		
Terrorist incidents		48	13	37	24	16	11	21	49	72	98	33
Deaths and injuries		150	25	135	71	5,639	1,507	344	635	690	898	651
Middle East												
MEPVs	4	3	2	3	3	4	4	5	4	4		
Deaths	103,000	53,000	3,000	3,000	4,000	4,000	4,000	4,000	4,000	4,000		
Terrorist incidents		78	79	100	116	45	45	37	31	26	20	29
Deaths and injuries		33	236	178	256	445	1,006	480	68	31	78	513
Europe												
MEPVs	2	3	5	6	5	5	3	4	4	5		
Deaths	1,000	10,000	61,000	61,000	51,000	51,000	1,000	11,000	8,000	9,000		
Terrorist incidents		199	113	185	88	272	121	52	48	85	30	17
Deaths and injuries		56	65	117	126	287	513	17	405	16	4	20

	1	2	3	4	5	6	7	8	9	10	11	12
MEPVs	2	3	3	3	2	3	2	2	2	1	2	3
Deaths	6,000	7,000	9,000	8,000	24,000	17,000	17,000	4,000	5,000	155,000		
Terrorist incidents	6	3	5	11	5	24	42	14	35	31	3	
Deaths and injuries	7	0	1	151	29	20	27	12	8	103	0	
Latin America												
MEPVs	5	4	4	4	5	6	5	4	3	3		
Deaths	16,000	11,000	11,000	11,000	24,000	25,000	24,000	6,000	3,000	3,000		
Terrorist incidents	229	143	97	58	92	84	128	111	122	192	194	
Deaths and injuries	68	374	66	329	46	16	18	11	195	20	16	
North America												
Terrorist incidents	2	1	0	0	0	13	0	0	2	0	4	
Deaths and injuries	1	1,006	0	0	0	7	0	0	0	0	3,315	
TOTAL												
MEPVs	37	42	37	38	40	41	38	38	33	36		
Deaths	270,000	224,500	214,500	298,000	746,500	239,500	211,500	193,000	173,500	334,500		
Terrorist incidents	375	437	565	363	431	322	440	296	304	426	348	
Deaths and injuries	317	730	2,516	988	6,454	6,454	3,132	928	6,510	1,125	1,205	4,205

Source: These figures are calculated from the Major Episodes of Political Violence Database at the Center for Systemic Peace, University of Maryland (URL). The casualty figures are conservative since the database uses a mean of different source to estimate the numbers of casualties. In this table, the number of casualties for each episode is further averaged over the duration of each episode. The figures on terrorist incidents are taken from the US Department of State (URL). The terrorist casualty figures include dead and wounded.

Mary Kaldor

A second factor is insecurity, which helps to explain the rise of the new militancy from below. The last two decades have been a period of dramatic structural change, with declines in state provision and public employment, rapid urbanisation, the growth of an informal criminalised economy and large-scale migration from countryside to town and from poor countries to the industrialised West. Nationalist and religious movements offer a sense of certainty in uncertain times, security in times of insecurity, and a narrative that provides psychological comfort when material comfort is missing. Many scholars emphasise the importance of marginalisation and exclusion as an explanation for the growth of these movements. Typical recruits to these movements are the restless young men, often educated for roles that no longer exist because of the decline of the state or of the industrial sector, often unable to marry because they lack income, and sometimes needing to legitimate semi-criminal activities in which they can find their only source of income. Membership in nationalist or religious groups offers meaning, a sense of historical relevance, and also adventure.

Related to the sense of insecurity is the encounter with globalisation, that is to say with growing interconnectedness, and the sense of impotence that arises when crucial decisions that affect everyday life are taken further and further away. The young men who committed suicide on September 11 were all educated in the West. This is typical of many religious militants, especially Islamic ones, who are often migrants, either from countryside to town or from South to West, who have experienced the loss of ties to their places of origin and yet do not feel integrated in their new homes.[4]

I use the term 'regressive globalisation' to describe the character of these new groups. By 'regressive globalisation', I mean groups which make use of and even promote globalisation when it is in the interests of a particular group, say a religious or nationalist group. These are groups which arise in response to globalisation. They are a reaction to the insecurities generated by globalisation as well as disillusion with the secular ideologies of the state. At the same time, these groups make use of the opportunities created by globalisation – the new media, especially television and the Internet, increased opportunities for funding from the Diaspora as well as from transnational criminal groups. To develop this argument, I will describe how they differ from classic terrorist groups, in ideology, tactics and organisation.

Ideology: A Modern Political Agenda with Anti-modern Symbols

The new global terrorism shares with classical terrorism the goals of state power and the idea of global struggle but at the same time the new groups claim to be explicitly anti-modern and backward-looking. Broadly speaking, it is possible to identify four main strands of ideological thinking.

They seek political power – generally control of the state

All the groups in Table 1 seek political power. Nationalist groups seek one of the following goals:

- Territorial expansion to include historic lands or lands inhabited by the ethnic nations, especially in Europe, where nationalist parties of Serbs, Croats, Hungarians or Romanians all espouse irredentist policies.
- Secession for minority groups who want their own state. This is the case for the Moros in the Philippines, the Aceh people in Indonesia, the Sikhs in India (Khalistan), the Tamils in Sri Lanka, Corsicans in France, or the Uighurs in China. The Basques argue both for secession and for expansion since they want to unite the lands where Basque people live. The same is true of Kurdish nationalist groups, who for the moment argue for secession or autonomy within Turkey and Iraq.
- Ethnically pure states and a strengthening of sovereignty. This is the case for Hindu nationalists who want to preserve Hindu culture in India and downgrade or eliminate Christians and Muslims.

Religious groups often share the same goals but they emphasise the importance of using state power to introduce religious practises. Groups like the Islamic Group and the Islamic Jihad in Egypt,

181

Mary Kaldor

Heizbollah in Lebanon, the Islamic Movement of Uzbekistan (IMU) or the Algerian Islamic Group (GIA) want to replace secular regimes with Islamic governments. Likewise in America, the Christian Right wants to build a Christian America that applies their version of Christian doctrine. Many of the nationalist groups described above are also religious groups. The Uighurs in China, the Moros in the Philippines, or the Aceh people all want secession in order to build Islamic states. Hamas, which means 'zeal' or 'enthusiasm', wants not just an independent Palestine but an Islamic Palestine.

Among Islamic groups, however, there are also those who see themselves a multi-ethnic and want to create a state that is the expression of Muslim unity. Thus Al Qaeda favours a Muslim caliphate for the whole of the Middle East, while Jemaah Islamiya, a network spread across Indonesia, Malaysia, the Philippines and Singapore, favours an Asian Muslim caliphate. The South Asian organisation Jamaat-e-Islami similarly wants to unite Muslims. It is other religions and religious practices they exclude rather than ethnicities.

It should be emphasised that all these groups have what might be described as a modernist view of the state. They still believe in state sovereignty and reject the conditionality that has accompanied globalisation. They believe that religions and ethnicities can somehow be kept within or excluded from bordered territory.

They see themselves as opposed to modernity

Many of the new nationalist and religious groups object to what they see as both the relativism of modernity and the claim that human reason is superior to other forms of human knowledge. They object to the doubt and questioning that characterises modern society. They insist that sacred knowledge is the superior form of knowledge, that there is a 'correct' interpretation of events that is given by God, which cannot be contradicted by human reason. Many nationalists also insist that their beliefs are God-given but even, for secular nationalists, at least extreme secularists, the assumption is that there is one model for society that has to be applied, whatever the obstacles. It is this emphasis on certainty and the unique character of divine knowledge that explains how so many fundamentalist groups can

182

hold extraordinary beliefs. Fundamentalist groups, say Marty and Appleby, want to 'scandalise':

> They catch the attention of the rest of us by scandalising (or amusing) us with preposterous claims about virgin births or hidden Imams or personified books. But the 'show' carries a lesson: there is another way of imaging the world, of understanding human destiny, of tapping the enthusiasms, hopes and talents of modern individuals.[5]

This refusal to accept the superiority of human reason also justifies the refusal to accept the fundamental equality of human beings; other religions or ethnicities are considered inferior. Some groups use animal terms to describe other groups; thus the Hutus of Rwanda described the Tutsis as cockroaches, while the Serbs described Kosovars as rabbits or eels (supposedly a reference to their breeding proclivities).

In particular, nearly all these groups object to what they see as changed gender relations that have accompanied modernity. They nearly all insist on traditional family values. Christian groups take militant positions on abortion. Islamic groups insist that women wear veils and, in some cases, the best known being the Taliban in Afghanistan or Saudi Arabia, they introduce what is essentially a form of gender apartheid. Most groups are also homophobic.

Emphasis is placed on the need to regenerate and unify a corrupt society

The notion of decline is common to many of these movements and acts as a powerful justification for their existence. Whether nationalist or religious, such groups are often backward-looking, nostalgic for a 'pure' past where religion was practised widely and according to ritual and/or where the nation was 'unpolluted' by foreigners, minorities, or mixed groups. Islamists, for example, propose a return to Islam's founding period 1,400 years ago and judge any state deviation from that golden age as *jahiliyya*, or pre-Islamic ignorance. Radical protestant sects, on the other hand, see themselves as returning to the arcadia of the early Christian Church.

Mary Kaldor

In effect these groups invent a past, based on a particular time and place, ignoring more recent history or, indeed, whatever historians have discovered about the period they pick that does not fit their preconceptions. For all fundamentalist and nationalists, places and dates are of critical importance. The Serbs claim that Kosovo is their holy land, like Jerusalem for the Jews, and they commemorate (actually only since the nineteenth century) the date in June 1389 when, in the famous Battle of Kosovo, the Serbs were defeated by the Turks. The Albanians are equated with the Turks despite the fact that, in the actual battle, Albanians were fighting on the same side as the Serbs. 'Fundamentalists', say Marty and Appleby, 'idealise sacred lands, "freezing" them at one time and place and lifting them out of their complex and changing historical context to serve as emblems of communal identity and as the raison d'être of political movements.'[6]

These groups are both traditional and anti-traditional. They insist on the reinvention of tradition, on reintroducing past rituals and practices even if these 'traditions' are quite at odds with the traditions of everyday life.

They believe they are part of a great struggle or war against an 'other'

Nostalgia is often linked to notions of struggle that are endemic in the ideologies of both groups. Indeed the notion of struggle may be the most important shared characteristic of religious and nationalist ideologies. Islamic groups insist on the importance of Jihad. Christian right groups talk about a 'civil war' in America. RAHOWA stands for 'racial holy war', which is the greeting and rallying cry in the World Church of the Creator, a group that undertook targeted racial killings in Illinois and Indiana in 1999. This emphasis on war is also characteristic of nationalist groups. Almost always, their narratives contain stories of great battles lost or won or even merely symptomatic of disorder (Kosovo, the Battle of the Boyne, the Mahabharat for example).

The notion of 'us' and 'them' is deeply embedded in the ideologies of such movements. The contrast with the 'other' becomes part of the definition of the group, whether it is another nationality or religion

184

or, in the contemporary period, secularity and/or cosmopolitanism. Religious leaders see their struggle as a 'Cosmic War' against 'evil' and promote the idea that every follower has to participate in that struggle. By doing so, their political causes are given sacred legitimacy and their members are given a sense of participation in something larger than every day life. Likewise, nationalist groups often claim to be avenging historic injustices.

Forms of Violence

Classic terrorism typically adopted tactics with very specific strategic goals aimed at the state apparatus or other high value targets – for example, attacks on state officials, high ranks of the civil service, or military and security officers. This was the tactic of European groups like the IRA and ETA, and also the GIA in Algeria. These specific and negotiable tactics still characterise some groups today. Some groups target foreign diplomats and businessmen in order to exercise pressure on their governments. Targeting the sources of state revenues has also been a much-used tactic: the oil and gas industry in Algeria, the tourism industry in Egypt and Spain, etc. In other cases, violence has been part of kidnappings, which have ended in demands for release of prisoners or ransom. Sometimes the aim is to provoke outside intervention. Thus the KLA targeted Serb policemen so as to provoke an exaggerated Serb response, which would mobilise international opinion.

The trend, however, is away from these more classic tactics and towards both symbolic and strategic violence aimed at the apparently random and senseless killing of civilians. Symbolic violence is a form of message, a way of making a statement. Terrorist attacks against civilians are typical of 'symbolic violence'. Violence is 'deliberately exaggerated' and often macabre. The Lord's Resistance Army in Uganda cuts off ears and lips. Hamas suicide bombers put nails in their bombs so as to kill as many people as possible. Juergensmeyer likens 'symbolic violence' to theatre – these are what he calls 'performance acts' – 'stunning, abnormal and outrageous murders carried out in a way that graphically displays the power of violence – set within grand

185

scenarios of conflict and proclamation.'[7] The targets of such attacks are often important symbols – the World Trade Center, the Federal Building in Oklahoma that symbolised welfare and gun control, the Mosque in Ayodha. These 'rituals of violence' carry with them an otherworldly significance and produce the sense of struggle, of Armageddon or Jihad, or of cosmic war. Those who took part in the nerve gas attack on a Tokyo subway, for example, in 1995, believed that this was the start of the world catastrophe predicted by Shoko Ashara, the spiritual leader of Aum Shinrikyo (the extreme Buddhist sect).

The theatrical character of much violence is illustrated by the way many of the perpetrators dress up for killing as though it is not they themselves who perform the acts. The notorious Frenki's Boys, who were responsible for atrocities in Bosnia and Kosovo, wore cowboy hats over ski masks and painted Indian stripes on their faces. Their trademark was the sign of the Serbian Chetniks and a silhouette of a destroyed city with the words 'City Breakers' in English. Joseph Kony, the leader of the Lord's Resistance Army, wears aviator sunglasses and dresses his hair in beaded braids hanging to his neck; sometimes he wears women's clothes.

But violence is not merely symbolic, not just 'letters to Israel' as one Hamas activist described the suicide bombers. In many of the recent armed conflicts, the aim has been deliberate elimination or indeed extermination of the 'other'. The Hutus in Rwanda wanted to get rid of the Tutsis, just as Hitler wanted to get rid of the Jews. The goal of the wars in the former Yugoslavia or the South Caucasus was to create ethnically pure territories. In these cases, exaggerated violence was aimed at making people hate their homes. Systematic rape, for example, was widespread in the former Yugoslavia. This was rape, not as a side effect of war, but as a deliberate weapon of war with the aim of making women, particularly Muslim women, feel ashamed and defiled so that they would not want to return to their homes. Likewise violence against symbolic targets was aimed at removing any trace of the culture of the 'other'. In Banja Luka, during the Bosnian war, two unique sixteenth-century Ottoman mosques were razed to the ground. They were blown up on a Friday, and on Monday the bulldozers came and grassed over the site so that you would never know they ever existed.

Both symbolic and strategic violence can be understood as a form of political mobilisation. This is the way that the extremist groups succeed in mobilising extremist sentiment. The killings and displacement in conflict like in Yugoslavia generate the very ideologies that were supposed to have been the cause of the conflict. Indeed this may be the point of the violence. It is difficult to explain the suicide bombings in Palestine as a way of achieving a Palestinian state, just as it is difficult to explain the brutal Israeli responses as a way of improving security. But if the goal is to strengthen extremist sentiment – support for Hamas or the extreme Zionist groups, what is happening is much easier to explain.

As I have argued elsewhere, this type of conflict is difficult to end and difficult to contain.[8] It is long-running conflicts like in Afghanistan or the Middle East or parts of Africa that produce 'black holes' characterised by lawlessness, extremist ideologies and endemic insecurity. And it is in these 'black holes' that the culture of violence is nurtured.

The weapons that are used in these new forms of violence are mainly small arms and conventional explosives. The application of science and technology to weaponry has meant that all types of weapons have become more accurate and easier to use and transport. The American literature has, in recent years, focused on the possibility that terrorist groups might be able to use weapons of mass destruction – 'dirty' bombs (conventional explosives coated with radioactive material), chemical and biological agents.[9] In practice, these weapons, though relatively easy to develop, are extremely difficult to disperse efficiently. Moreover, acquiring the capability to disperse such weapons is extremely expensive and few nationalist and religious groups, let alone states, have access to the kind of scientific infrastructure required.

The example that is often cited is Aum Shinrikyo. But on closer inspection, this is the exception that proves the rule. Aum Shinrikyo had more than 60,000 members at the time of the nerve gas attack, with offices in New York, Germany, Australia, Sri Lanka, Russia and Japan. It had assets of over $1 billion; it recruited scientists and engineers from Japan's leading universities and supplied them with lavish state-of-the-art laboratories. When the police raided the group's laboratories after the attack, they found enough sarin to kill an estimated 4.2 million people and they discovered that Aum had already produced or had plans to produce nerve gas agents like VX, tabun and soman, other chemical agents like mustard gas and sodium cyanide, biological agents such as anthrax, Q-fever, and possibly Ebola. They also had plans to develop a nuclear capability, as well as large amounts of conventional weapons. But Aum had enormous difficulty in operationalising this capability. On at least nine occasions they tried to disseminate anthrax bacteria and botulinal toxin but their attempts failed either because they had developed the wrong strains or because the mechanical sprayers became clogged. Even the attack on the Tokyo subway achieved far less than the group anticipated, even though twelve people were killed and many more injured either physically or psychologically. To disseminate the gas they used plastic trash bags that had to be poked open with umbrella tips.[10]

Even if other groups had access to assets on a similar scale, they would be likely to conclude that funds are better spent on mobilisation (media and education), communication and conventional weaponry. After all, nowadays, you do not need weapons of mass destruction to inflict mass destruction. What is required is modern communications, and, in some cases the vulnerability of global infrastructure. The genocide in Rwanda was committed with machetes and co-ordinated through radio; the attack on the World Trade Center required no weaponry at all but was equivalent to a small nuclear weapon. Above all, terrorism, or suicide bombers or other attacks against unprotected civilians are the weapons of the weak, not the technologically powerful.

Organisation, Media and Funding

The new global terrorism differs from 'old' terrorism in organisation, in the use of media and in methods of funding.

First of all, the increasing transnational character of these movements has led to a shift from vertical forms of organisation to more horizontal network-like structures. Probably only Al Qaeda is a truly global network. Nevertheless, many groups, even if their political goals are very local, like Hamas, have cells in many different countries. According to Bruce Hoffman, a terrorism expert from the RAND corporation, this is part of a general trend away from the pyramidal structure of terrorist organisations of the 1970s and 1980s to today's flexible network:

> These movements also tend to operate on a linear rather than hierarchical basis. Hence, instead of the classic cellular structure that was common to previous generations of terrorist organizations, some contemporary groups are more loosely connected or indirectly linked through networks comprised of both professional terrorists and amateurs.[11]

Linked to the horizontal network is the absence of publicly identifiable command structures and the tendency for anonymity, even though charismatic leaders like Osama Bin Laden remain important. 'Old' terrorists always claimed responsibility for their acts. Even today, no one has claimed responsibility for the attacks of September 11.

Secondly, many of these groups are part of a family of organisations. It is often the case that nationalist and religious groups organise what might be described as parallel societies, a sophisticated organisational infrastructure with political, military, educational, welfare and publishing components. A typical phenomenon in recent years has been the spread of religious schools, often linked to extremist groups. Christian schools have increased dramatically in the United States, as have Madrassahs, particularly in Pakistan and Afghanistan, and Hindu schools, especially in tribal areas. Humanitarian NGOs also play an important role, especially for Islamic groups; it is these religious NGOs that often provide the only form of welfare for newly arrived immigrants in cities.

All of these groups make use of the 'new media' – television, Internet, video-cassettes. Symbolic violence is important because it is often performed for audiences of millions. The mesmerising pictures of the collapse of the World Trade Center beamed over and over again on all global TV channels were perhaps the most successful media event of all times. Many groups have their own TV or Radio Channels. Hindu nationalists benefit from the new Satellite Channel, Star TV. Serbian television paid a critical role in the years leading up to the Yugoslav wars in promoting nationalist propaganda, inter-changing contemporary events with the Second World War and the 1389 Battle of Kosovo. Television and radio reach out to people who do not have the reading habit. In Africa, the radio is literally magic, and it was Milles Collines Hate Radio that incited the genocide in Rwanda.

The use of the Internet and e-mail has been particularly important in building transnational networks. Since September 11, points out Rohan Gunaratna, 'sympathetic websites (to Al Qaeda) are prolifer-ating – many of them operationally unconnected but ideologically sympathetic to the group'.[12] Where known, the web-sites are given in Table 1.

Traditionally, the main sources of funding for terrorists were donations from supporters, crime and state sponsorship. The first two remain important sources of income although they are more transnational than before. But state sponsorship has declined while Diaspora support has increased. Many groups, as in the past, levy 'taxes' on their supporters, especially those abroad. Some groups, like Al Qaeda, or the Christian Right, benefit from wealthy individuals.

In addition, many groups engage in illicit commercial activities, especially transnational activities. Loot and pillage, extortion and kidnapping are the typical forms of funding for armed groups. Some engage in both illegal and legal activities. Hence, we have the case of the Japanese Aum Shinrikyo which funded itself not only through a lucrative series of noodle shops, estate agents, computer shops and pharmaceuticals but also through land fraud and drug trafficking. One of the most notorious Serbian paramilitary leaders, Arkan, had a string of pizza parlours that were a cover for the drug trade. The 'right to be the first to loot' was payment for the atrocities committed by his paramilitary groups, the Tigers. In recent years, human traf-ficking has become an important source of income for Balkan groups.

A third and increasingly significant source of income is Diaspora support. Diasporas provide money, ideas, skills and even volunteers. Far away from what they see as their homeland, Diaspora groups are often vulnerable to the appeals of extremist groups and to the imagi-nary depiction of struggle that is supposed to be happening at home. Hence Diaspora support is increasingly important for all South Asian groups, for Serbs, Croats, Kosovar Albanians, as well as Kurds. Many people in the Diaspora support charitable organisations. Whether knowingly or not, funds to extremist groups are often channelled through religious NGOs. Islamic NGOs were one of the first targets of the FBI after September 11 in their efforts to crack down on terrorism.

The Case of Al Qaeda

Many of the groups I have described are a mixture of old and new groups. Al Qaeda is in a class of its own – more global and net-worked than probably any other violent religious or nationalist group. The infrastructure of Al Qaeda has many parallels with the infra-structure of international NGOs or civil society networks.[13]

Al Qaeda is a cross-border network, involving hybrid forms of organisation. Al Qaeda (The Base) itself is a coalition involving a number of constituent organisations: the most well-known are the Egyptian groups Islamic Jihad and Jemaah Islamiya (Islamic Group of Egypt) and the Groupe Islamique Armé (GIA) of Algeria, but there are also organisations from Pakistan, Chechnya, Sudan, Somalia and the Philippines among others. These organisations come together in the Shura Majlis or Consultative Council, which is thought to have four committees (Religio-Legal, Military, Finance and Media).[14] Al Qaeda is also involved in partnerships and different forms of co-operation with other Islamic terrorist groups, although this may be exaggerated by Western sources. Al Qaeda has many local branches, known in the West as operational cells, often linked to Mosques and Muslim charities and NGOs. There are operational cells in perhaps as many as ninety countries, including Western Europe and North America.

What holds the network together is the mission, just as is the case for networks like Jubilee 2000 or the Land Mines Coalition. In the absence of traditional, vertical forms of organisation, individual com-mitment is a key organising tool. In this case, the mission is to restore the Muslim Caliphate in the Middle East, abolished in 1924, and reinstate Islamic control over the holy sites, especially the Al Aqsa

Mary Kaldor

Mosque in Jerusalem and the mosques in Mecca and Medina. In 1998, Al Qaeda established the 'World Islamic Jihad Against the Jews and Crusaders'. The constituent organisations are all signatories to the founding statement, which included the following *fatwa*:

> The ruling to kill the Americans and their allies – civilians and military – is an individual duty for every Muslim who can do it in any country which is possible to do it, in order to liberate the Al Aqsa Mosque and the Holy Mosque (Mecca) from their grip, and in order for their armies to move out of all the lands of Islam, defeated and unable to threaten any Muslim.[15]

Like global civil society groups, Al Qaeda have pioneered new forms of action. The main form of action is the 'raid'. In the last ten years before his death, the Prophet redefined the notion of a 'raid', which had been characteristic of pre-Islamic nomad groups, as part of Jihad, to mean a raid aimed at the benefit of the whole community and not individual gain. Al Qaeda have resurrected the term and it was used to describe the attacks on the World Trade Center and other operations.[16] In the founding statement quoted above, Al Qaeda calls on 'Muslim *Ulema*, leaders, youths and soldiers to launch a raid on Satan's US troops and the devil's supporters allying with them, and to displace those who are behind them so that they may learn a lesson'.[17]

Two mechanisms are important for holding the network together and sustaining the mission. These are training camps and new forms of communication. The main training camps were in Afghanistan but there were, and perhaps still are, also training camps in Sudan, Pakistan and Bosnia. According to the International Institute for Strategic Studies, some 20,000 jihadists were trained in the Afghan camps between 1996 and 2001.[18] The Americans in Afghanistan unearthed the Encyclopaedia of Jihad, some 1,000 pages stored on computer diskettes, and the Manual of Military Studies of Jihad. Some courses are quite short (15 days) – like staff training or summer schools for NGOs. As well as military training, the camps conduct courses in religious knowledge and theory of Jihad, and training in operational principles – writing reports, using computers, fundraising and budgeting. Video cassettes seem to be widely used in the organisation: as a form of communication and propaganda (Bin Laden's speeches as well as speeches by favoured religious scholars); as a method of dialogue (the Americans seem uncannily to discover videos of discussions about proposed operations); for identifying targets and planning (this was very important in the Kenya and Tanzania Embassy bombings as emerged in the trials); and for demonstrating the success of actual operations and learning lessons.

Al Qaeda has a range of funding sources. Bin Laden himself is personally very wealthy; his inherited fortune is estimated at $300 million and he owns a range of businesses, including banks, farms and factories throughout the world. Nevertheless, the network seems to be engaged in perpetual fundraising. First of all, operational cells appear to be self-sufficient. Members of the cells are mostly volunteers; their livelihoods are salaries or scholarships for students. They engage in their own fundraising, which includes legitimate businesses, like home repairs or restoring second-hand cars, as is the case for one cell broken up in Germany, and criminal activity, such as credit card fraud (very frequent), burglaries and bank robberies, kidnapping for ransom. In all Al Qaeda statements, 'plunder' is frequently mentioned. In the founding statement, Al Qaeda calls on every Muslim 'to kill Americans and plunder their money wherever and whenever they find it'.

The most likely explanation for the self-sufficiency of the operational cells is that, as with local branches of civil society networks, they are autonomous spontaneous groups, sympathetic to Al Qaeda but self-organised. Another explanation is security. The FBI argues that the way to catch Al Qaeda is to 'follow the money'. But if the cells are self-sufficient, it is much more difficult to trace financial links. Also, self-sufficiency helps to create a self-sustaining organisation. The cells appear to have a remarkable capacity to replicate themselves, even after being broken up by security services.

A second source of funding is banks and Islamic charities. In 2002, the United States and its allies in the global coalition froze the assets of two banks, Al-Taqwa and Bakarat, that manage hawala transfers (non-recorded transfers of remittances). These transfers amount to some $5–6 billion annually. They are mostly legitimate – Gulf workers, for example, transferring money to their relatives. But the bank makes a 5 per cent commission and this can be used for transfers within the network. Bakarat seems to have branches in many countries but it is particularly important to Somalia, where it acts unofficially as the central bank. (It is not clear whether Al Qaeda exploited the informal nature of the hawala system to its own ends or whether these banks actively supported the organisation.) Likewise, Islamic NGOs like the Texas-based charity, the Holy Land Foundation for Relief and Development, or the International Islamic Relief Organisation (IIRO) are said to be used, according to the FBI, both as methods for channelling funds, and as a support infrastructure for terrorist activity.[19]

Clearly, some groups are directly funded by Bin Laden through these mechanisms. Perhaps Bin Laden provides 'match funding' or 'start-up' funds. A recent trial of Mohammed Al-Tahiti, a Saudi national, in Morocco after an unsuccessful attack sheds light on Al Qaeda's way of working. He had visited Afghanistan in 1999 and requested a martyrdom mission; he was told to come back when he had a plan. He then went to Morocco and recruited some young men and afterwards returned to Afghanistan where he obtained funding.[20]

Since 2001, the FBI has frozen some $125 million in assets; some 2,700 known or suspected operatives have been arrested, and perhaps a third of the leadership has been killed; nevertheless, according to all accounts the organisation continues to grow, with 'raids' this year in Saudi Arabia, Morocco, Pakistan, Yemen and Kenya. What is important is the ability to recruit young men to the cause; that is what makes possible the multiplication of cells. As Jason Burke has put it:

> Al Qaeda can only be understood as an ideology, an agenda, a way of seeing the world that is shared by an increasing number of young predominantly male Muslims.[21]

Implications for Policy

The groups I have described differ from classic terrorists in their goals (anti-modernist religious and national rather than left or right); in the forms of violence mainly directed against civilians and symbolic targets rather than state or high value economic targets; in their forms of organisation, which tend to be transnational networks rather than hierarchical command structures; in their use of the new media and the Internet; and in their forms of funding, which tend to be transnational and criminal. Above all, these groups share a commitment to the idea of violent struggle, of war between good and evil.

I have tried to show that these groups can be described as 'regressive globalisers'. On the one hand, they respond to and feed on the insecurities generated by globalisation and they are organised as global networks in ways that are similar to other global organisations in civil society or the business world. On the other hand, their goals are rather traditional – they want to capture state power or construct new states (for example, new regional states, as in the case of Al Qaeda or Jemaah Islamiya or new secessionist states) and they envisage states in traditional terms as 'bordered power containers'.[22] In other words, they want to roll back globalisation, while making use of the instruments of globalisation.

If this analysis is correct, these groups are likely to grow both because of growing insecurities and because they are only now beginning to exploit fully the organisational opportunities provided by globalisation. But in the context of globalisation, their political goals are fundamentally contradictory. The goal of achieving ethnically pure or religious states is more elusive than ever. Perhaps these groups do not expect to achieve their stated goals; it is the struggle on which they thrive and the difficulty of achieving their stated goals will make the struggle even more plausible. If so, the prognosis is gloomy.

For those who could be described as 'progressive globalisers', that is to say those who favour globalisation when it benefits the many rather the few, and press for the reform of global institutions in order to bring this about, it is very important to develop a strategy for countering the growth of these groups that is based on law and morality rather than war, even though such a strategy will probably have to involve military means. It may never be feasible to eliminate these new groups but it might be possible to reduce their recruiting power and to minimise the damage they are able to inflict. If the aim is to reduce the insecurities that provide a breeding ground for extreme ideologies, then such a strategy ultimately amounts to a global agenda for progressive governance. But it is possible to draw out some strands of policy that relate specifically to the analysis provided in this paper.

First of all, such a strategy has to involve the protection of civilians and the capture and arrest of criminals responsible for violence in order to deal with the immediate risks. And this applies to all forms of illegal violence (war crimes, crimes against humanity, genocide, massive violations of human rights, as well as privately organised crime) not just terrorism. But it is very important that countering violence is treated as law enforcement not war. The big risk of using the language of war and attacking states which sponsor terrorism, as the Bush Administration is doing, is that this feeds into the terrorists' own perception of struggle. War implies legitimate killing by agents of the state whereas terrorism is viewed as criminal violence by non-state actors. But there is a fine line between heroes, who kill in war, and murderers. The problem is that the terrorists themselves define what they are doing as war. Thus, the language of war and, above all, the destructiveness of war can perversely end up legitimating the actions of the terrorists. For example, the Palestinian groups – Hamas, Islamic Jihad, or the Al Aqsa Brigades – are all included in the State Department's list of international terrorist groups; since the beginning of the Second Intifada, they have killed 781 Israelis. On the other hand, the Israeli forces, who are state actors and therefore considered legitimate, have killed 2,085 Palestinians, mostly civilians.[23] The Israelis (and the Americans) may regard the Palestinian groups as terrorists, but for the latter this is considered a war of self-defence and each Israeli strike adds further to their perception of legitimacy. In much the same way, Iraqi casualties in the recent war in Iraq are cited as justification for joining extremist anti-Western groups.[24]

War feeds into the terrorists' notions of perpetual struggle. It may be necessary to use military means, for example in destroying terrorist camps, but any military action must be viewed as law enforcement rather than war. This is not just a matter of procedure, that the use of military force should be approved through due process – for example the United Nations Security Council – it is also a matter of means. Law enforcement starts from the assumption of human equality. The lives of soldiers cannot be privileged over the lives of the civilians they are supposed to protect. Hence, military force must be used on the same principles as policing; soldiers are expected to risk their lives to save others.

The importance of means also applies to intelligence, policing and other legal procedures. The various forms of counter-terrorist legislation in Britain and the United States allow procedures to be adopted, such as detention without charges, that potentially contravene human rights. Indeed, the recent report of the Office of the Inspector General in the US Department of Justice makes alarming reading. It details detention without charges on a large scale, the use of immigration charges to investigate criminal activities also on a large scale, blanket refusal of bail, physical and verbal abuse, restrictive conditions of detention including small cells illuminated round the clock and information black-outs.[25] The term 'terrorist' has also been used to legitimise repressive behaviour in a number of countries; it is used for example in Australia against asylum-seekers, or against various secessionist movements in different countries.[26]

The risk is not just that this behaviour can further fuel anger and resentment among potential recruits to extremist causes, it is also the challenge to our own civil liberties and our claim to offer an alternative ideology. How to balance the needs of counter-terrorism with civil liberties does require much more careful attention both by scholars and policymakers.

Secondly, it is of key importance to counter the ideology of these groups and do so through grass-roots political mobilisation. This means support for and dialogue with civil society groups especially in areas, like the 'black holes' created by conflict, which are the most likely recruiting areas for these groups. Women's groups are particularly important in countering the gender discrimination of extremist ideologies.

The global mobilisation against the war in Iraq represented an opportunity to build an alternative popular mobilisation because it involved both Europe and the Arab world and, for the first time, brought immigrant communities into the political process. This was particularly important in Britain, where Hindus and Sikhs as well as Muslims joined the demonstrations. At the moment, however, these groups do not have serious, formal political representation and there

Mary Kaldor

is a real need for progressive elected representatives to reach out to them. It is true that many of the individuals and groups that took part in the demonstrations were rejectionist (against globalisation) or regressive and this is particularly true of many of the spokespeople, who were often remnants of the old left, or even Islamicists. But there are thousands of young people who are being politicised by the movement and who are open to, and indeed hope for, a more constructive reformist agenda.

Thirdly, such a strategy has to counter the sophisticated organisational infrastructure of these groups. I would emphasis four factors:

1   Education. Universal primary education would be very important in reducing the incentive to send children to religious schools. Education of girls is especially important.
2   Media. There needs to be much greater investment in global public (but not state) radio and TV. Independent community radio is especially important in countering extremist propaganda, as has been shown in Serbia and parts of Africa.
3   Welfare. The decline in social services has provided openings for humanitarian NGOs which also bring with them a political message.
4   Jobs. Unemployed or criminalised young men are the main breeding ground for these ideologies. Development needs to give priority to legitimate ways for these young people to make a living.

All of these four factors are part of a wider strategy to reduce global insecurity. Perhaps the most important element of any strategy is to deal not with terrorism *per se* but the 'black holes' that generate the culture of violent struggle. This requires an enormous commitment not just of resources but also of will. It means behaving and not just speaking in cosmopolitan terms. The most important challenge is cognitive; how to take seriously the principle that all human beings are equal.

President Clinton made the point in his speech to the conference on progressive governance that the right thrives on enemies and attacks, while the left has to depend on debate and evidence. This assertion applies very well to extreme nationalist and religious movements, which thrive on notions of struggle and insecurity. There is a real risk that regressive globalisers, whether we are talking about American neo-conservatives or the movements that generate global terrorism, will feed on each other, squeezing the space for progressives, that is to say, the space for debate and evidence.

Notes

1 This paper relies heavily on research undertaken for the global civil society programme at LSE. I am particularly grateful to Diego Muro, who co-authored the chapter on religious and nationalist militant groups for *Global Civil Society 2003*, published in autumn 2003, and who is responsible for some of the information in this paper.

2 *Doctrine of the International Community*, 22 April 1999, Hilton Hotel, Chicago, Illinois.

3 Nationalist parties captured power in the Balkans, for example, or in India. Islamic parties are ruling in Iran and Turkey and have done well in elections in Pakistan and Algeria, where electoral victory led to a military coup. In Western Europe, right-wing anti-immigrant parties have increased their share of the vote and in the United States Christian fundamentalist and Zionist groups are increasingly influential in the Republican Party.

4 Mark Juergensmeyer describes a young Muslim activist in New York, one of the group that tried to blow up the World Trade Centre in 1993. He says he was 'lured' by secular life in Germany and America but began to realise that he was losing his soul and therefore volunteered for Afghanistan. *Terror in the Mind of God*, University of California Press, Berkeley, 2000.

5 Martin E. Marty and R. Scott Appleby, *The Glory and the Power: The Fundamentalist Challenge to the Modern World*, Beacon Press, Boston, 1992, p. 24.

6 *Ibid.*, p. 184.

7 Juergensmeyer, *op. cit.*, p. 122.

8 See Mary Kaldor, *New and Old Wars: Organised Violence in a Global Era*, Polity Press, Cambridge, 1999.

9 Central Intelligence Agency, Directorate of Intelligence, *Terrorist CBN: Materials and Effects (U)* CTC 2003–40058, Washington, May 2003.

10 See Bruce Hoffman, 'Change and Continuity in Terrorism', in *Studies in Conflict & Terrorism*, 24: 2001, pp. 417–28.

Mary Kaldor

11 *Ibid.*, p. 418.
12 Rohan Gunaratna, 'Still Threatening', *The World Today*, 59: 1, January 2003, p. 20.
13 What we know about Al Qaeda comes primarily from Western sources – evidence provided at trials of Al Qaeda associates and documents retrieved by the FBI and other Western agencies; this should be borne in mind when assessing information.
14 'Blowback', by Phil Hirschkorn, Rohan Gunaratna, Ed Blanche, and Stefan Leader, *Jane's Intelligence Review*, 1 August 2001.
15 Bin Laden, Osama (1998), *World Islamic Front Statement urging Jihad Against Jews and Crusaders* (http://www.fas.org/irp/world/para/docs/980223-fatwa.htm).
16 See Hassan Mneimneh and Kanan Makiya (2002) 'Manual for a "Raid"', *New York Review of Books*, January 17.
17 Bin Laden, *op. cit.*
18 International Institute for Strategic Studies, *Strategic Survey 2003*, London 2003.
19 See FBI, Dennis M. Lormel, Chief, Financial Crimes Section, Federal Bureau of Investigation, *Statement for the Record*, House Committee on Financial Services, Subcommittee on Oversight and Investigations, Washington DC, 1 February 2002, see www.fbi.gov/congress/congress02/lormel021202.htm
20 See Jason Burke, 'Terror's Myriad Faces', *Observer*, 18 May 2003.
21 *Ibid.*
22 Anthony Giddens, *The Nation-State and Violence*, Polity Press, Cambridge, 1985.
23 Ze'er Schiff, 'Summit Analysis', *Haaretz*, 5 June 2003. These are Israeli figures and probably understate Palestinian casualties.
24 The Coalition forces put great effort into minimising civilian casualties. This is probably true, although in war it is not possible to avoid civilian casualties. The best figures we have for Iraqi civilian casualties, drawn from individual press reports, are a minimum of 5,500 and a maximum of 7,200 (Iraqbodycount.net). An NGO called CIVIC (Campaign for Innocent Victims in Conflict) is currently conducting an inquiry into civilian casualties through house-to-house interviews and the initial results suggest much higher numbers. For comparison, the total number of deaths in terrorist incidents in 2002 was 725 and the total number of dead in the World Trade Center attacks was 1,440 people.
25 United States Department of Justice, Office of the Inspector General, 'The September 11 Detainees: A Review of the Treatment of Aliens held

200

on Immigration Charges in Connection with the Investigation of the
September 11 Attacks', Report, June 2003; Human Rights Watch Report, 'Presumption of Guilt: Human Rights Abuses of Post-September
11 Detainees', August 2002 http://hrw.org.
26 Human Rights Watch, Opportunismwatch http://hrw.org.

8

Technology, Risk and the Environment

Rebecca Willis and James Wilsdon

'Humanity, get down on your knees!'
So screamed the billboards for Michael Crichton's latest novel *Prey*. Crichton, who did much to popularise concerns about biotechnology in *Jurassic Park*, has now turned his attention to a new generation of technologies. In *Prey*, he describes an experiment at the frontiers of nanoscience, which goes badly wrong, causing clouds of self-replicating nanobots to swarm out of control.

This could be read as harmless science fiction: a modern-day fairy story designed to leap off the shelves of discount bookshops. Yet in an introduction to the novel, Crichton signals that he intends it to be taken as a serious warning of what lies ahead. He predicts, 'Sometime in the twenty-first century, our self-deluded recklessness will collide with our growing technological power. One area where this will occur is in the meeting point of nanotechnology, biotechnology, and computer technology'.[1]

Crichton is not alone in expressing such concerns. In January 2003, the ETC Group, a Canadian Non-Governmental Organisation (NGO), hit the headlines with its assessment of the dangers of nanotechnology. Demanding a moratorium on commercialisation, the report warns of a 'Pandora's Box' of potential hazards, ranging from 'nanoparticle contamination to grey goo and cyborgs, to the amplification of weapons of mass destruction'.[2] Then in May, the Prince of Wales was

Technology, Risk and the Environment

reported to have serious concerns about grey goo, sparking a fresh wave of media interest.[3]

Nanotechnology may be a new field, but the battle lines of debate already being drawn up around it appear depressingly similar to earlier controversies over nuclear power, GM crops and mobile phone masts. Lining up on one side are those who see nanotechnology as an area of exciting potential for the economy, society and the environment. Opposing them are those who remain sceptical about the vested interests that lie behind the science, and the risks that may be unleashed by its application.

And nanotechnology is only one of a cluster of innovations that will have a major impact over the next decade. Others such as cloning, pervasive computing, artificial intelligence and virtual reality will give rise to fresh ethical and political dilemmas.

As the pace of innovation accelerates, progressives face a mounting challenge: how can the potential of new technologies be harnessed to wider projects of economic and social renewal without continually giving rise to such negative and polarised responses? Are there new approaches to the development and diffusion of new technologies that are more responsive to social and ethical concerns, and can move the site of public debate further upstream within research and development processes?

In this chapter, we start by arguing that progressives have sometimes displayed an uncritical technophilia, with insufficient reflection on the wider social and environmental questions raised by new technologies. Environmentalists, on the other hand, have tended to adopt inconsistent approaches, decrying new technologies like genetic modification, whilst relying on others such as renewable energy to deliver a more sustainable future.

Both sides are now edging towards a more nuanced account of the technology–society relationship, and there is a growing recognition, in particular, of the need for more proactive public involvement. Yet there is little evidence that the lessons of recent controversies are being applied systematically. In section two, we outline emerging models for managing risk. We explore the limits of deliberative models of public engagement, and reflect on some of the wider

203

institutional and regulatory questions that need to be addressed if public trust in new technologies is to be restored.

In the third section we argue that an excessive focus on new technologies can blind us to the environmental opportunities of technologies that already exist. A key dimension of the progressive approach will be to accompany new approaches to risk with a more rounded account of the role of technology within wider systems of social, political and institutional innovation.

Finally, we outline some initial thoughts on a more progressive approach to emerging technologies, and offer some practical steps forward, using nanotechnology as a test case.

The New Luddites?

In 1811, a revolutionary force shook England. Across five counties, bands of weavers and artisans rose up in protest against the social impact of new technologies. Taking their name from the mythical Ned Ludd, these rebels were highly organised, posing a genuine challenge to the political economy of Britain at the start of the 19th century. They protested through the most direct means possible – the destruction of the machines that were symbols of what they saw as the dehumanising effects of industrialisation.

Nearly two centuries later, the term 'Luddite' is still flung as an insult towards the green or anti-globalization movements. Yet the pivotal role that Luddism played in the emergence of trade unionism and the labour movement is largely forgotten. Alongside the direct action for which the Luddites are well known, they also lobbied in favour of a minimum wage, controls on child labour, and the right to trade union membership. As E. P. Thompson writes in his account of that period:

> All these demands looked forwards, as much as backwards; and they contained within them a shadowy image ... of a democratic community, in which industrial growth should be regulated according to ethical priorities and the pursuit of profit be subordinated to human needs.[4]

204

Today, politicians of all complexions rush to embrace science and technology, and place them at the centre of their visions of renewal, progress and prosperity. This is not in itself problematic. But it is a short step from enthusiasm to unquestioning devotion; to a caricature of science as a provider of absolute certainty. In the onward march of progress, science and technology are often forced into a role that neither the scientists nor the public want.

This temptation to slip into an uncomplicated account of new technologies is one of the reasons why many progressives have found the environmental agenda difficult to navigate. In his assessment of New Labour's first term, Anthony Giddens writes that, 'some of [their] biggest difficulties came in the environmental field, including the continuing problems of BSE, genetically modified crops, coping with abnormal weather patterns and floods, fuel protests and turmoil in the railway system'.[5] In each of these areas, we can see risk and scientific uncertainty at work.

In developing new approaches, there is a case for drawing lessons from the Luddites. Look beyond the insults to the actual history, and it is clear that theirs was a sophisticated protest – not a blind opposition to technology, but a moral and ethical objection to the social trajectory of the new machines and the patterns of life they undermined. Today, we see ripples of 'new Luddism' in the controversies over GM foods, nuclear power, gene cloning, and in the rhetoric of the anti-globalization protestors.

Rather than dismissing these responses, we should recognise that they contain important lessons for progressive politics. If new technologies are to realise their potential contribution to social and economic modernisation, we need to understand far more about the distinctive values and assumptions embedded in their development. We need to work with, not against, the impulses of new Luddism, to construct a reflective account of emerging technologies that places society alongside science.

Are there further lessons to be drawn from the environmental movement? Traditionally, green thought has been suspicious of new technologies and the enlightenment rationality on which they are based. There are numerous green critiques of technology, from writers in both the developed and the developing worlds. To take just one example, the Indian ecologist Vandana Shiva writes that 'the act of living and conserving life in all its diversity . . . seems to have been sacrificed to progress, and the sanctity of life substituted by the sanctity of science and development'.[6] But most greens are more ambivalent, and more contradictory. They welcome some technologies, whilst resisting others.

This ambivalence is reflected in the actions of pressure groups such as Greenpeace. In the summer of 1999, Lord Melchett, executive director of Greenpeace UK, risked arrest by donning a contamination suit and ripping up a field of genetically modified crops. Yet Greenpeace are also cheerleaders for renewable technologies such as solar photovoltaics. Critics like Charles Leadbeater point to the apparent inconsistencies, arguing that many environmentalists '. . . are selective Luddites. They use new technology to organise their protest networks and media campaigns but champion low-tech solutions'.[7]

Of course, there are many examples of Greens taking a simplistic campaigning stance against a particular technology – just as there are examples of governments promoting technology unquestioningly. Neither approach is useful. But there are lessons to be learned from the Green movement's more ambivalent attitude toward technology.

First, different problems require different solutions – some technical, some political. Tackling a problem as complex as climate change will require both political and technological solutions. Hence Greenpeace's support for renewables alongside energy taxes, as part of an overall package for a low-carbon economy. But Greenpeace argues that GM food is an inappropriate and unnecessary technology, masking the tough political decisions needed to secure more sustainable agriculture.

The second is that Greenpeace sees GM as a 'manufactured' risk, imposed by humans rather than by the natural world. Ulrich Beck explains this category of risks in his analysis of the BSE crisis: 'these risks are not fate, but the results of decisions and options that were taken in industry, science and politics . . . they are the results of efforts to control risk'.[8] Greenpeace, therefore, takes a moral stance that man-made technological risks should be avoided if there are low-tech political solutions.

As with the Luddites, the centre-left can learn from the best thinking within the environmental movement to develop a richer account of the societal benefits and costs of new technologies. This becomes clear in the next section, where we discuss new approaches to managing the risks and benefits brought by such technologies.

New Approaches to Risk Management

Crises such as the ongoing row over genetically modified foods have hastened the end of traditional approaches to risk. The 'old school' of risk handling was characterised by stating fact, asserting authority and seeking solace in science. This no longer works with modern, complex risks, or with modern, complex societies. Consequently, from all sectors – government, the private sector and NGOs – new models of public engagement are springing up, shifting the emphasis away from authority to involvement, facts to values.

This turn towards openness and public deliberation could represent a fundamental shift away from the traditional model. In the past, risk was seen as a technocratic issue – something for experts to assess and manage. A typical approach ran as follows: define the potential risk, using scientific analysis; define the scope of that risk, using assessment methodologies; decide how to proceed, using cost-benefit analysis; and finally, defend the decision to the public. Increasingly, though, this approach has been found to be inadequate. As Robin Grove-White writes,

> Industrial innovation plunges ahead in areas of relative scientific ignorance. Regulators and ministerial advisory committees stumble along behind, discovering by trial and error the implicit pitfalls, seeking to contain and mitigate them. Meanwhile, Ministers lean on the absence of conclusive proof or evidence of harm, and the inherited (but increasingly brittle) social authority of a particular positivistic view of science, to keep the show on the road.[9]

The new approach does not follow the simple stages set out above, of identification, assessment, management and communication. Rather,

Rebecca Willis and James Wilsdon

all stages are seen as subjective, open to interpretation, and inherently linked to each other.

Box 1: New approach versus traditional approach to risk management

New approach
Acknowledgement of uncertainty
Public involvement
Wider context to decisions
Choices about the future

Traditional approach
Denial of uncertainty
Public information
Narrow framing of decisions
Objective approach to future

An ability to accept uncertainty – to say 'we're not sure' – is an essential component of the new approach to risk. Yet it remains one of the hardest things to get right.

First, it requires an understanding of the difference between a strict 'risk' and uncertainty. A straightforward risk involves knowledge of both likelihood and potential effect – like tossing a coin. Yet many environmental and health risks are not 'risks' in this strict sense. There is limited knowledge about the likelihood of adverse effects, or what these adverse effects might look like. Standard tools of risk assessment are inadequate in such situations.

Secondly, there is a need to accept that you may never have the full picture. As the conclusions of a major ESRC research programme on risk state, 'Uncertainties . . . are often inherent in the object of the research itself: indeterminacy is a frequent occurrence in nature. Environmental systems can involve unpredictable changes or are too complex to be fully understood.'[10] In other words, we cannot always wait until we have all the information we need, because that moment may never arrive.

Lastly, saying 'we're not sure' requires a considerable amount of courage. Governments worry that, if they admit they don't know the 'truth', they will face a public and media backlash. In the middle of a crisis, conceding uncertainty can appear irresponsible. There is a fear that the public cannot deal with risk, and need to be presented with hard facts and absolute certainties. In reality, the public are more sophisticated. Research increasingly shows that the public understand scientific uncertainty and are prepared to deal with it.[11]

To take a recent British example, when asked to examine the health risks of mobile phones, an independent expert panel concluded that 'the balance of evidence to date' did not suggest serious risks, but at the same time recommended some precautionary measures to reduce any potential harm, particularly to children.[12] The report's findings were widely publicised, but most people have continued to use their phones, on the basis that the actual benefits outweigh the potential risks.

The reality is that individuals make complex decisions about risks, benefits and uncertainties every day. They factor a whole range of issues into their decisions, asking questions like, 'What is the evidence? What are the uncertainties? Who is providing the information, and what are their interests?' People are willing to live with risk if they understand it. What causes alarm is often not the risk itself, but the denial of it. People are very sensitive to attempts to cover up risk or uncertainty, and it is the denial of uncertainty that corrodes trust.

The Deliberative Turn

In 1999, a group of citizens in South Korea protested at what they saw as a lack of opportunity to get involved in decisions about science and technology. They issued a public statement which read '. . . civil society has so far been passive in accepting results of science and technology. We believe that dialogue between the scientific community and civil society needs to take place now.'[13]

Who were these people? Not anti-globalization activists or members of Friends of the Earth, but a schoolteacher, a housekeeper and an official of the Korea Electric Company, who were taking part in a groundbreaking consensus conference on the impacts of cloning. The panel cross-examined experts from biomedical science, ethics, theology, law and science policy, as well as representatives of NGOs, before formulating recommendations on how government should regulate cloning technology.

At the heart of the new politics of risk are these new approaches to public involvement. There is now a growing recognition that participatory approaches are an essential part of good decision-making, and of rebuilding trust in the regulatory system.

The traditional – and still influential – view is that the public cannot cope with risk because they do not understand the science. This view, often called the 'deficit model', assumes that 'experts' have all the information necessary, whilst the public suffer from a 'deficit' of information or understanding. It follows that if people are educated, or given better information, they will see things differently. It is this thinking which underpins programmes to promote the 'public understanding of science'.[14]

Yet it is increasingly recognised that the problem is not lack of information, so much as lack of involvement. When people have concerns, they do not want to be presented with a one-way information flow. They want to feel that, either individually or through representatives, they can influence the outcome of the decision – that it is, in some sense, a two-way interaction.

Furthermore, public involvement tends to result in better decisions. People may not possess 'expert' knowledge, as traditionally defined, but they are often able to triangulate, by looking at where information is coming from and at the agenda of the information source, and weigh up their decisions accordingly. In the Korean consensus conference, the participants recommended a ban on human cloning, but a go-ahead for animal cloning under certain conditions. Theirs was no knee-jerk opposition to technology.

Public involvement also encourages debate about the wider issues surrounding any particular technology. Assessing risks is only half the equation. There is also a need to focus on the benefits, to ask 'what can this technology do for us?' Many opponents of GM focus their concern not on the technology but on its implications for the industrialisation of agriculture, as a recent pan-European study shows: 'GMOs were perceived as possibly representing "a step too far" in an ongoing trajectory' of further industrialisation of food production.[15]

Slowly but surely, there is a consensus emerging around this new approach to risk. In Denmark, it is reflected in the Danish Board of Technology, an independent body established by the Danish Parliament in 1995, 'to further the technology debate, assess technological impacts and options and advise the Danish Parliament and the

Government'.[16] In the UK, it can be seen in a recent report by the Government's Strategy Unit, which argues for 'decisions that better reflect public attitudes and values, based on earlier identification of concerns about potential risks and on a more proactive two-way communication process'.[17]

But this new consensus is fragile. When an issue becomes politically controversial, such lessons tend to be forgotten. The recent controversy in the UK over the MMR vaccine shows just how easy it is to slip back into the old approach. When new research suggested a possible link between the MMR vaccine and autism, the UK government was quick to follow the classic pattern of defence and denial. The scientific uncertainty was played down, the infallibility of experts was played up, dissenters were silenced – and the result was a public outcry, fuelled by the media.

The scientific consensus on MMR appears firmly in favour of the vaccine. But the government rubbished all attempts to express the slightest concern – and it was this, not the science itself, which caused the uproar. An ICM poll showed that 73 per cent of parents believed the vaccine was safe[18] – and still they objected, because of the government's heavy-handed, paternalistic stance. In the face of ever more vehement statements of certainty from government, it is hardly surprising that the newspapers filled up with accounts of parents who were unsure. 'I've read it all, digested all the evidence, the arguments and the heartfelt stories and still it's not going to be any easier', said one journalist about the impending decision to vaccinate her child.[19]

The MMR controversy illustrated a chronic lack of trust in government institutions. The same ICM poll showed that people did not trust the government to decide in their interest – 79 per cent believed that there should be an independent public enquiry to examine the issue. MMR points to a need for institutions to demonstrate much more openly that they are making decisions in the public interest – and this means opening up to debate and dissent.

The limits to public dialogue

The MMR story shows how difficult governments find it to involve the public in decision-making. Too often, when there have been innovative attempts at public involvement, like consensus conferences or deliberative polls, they have taken place at some distance from the actual decisions at stake. Building new forms of public involvement requires fundamental changes to the process and institutions of policy-making. Both government and advocates of the new approach have tended to play down the far-reaching implications of this shift.

However, even if governments embrace public involvement with more enthusiasm, it will not provide a total answer to the problem. Some fundamental questions remain.

First, there are questions about the proper role of government. Does a dialogue-based approach encourage governments to abdicate responsibility for difficult questions? What role do corporations, who often have a massive stake in new technologies, play within the dialogue process? What weight do we give to different voices? Who takes the final decision? A dialogue-based approach has a great deal to say about process, but leaves unanswered many political issues.

The most enthusiastic advocates of dialogue-based solutions portray them as a new form of democracy, akin to Athenian models of direct democracy. Elected representatives are bypassed in favour of decisions made by the people themselves. The 'stakeholder dialogue' model, a favourite of large corporations and professionalised by organisations like the New Economics Foundation and the Environment Council, works on the assumption that, if you put all the parties concerned with a particular issue (whether radioactive waste or climate change) in a room for long enough, with a team of facilitators and a lifetime's supply of Post-Its, a consensus will emerge. This ignores the entrenched interests and radically different worldviews that participants will bring to the table. Greenpeace activists and nuclear energy representatives are unlikely ever to see eye-to-eye – why try to make them? The task of government is, after all, to arbitrate between different, and often conflicting, interests. As politicians are fond of saying, there will always be difficult decisions – and there will always be winners and losers.

Secondly, there is the tricky issue of who becomes involved in dialogue processes. Public meetings and other deliberative processes often attract a self-selecting group with a strong vested interest in a particular outcome. The recent GM public debate in the UK consisted of six public meetings held in various towns across the country. But a journalist observing one of these meetings described the participants as 'a few dozen Greenpeace types, assorted yogic flyers from the Natural Law Party, a handful of pensioners and perhaps the odd scientist or farmer', which hardly offers the prospect of a representative debate.[20] As Henry Rothstein points out, 'Simply involving public interest groups in policy processes, *per se*, does not necessarily mean that the public interest is represented.'[21]

Advocacy of deliberative approaches needs to be accompanied by a clear understanding of the relationship between people and government. The rush towards greater public involvement should not mask political realities. It is politically naïve to assume that deliberative processes will make a decision for you. Decisions still have to be made, and elected politicians have to make them. But greater public involvement can help government to make better decisions, through providing government with the forms of 'social intelligence' needed to better understand an issue, and make an informed decision.[22] By bringing a greater range of views, and a better understanding of values, into the frame, government decisions will be better and more durable.

Finally, there are questions about the compatibility of public engagement with increasingly globalized economies, and increasingly (though imperfectly) globalized systems of governance. It is always possible to hold a citizens' jury on GM foods in Birmingham, Brisbane or Berlin, but how helpful are such deliberative processes when the real decisions about GM are being taken at the level of the EU or the WTO?

A dialogue-based approach is at odds with the normal workings of international law and politics. This is partly because these approaches are context-bound, and best suited to small-scale government, at local, regional or possibly national level. A global citizens' jury seems unlikely. But it is also because multilateral organisations and agreements, such as the World Trade Organisation, tend to frame issues in a narrow, technocratic way. The WTO's systems struggle to cope with uncertain science, with unknowns and indeterminacies.[23] Under WTO rules, the US has recently launched a case against the EU's ban on GM crops. The US wants the WTO to rule that the EU ban has no scientific basis. Arguing that there is too much uncertainty, or that the citizens of Europe find GM foods unacceptable, is not deemed a sufficient reason to restrict trade.

Similarly, the UK's 'public debate' on GM is being carried out in parallel with engagement in the EU's consents procedure for GM crops, which is based on different decision-making procedures. If the UK government were to use the outcome of its public debate to argue for restrictions on GM crops at either EU or WTO level, they would have a real battle on their hands. As Rothstein notes, there is a paradox in the dialogue model where: 'participative reforms that come closest to meeting democratic ideals, for example by directly involving the public in nationwide debates . . . tend to be the furthest away from actual policy making'.[24] There is an urgent need to bring the new approach to risk to international as well as national governance. We will return to this in the conclusion.

Smart Technologies Need Smart Institutions

With so much focus on emerging technologies, it can be easy to forget the environmental and social potential of the ones we already have. The most efficient vehicle known to man is not the hydrogen fuel-cell car, nor the high-speed train – it is the bicycle. As governments everywhere are learning through bitter experience, environmental problems will not be solved by technological innovation alone – they are knotty problems requiring multiple forms of innovation. It is easy to throw money at the technological end of the problem. But new technologies will never achieve their full potential unless they are accompanied by social and political innovation that alters the framework within which economic choices are made. Charles Leadbeater makes this point well in the context of transport:

> New, more sustainable forms of car transport will require scientific and technological innovation, such as new fuel sources for cars. But the true potential will not be realised without social innovation to create new patterns of car use, and even ways for consumers to share and own cars through leasing schemes. It will require regulatory innovations such as

road pricing, which may well only be possible if we have political innovations to give cities more powers to control their own transport taxation.
We need to imagine not just new technologies, but whole new social systems for transport.[25]

The 19th century, argues Leadbeater, was remarkable not just for
its technological innovation in the form of the industrial revolution,
but because of radical institutional innovations too – extended democracy; a professional civil service; local government; building societies and insurance schemes. Today's approach is a marked contrast:
'We are timid and cautious where the Victorians were confident and
innovative . . . we are scientific and technological revolutionaries, but
political and institutional conservatives.'[26]

A progressive approach should involve not just a more rounded
assessment of new technologies, but also a more realistic account of
the social and political innovation needed to make the most of existing technologies.

Take the example of energy. It is clear that we will need to decrease drastically our use of fossil fuels if we are to slow the pace of
climate change. We have a good idea of the technologies needed to
get us there: solar power, wind power, possibly wave and tidal power
too. Yet most renewable technologies are still finding the European
energy market a cold and inhospitable place. And there is little or
no incentive for the best (and most low-tech) solution of them all –
energy efficiency – which enables us to use less in the first place.

This point is understood, implicitly at least, by political leaders,
who tend to enthuse about renewable energy technologies, only to
wring their hands at the difficulty of bringing them into mainstream
use. In 2001, the G8 Renewables Taskforce produced an upbeat assessment of the potential of renewables and called for world leaders
to rally behind them. Yet the initiative ran into the sand as politicians
realised that proper support for renewable energy would involve
a lot of messy and difficult non-technological innovation, such as
increasing the price of fossil fuels, and restructuring the European
energy market.

So what would whole-system innovation look like in the energy
field? Of course, it would require significant technological innovation

215

– there is still much to be done to make renewable energy cheaper and more reliable. But success will also rely on social and institutional innovation. Catherine Mitchell argues that subsidy to renewable technologies is not enough, because the system is so stacked against them. She criticises the expectation that:

> ...a diverse set of new technologies, with very different operating characteristics from conventional technologies and which have had very little R&D, will be able to compete against conventional technologies, which have had generous R&D over the years, in a competitive marketplace where the market rules value the characteristics of the conventional technologies.[27]

As Mitchell argues, 'a sustainable energy future requires a system change'.[28] This is obvious if one compares the current energy system with a possible future one. On the supply side, the current system consists of large, centralised energy 'factories' in the form of power plants. On the demand side, consumers play a passive role, with little control over the energy they use, and little incentive to change their behaviour. A sustainable system would, in marked contrast, consist of lots of different sources of supply. Every building could generate its own electricity, through solar panels or combined heat-and-power systems. There would still be big power plants, but these would be supplemented by smaller, more embedded generators – small-scale wind turbines, wave power and so on. In this system, the boundaries between supply and demand would be broken down. Every consumer would be a supplier as well, selling electricity back to the grid when they were producing more than they needed. And every supplier could help consumers to consume less, if they were incentivised to help with energy efficiency measures.

This vision is not utopian. But current incentives, pricing structures and regulations all work in favour of the established, conventional system. The brave few who pioneer smaller-scale, more flexible alternatives soon find themselves struggling – the system works against them. Economic incentives, like grants for installing solar panels, are rarely enough. Whole-system innovation is needed if we are to get the sort of approach to energy we need.

In thinking about how we get from here to there, there may be lessons to draw from the current debates on public service reform. Progressives have, after all, spent far more time thinking about how to structure public services than how to structure energy systems. Recently, there has been much discussion of an approach to public services based on 'co-production'. Apply the same idea to energy, and a radically different energy system appears: one in which people have an active incentive to reduce their energy use, generate their own power, and to sell any excess back to the grid. The national grid then becomes an enabler, not a provider.

There is a parallel here with the changes we are advocating for the assessment and use of new technologies. Both involve an active role for people and government, working in tandem to assess, understand and use technology in ways which maximise its social benefit.

A Progressive Agenda for Technology, Risk and the Environment

Our analysis points to the need for a better understanding of the complex, dynamic relationship between technology, society and the environment. But what does this mean in practice? How should progressive politics approach the next set of controversial technologies that leap out of the laboratories? In the final section, we apply our analysis to a specific example – nanotechnology – in order to suggest some practical ways forward.

Nanotechnology promises to be one of the defining sciences of the 21st century. It is based on the ability to measure, manipulate and organise material on the nanoscale – 1 to 100 billionths of a metre. Yet nanotechnology is not just another step toward miniaturisation – it is a radically new approach to manufacturing, set to have a drastic and potentially disruptive impact on materials science and engineering. Envisaged breakthroughs include medical applications like biocompatible materials that will change the way that we repair nerves and tissues; telecommunications advances such as sensors allowing ubiquitous monitoring; and pollution control at the nano-level.

Rebecca Willis and James Wilsdon

But there may be downsides. Concerns have already been voiced about the potential for self-replicating nano-machines to smother the world in 'grey goo'. Scientists have also expressed worries about the potentially carcinogenic effects of nanoparticles.[29] It seems that even before debates over GM have approached any kind of resolution, NGOs, consumer groups and journalists are moving on to nanotech as the focus of the next battle between science and society.

Yet before we all get carried along on the next wave of media-inspired panic, it is important to remember that nanotechnology is at an equivalent stage in R&D terms to biotechnology in the late 1970s. The forms and eventual applications of the technology are not yet determined. We still have the opportunity to intervene and improve the social sensitivity of innovation processes at the design-stage – to avoid the mistakes that were made over GM and other technologies.

Science in context

Progressive governments will, quite rightly, support and channel research funds into nanotechnology, as a potentially rich source of economic and social innovation. But in doing so, they must not become uncritical cheerleaders. When ministers announce nanotech initiatives, they should acknowledge some of the profound misgivings that exist. Funding should be directed not only towards the technologies themselves, but also towards social science research into wider social and political consequences. It should look at whole-system innovation – as we describe above – and ask uncomfortable questions. For example, what problems will nanotech solve? What new problems could it create? Does it represent a techno-fix, or are there social or political solutions to the same problems?

Moving public debate upstream

Now is the time to get people talking about nanotech. Arguably the main problem with the current public debate on GM in the UK is that it is taking place ten years too late. Developing the technology needs to become a more cooperative undertaking between researchers, people and government. Of course, it is impossible to predict the

218

precise ways in which nanotechnology will be used. As we have seen with mobile phones, it is only through using a technology that we begin to identify its full potential. It would be wrong to jump to any conclusions so early in the process.

Yet equally, there is nothing to be gained – and plenty to be lost – from secretive, rarefied research into nanotech, removed from wider processes of social scrutiny. Involving wider voices from the start will help shape the technology in ways which can contribute to the public good. There is much to learn from the open-source movement in software development, where operating systems like Linux are developed and improved through constant interaction between developers and end-users.

For nanotech, this does not mean just conducting a 'public debate' in isolation from the actual processes of scientific innovation. The two must be interwoven. There is a need for new forums in which the scientists and companies involved in nanotech R&D can get together with citizens' groups and politicians, to debate the direction of the technology. Companies and government should collaborate to commission research into social impacts and reactions, using methodologies such as citizens' juries. Social engagement of this sort should be a requirement for all publicly funded research, and a condition of regulatory approval. In the UK, the recent announcement of a government-backed inquiry into the wider impacts of nanotech (being led by the Royal Society and the Royal Academy of Engineering) is an important and welcome first step, but this should mark the start rather than the end of the dialogue process.

Institutions with integrity

It is partly through this sort of public involvement that we will build institutions with greater integrity. As we show in our discussion of the MMR vaccine controversy, people do not necessarily object to a technology *per se* – they object to the way that it is being handled by government. They ask whether regulatory authorities are willing to regulate, and capable of counterbalancing the demands of the developers of the technology. They ask whether potential long-term consequences have been assessed, and who will be held responsible if things go wrong. It is the job of government to show, in an open and straightforward way, that they understand and act on these questions.

In practical terms, this means establishing institutions and regulatory regimes for nanotechnology which do not rely simply on an assessment of the established science. Instead, such institutions should also acknowledge uncertainties, look at the potential social and distributional impacts (which could be positive or negative), and use this information to decide whether or how to proceed with commercialisation. In short, they should demonstrate that they are acting in the public interest. This is a more complex process of regulation – but it will provide a better climate for innovation if it prevents the polarisation of views between gung-ho governments and scared citizens.

Beyond the national

As we have seen with GM, efforts to assess new technologies at the national level are often thwarted by international trade regimes and regulatory systems. The current WTO dispute between the US and the EU over GM is a case in point. The WTO's insistence on science as sole arbiter is no solution. Progressives should extend new approaches into international forums. One potential solution could be the Swedish proposal for an 'International Convention for Socioeconomic and Environmental Evaluation of New Technologies'. Under United Nations auspices, this would 'ensure independent assessment of emerging technologies through processes that guarantee public participation'.[30] This Convention would have to have political and legal weight alongside existing international law, particularly trade law. For nanotechnology, progressive governments should be laying out their stall now, arguing for a consideration of the social and ethical implications of the technology in international law and process.

The politics of technology

In technology, as in politics, answering one question inevitably raises others. The process of enquiry and learning is endless. We should know that no matter how well we handle one new technology, controversy is not about to disappear. For example, as nanotech

220

develops, the potential changes to the way we organise and manage our economies and our lives are so profound that there will always be radically different views on how we should proceed. We cannot hope to reach the mythical end-point of consensus, the middle ground of prudent progress behind which everyone can rally.

Our challenge as progressives is to recognise that we rely on this constant questioning and the innovation that drives it. Instead of shrinking from scientific and technological endeavour for fear of the uncertainty that accompanies it, we should embrace the challenge of creating the conditions for science and technology to thrive. But the simultaneous challenge is to generate new approaches to the governance of technology that can learn from past mistakes, cope more readily with complexity and uncertainty, and harness the drivers of technological change for the common good.

Notes

1 Crichton, M., *Prey*, London, 2002.
2 ETC Group, *The Big Down. Atomtech: Technologies Converging at the Nano-scale*, Winnipeg, 2003.
3 *Daily Telegraph*, 'Prince asks Scientists to look into Grey Goo', 5 June 2003.
4 Thompson, E. P., *The Making of the English Working Classes*, London, 1963.
5 Giddens, A., *Where Now For New Labour?*, Cambridge, 2002.
6 Shiva, V., *Staying Alive*, London, 1988.
7 Leadbeater, C., 'A Credible Centre-left Optimism', *Progressive Politics*, September 2002.
8 Beck, U., 'Global Risk Politics', in Jacobs, ed., *Greening the Millennium? The New Politics of the Environment*, Oxford, 1997.
9 Grove-White, R., 'Risk Society, Politics and BSE', in Franklin, ed., *The Politics of Risk Society*, Cambridge, 1998.
10 ESRC Global Environmental Change Programme, *Risky Choices, Soft Disasters: Environmental Decision-making Under Uncertainty*, Brighton, ESRC, 2000, and http://www.gecko.ac.uk
11 For a more detailed discussion of these issues, see the work of Brian Wynne, Professor of Science Studies at Lancaster University – for example, Wynne, B., and Irwin, A., eds, *Misunderstanding Science?*, Cambridge, 1996.

12 Independent Expert Group on Mobile Phones, *Mobile Phones and Health*, London, 2000, http://iegmp.org.uk. For a further discussion of this issue, see Green Alliance, *Decision-making Under Uncertainty: The Case of Mobile Phones*, 2001, http://www.greenalliance.org.uk

13 The second Korean consensus conference on cloning, organised by the Korean National Commission for UNESCO, March–September 1999, Seoul, Korea. See http://www.unesco.or.kr/cc/eng.html

14 See the House of Lords report, *Science and Society*, for a further discussion of these points. House of Lords Committee on Science and Technology, *Science and Society*, 2000.

15 PABE research project, *Public Perceptions of Agricultural Biotechnologies in Europe*, 2002, http://www.pabe.net

16 See the Danish Board of Technology website, http://www.tekno.dk

17 Strategy Unit, *Risk: Improving Government's Capacity to Handle Risk and Uncertainty*, London, 2002.

18 BBC Radio Four, 'MMR Vaccine – Should we be Given the Choice?', http://www.bbc.co.uk/radio4/today/reports/science_nature/mmrvaccine.shtml, February 2002.

19 BBC, 'My Worries over MMR', http://www.news.bbc.uk/1/low/health/1803928.stm, February 2002.

20 *The Times*, 'Who Cares what "the people" think of GM Foods?', 13 June 2003.

21 Rothstein, H., *A Short Note on Some Problems of Risk Governance for the Working Group on Science, Risk and Technology*, 2003.

22 Phil Macnaghten, personal communication, March 2003.

23 Robin Grove-White, from Progressive Governance working group discussion, March 2003.

24 Rothstein, H., *A Short Note on Some Problems of Risk Governance for the Working Group on Science, Risk and Technology*, 2003.

25 Leadbeater, C., *Mind Over Matter: Greening the New Economy*, London, 2000.

26 *Ibid.*

27 Mitchell, C., *System Change: Drivers and Requirements for a Sustainable Energy Policy*, Warwick, 2002, http://www.wbs.ac.uk

28 *Ibid.*

29 'Nanotech is Not so Scary', in *Nature*, 421: 299.

30 Ministry for the Environment, Sweden, *Stockholm: Thirty Years On*, conference proceedings, June 2002, http://www.miljo.regeringen.se